# POLICY AND PROVISION FOR SPECIAL EDUCATIONAL NEEDS

# Policy and Provision for Special Educational Needs

## Implementing the 1981 Education Act

*Brian Goacher*
*Jennifer Evans*
*John Welton*
*Klaus Wedell*

Cassell Educational Limited
Artillery House
Artillery Row
London SW1P 1RT

**British Library Cataloguing in Publication Data**

Policy and provision for special educational
  needs : implementing the 1981 Education Act.
  1. Great Britain, Education Act 1981
  2. Educational law and legislation—
  England
  I. Goacher, Brian
  344.204'791      KD3605

ISBN 0-304-31461-7

Typeset by Inforum Ltd, Portsmouth
Printed and bound in Great Britain by Mackays of Chatham Ltd

First published 1988

# Contents

# Background Papers to Main Research Report*

\* Copies of this separate volume are available for reference in the library of the University of London Institute of Education, 11–13 Ridgmount Street, London WC1.

# Preface

This research built upon a pilot project, commissioned by the Department of Education and Science at the University of London Institute of Education, into procedures for assessing and making provision for children's special educational needs. The pilot project sought to identify those aspects of administrative and professional practice to be taken into account in designing and implementing the proposed new legislative framework for special educational provision.

In reporting on that project, we noted that the 1981 Education Act was the manifestation in statute of changes in thinking about the special educational needs of children and young people, and of the way in which provision would be made for them. Neither the Act of Parliament, nor the Warnock Committee report (1978) which it followed, arose from a vacuum or created entirely new forms of practice. The pilot project led us to question the extent to which fundamental change in the nature of special provision and practice was likely to occur following the Act. We noted that it was unlikely to occur without simultaneous developments in the administrative structure and in relationships between professionals, administrators and users (parents and children) or without changes in ideas, attitudes and practice. A major finding of the pilot project was that the most specific aspects of the SE (Special Education) procedures instituted following Circular 2/75 were not generally implemented as its authors had intended, but became either adapted to local use or 'ritualized' as a *post hoc* means of recording and justifying decision-making.

Working on the pilot project at the same time as the Education Bill was passing through both Houses of Parliament, and while draft circulars and regulations were being prepared, we were very aware of the processes of negotiation, bargaining and compromise which are, in fact, characteristic of all policy-making. These processes involved a wide range of professional and administrative interest groups as well as parent groups and other voluntary organizations.

Fundamental to our approach to the study of policy-making and implementation is the view that a change in legislation is only one, albeit very significant, event in the process of service and policy development. By and large, the same actors and agencies who were involved in the creation of new legislation are involved in its service development and implementation.

As we discuss in Chapter 1 of this report, the 1981 Education Act represented, in law, fundamental changes in the principles concerned with the nature of special educational needs: principles concerned with the rights of those with special educational needs (and their parents), and with the effectiveness of identifying, assessing and meeting special educational needs. Research for the pilot study suggested that not all professionals and administrators would find it easy to adapt to these principles. However, while some professionals and administrators might set a process of 'tissue rejection' in motion by not accommodating the Act's underlying model of practice, that model might be protected by the 'immune response repressants' injected by the Act's concern for professional and administrative accountability, by the newly established rights of parents, by the continued political activities of the voluntary organizations and by the conflicting pressures of supply and demand.

The present project built on the pilot project, examining the process of policy implementation in local education authorities, social service departments and district health authorities in England, for the first three years after the Act was brought into force. The research covered developments in administrative and professional policy, and the way in which these developments conformed to the principles of the Act.

In Chapter 2 the conceptual framework for the analysis of policy-making and implementation is outlined. By adopting a model of the policy process as a 'policy-implementation chain' within which ideas, intentions and practices are progressively defined and redefined, we are reminded that three years is a very short time in which to identify what the real impact of the Act on policy and provision for special educational needs will be. Chapter 3 describes the research methodology and Chapter 4 describes the contextual factors which influenced the way in which local authorities set about implementing the provisions of the 1981 Education Act. Chapter 4 (and later chapters) also describes the great variety of policy, provision and practice found both within and between local authorities. It is not possible to generalize in simple terms about the extent and nature of change across the whole country. However, we identify and seek to explain a wide variety of response to the Act in terms of both change and lack of change.

The findings of our pilot project led us to predict that some professionals would have difficulty in accommodating the new paradigm of special educational needs. In Chapter 5 we consider the ways in which local authorities and health authorities have understood and interpreted the Act. Chapter 6 describes the way in which local authorities established and sought to implement policies relating to the Act.

Much of the model of 'good practice' underlying the Act is made explicit in its accompanying circulars of guidance rather than in the Act itself which, after the first three sections, is concerned mainly with specifying various procedural matters, particularly those concerned with the statutory assessment required to make and review a Statement of Special Educational Need. Chapter 7 describes the ways in which local authorities responded to the new statutory framework concerning the decision-making process about children's special educational needs.

A key to understanding the way in which the policy process develops is the behaviour of interest groups which crystallize around common causes or needs. Ultimately, the key indicator of the outcome of the policy process is the way in which individual clients experience the service, i.e. the way in which their needs are met. Organizational structures and procedures are the continually evolving product of the experience of, and negotiations between, individuals and interest groups. Chapter 8 is concerned with the feelings and evaluations of those who have been involved in the operation of the 1981 Education Act at the local level: parents and children, professionals, administrators and other local and health authority officials. Members of voluntary organizations and pressure groups which stand outside the statutory services, but have an integral part to play in supporting the meeting of special educational needs, are also included.

Chapter 9, the first of two concluding chapters, reviews our findings on the effects of the Act on special education policies and practices in local and health authorities, and suggests ways in which the difficulties experienced in implementing some aspects of the legislation might be overcome. Chapter 10 adds a postscript on the role of legislation in changing policy and practice.

In preparing this report, we have drawn from the wide range of sources on research methodology described in Chapter 3. A second volume of background papers summarizing much of the supporting research evidence is being produced to accompany this report (see page vi).

Policy-making and implementation is the 'art of the possible'. Stepping aside from our role as researchers and commentators, we view the future of the services for children with special educational needs with optimism. Despite low morale generally in the education service and difficulties over both the level and disposition of resources for children with special educational needs, we have found that overall there is widespread eagerness and willingness for change among those providing services in local authorities and health authorities.

One of the main obstacles to change in any set of structures is the in-built inertia which most systems or organizations acquire. Old solutions to problems continue to be adopted, even when they are no longer appropriate. The new statutory procedures for the assessment of children with special educational needs have forced changes in the nature of special educational administration. However, it is difficult to assess whether changing the procedures for ascertainment has yet led to any fundamental changes in thinking about special needs, professional behaviour, or patterns of provision.

Despite the difficulties inherent in making radical changes, especially in a time of limited resources, some authorities have achieved a great deal. We are glad to have been able to share in the experience of committed and energetic officers, professionals, parents and members of voluntary organizations who have tackled the problems of change, instead of using them as a rationalization for doing nothing.

*Chapter 1*

# The 1981 Education Act: Principles and Content

## INTRODUCTION

This chapter sets the scene for the subsequent data-related chapters. We consider the development of the concepts and principles which represent the context in which the 1981 Education Act and its attendant Regulations and Circulars were formulated. We also consider the *principles underlying* the Act, which have evolved as part of a general change in attitudes towards handicap and the education of children with special needs, and the *representation* of these principles in the Act, Regulations and Circulars. We assume that the intention of the legislators was to offer a model of 'good practice' and consider the extent to which this has been achieved.

This chapter, therefore, offers a broad critique of the Act in its historical perspective. Those wishing for more detail of the history of special education are directed to Chapter 2 of *Special Educational Needs*, the report of the Warnock Committee (HMSO, 1978). Accounts of more recent thinking are contained in *Educational Opportunities for All?*, the report of the Fish Committee (ILEA, 1985), and in Adams (1986).

It is important to identify the principles underlying the Act because they are the basis for the subsequent evaluation of local interpretation and implementation in the main part of this research report. The extent to which the Act and the Circulars provide models of 'good practice' derived from these principles and the extent to which these models have been adopted in local authorities are the fundamental questions which will be addressed in this book.

The principles can be grouped and explored under three main headings:

(a)  principles concerned with the *nature* of special educational needs
(b)  principles concerned with the *rights* of those with special educational needs (and their parents)
(c)  principles concerned with the *effectiveness* of identifying, assessing and meeting special educational needs.

## THE CONCEPT OF 'GOOD PRACTICE'

Before considering the principles outlined above in more detail, it may be useful to explore the concept of 'good practice' and to consider why it is such an important issue in the implementation of the 1981 Education Act. The importance of the issue derives from the nature and structure of the administration of the British education system as well as from the nature of professional responses to the problem of handicap.

The administration of education in England and Wales is carried out through a delicately balanced partnership between central and local government; between the Department of Education and Science (DES) and 104 largely autonomous local education authorities (LEAs). In the case of special education, the partnership is further complicated by the involvement of education, health and social services at both central and local levels. The complexities of these relationships are explored in more detail in Chapters 2 and 4. However, in general terms, if an Education Act is to achieve its intended or expected results, goodwill is essential from all parties. While the 1981 Education Act, through its relationship with the 1944 Act, includes within its framework the possibility of sanctions against non-compliant LEAs, it is not at all clear what form such sanctions would take and even less clear what consequences their imposition might bring about. Therefore, essentially, the Act is enabling rather than coercive. Inherent in such a system is the assumption of 'good practice' as well as that of goodwill.

The duties imposed by the Act are supported by sets of rules, representing the 'letter of the law', which appear specifically in the case of the 1981 Education Act as the Education (Special Educational Needs) Regulations (1983). The Act's underlying principles of good practice are described in more detail in the Circulars of Guidance 1/83 and 8/81 which provide guidelines and advice for appropriate implementation. The distinction between these two facets of the legislation is quite explicit. Instructions within the Regulations are framed in terms of what the LEA has a legal obligation to do, as distinct from the more persuasive approach of the Circulars which are presented with the codicil:

> A Circular cannot be regarded as providing an authoritative legal interpretation of any of the provisions of the Act as this is exclusively a function of the Courts.

It is apparent, therefore, that the Act and Regulations represent different levels of specificity and carry different degrees of legal force from the Circulars. Acts of Parliament can only be amended through the introduction of further legislation. Regulations, on the other hand, can be laid before Parliament by the Minister and do not have to be debated. New Circulars can be issued by the Department without reference to Parliament. Despite these distinctions, it is important to note that the 1981 Education Act, the Regulations and the Circulars were drawn up in relation to the three groups of principles outlined above.

The Act was formulated in the context of the thinking which prevailed during the late 1970s; its present interpretation must take account of later developments in thinking about special education and a very different political and economic climate. The Act and Circulars thus provide the framework within which current ideas of 'good practice' have to be applied.

Notions of what constitutes 'good practice' reflect current thinking; therefore, they change with time. Whether the Warnock Report and the 1981 Education Act, which embodies some of its fundamental ideas, represent a major shift in the prevailing concept of special needs (a shift of paradigm), a small step along a path or, as has been claimed by Tomlinson (1985), for example, merely 'more of the same' remains an issue to be clarified as new patterns of practice become established. Given the range of practice existing in LEAs prior to the Act, and the non-prescriptive nature of the legislation (apart from the detailed statutory assessment procedures), it is likely that obtaining a uniform and consistent standard of 'good practice' in LEAs will be a difficult task. However, the legislation is intended as a statement of intent on the part of the government, and the Circulars make explicit what the government's view of 'good practice' entails. It is likely, therefore, that LEAs will attempt to alter their practices in line with the government's wishes, particularly in view of the fact that the principles embodied in the Act and the formulations of 'good practice' given in the Circular were heavily influenced by the thinking amongst professionals and others working within local and health authorities.

## THE PRINCIPLES

### The nature of special educational needs

*The origins of the concept of special educational needs*

Before the 1981 Education Act came into force on 1 April 1983, the provision of special educational services in England (and Wales) was based, as is the administration of all other aspects of education, upon the 1944 Education Act. Accepting that, it was still possible for Jones (1982) to identify 17 other 'Acts, Reports and documents relating to special education', many of which clearly represented quite major changes in direction for either special education as a whole or some aspect of the service.

The 1944 Education Act had in turn replaced the 1921 Education Act, which offered four categories of children for whom local authorities were to make provision: the blind; the deaf; the defective, both physical and mental; and the epileptic. Children adjudged to be 'idiots' or 'imbeciles' were required to be 'ascertained' and 'certified'. The 1944 Education Act extended the duty of LEAs to ascertain which children required special treatment to all 'pupils who suffer from any disability of mind or body'. A continuity with the previous categorization of 'idiot' was, however, maintained within a group identified as 'ineducable' and excluded from the population for whom LEAs were given a duty to provide. This distinction was not to be eradicated until the 1970 Education (Handicapped Children) Act transferred the responsibility for severely mentally handicapped children from the health to the education authorities.

In practice, the 1944 Act extended the duties of LEAs greatly by defining, in the Handicapped Pupils and School Health Regulations, 11 categories of pupil for whom provision should be made. Two categories, 'maladjusted' and 'speech defective', were new; partial states of blindness and deafness were extensions of previous categories; and 'delicate' and 'epileptic' children had formerly been included under the umbrella term of 'physical handicap'.

Subsequent evaluations of special education disclosed no decline in the proportion of children receiving special educational 'treatment', but demonstrated an increasing diversity of opinion and a greater degree of uncertainty concerning the value and outcome of separate specialist provision. Studies of compensatory education and the effect of early developmental influences provided a range of new evidence about the causes of special educational need. The developments in thinking were reflected in the reports of the Plowden Committee (DES, 1967) and the Newsom Committee (DES, 1963), as well as providing one basis for the recommendations of the Warnock Committee.

The Warnock Committee pointed out in its report that children could not be fitted neatly into handicap categories, and that their special needs were often more complex than a single category would indicate. Furthermore, the educational needs of a child could not usually be derived from a given category of handicap.

The designation of 'disability of mind or body' in the 1944 Education Act indicated the weight given to 'within-child' factors as the cause of a need for special education. From this position there has been a gradual, but continual, movement towards a more interactive view of special needs, derived from a variety of sources, including studies of compensatory education, and environmental influences in general, as indicated in the Plowden (DES, 1987) and Newsom (DES, 1963) Reports. As a result, thinking about categories of handicap began to be replaced by the idea of a continuum of special educational needs. In this view, an individual's special needs are seen as the outcome of the interaction between factors within the child and within the environment (Wedell, 1981).

There was also evidence of the recognition of education as a compensatory resource in this interactive process, in the campaign by parents of severely mentally handicapped children, those deemed 'ineducable' under the 1944 Act, to force the government to provide education for their children. The extension of education to developmental programmes for children with severe mental handicap had been carried out in the United States and also in this country, particularly by the Hester Adrian Centre. The parents' campaign culminated, in 1971, in the transfer of responsibility for these children from the health authority to the education authority. This represented the acceptance of the principle that no child was ineducable.

For these and other reasons, such as the recognition of the 'labelling' effect of categories, the Warnock Committee recommended that the system of handicap categories should be replaced by a more flexible and interactive definition of special educational need.

## The degree of special educational need

Within such a view of special educational need, the degree of need can be considered from a number of different viewpoints (Wedell, 1983). For example, the degree of special educational need can be considered in relation to:

- a normative perspective
- an individual professional's perception of his capacity to 'cope' with a child's needs
- priority of access to available provision.

The first of these views focuses upon the gap between individual achievement and the curricular expectations. As far as the educational thinking of the time was concerned, this view was reflected by the Warnock Committee in its statement that the aims of education were the same for all children and young people.

The second perspective reflects the views of teachers and other professionals contributing to the development of the child. It is framed in terms of continuous assessment, focusing upon the capacity of those involved in the day-to-day care of children to cope with their special educational needs, and in terms of other professionals' views of whether those needs are being met effectively.

The third view reflects on the relationship between children's needs and available resources. Where resources are scarce (reflecting the community's willingness to provide as well as demands upon local politicians and officers to make efficient use of resources), access to them must necessarily be restricted. From such a perspective, the degree of need becomes, inevitably, related to the number of available 'places' and degree of need comes to be interpreted as priority of access to provision.

## Principles related to the rights of those with special educational needs — and their parents

Within the area of rights, changes have been equally dramatic and their evolution has been even more rapid than those concerned with the nature of special educational needs.

The Green Paper, *Education after the War*, which preceded the 1944 Education Act, included for the first time the suggestion that provision for most children with problems of sight or hearing, and mentally defective and delicate children, should be made in ordinary schools. A thorough review of the education of handicapped children and the certification of defective children was also recommended, although, as the Warnock Report recorded, in the subsequent White Paper *Educational Reconstruction* (HMSO, 1943) handicapped children 'were dealt with in two sentences', concluding with the need for 'a substantial modification of the prevailing legislation'. The extent to which this represented a further legitimation of the concept of 'normalization' — that the handicapped should be seen as part of the continuum of normality — is more difficult to determine at such a distance.

What constituted acceptable standards of behaviour towards children with disabilities, and principles concerning equal opportunity, was determined by changing attitudes towards social minorities whether of race, sex or disability. Within education, much attention in this area focused on the opportunity provided for children with special educational needs to be educated with their fellow pupils. Such a principle was commonly expressed in terms of 'integration' or framed in terms of the right for children to receive their education in the 'least restrictive environment'. In one sense, this trend is part of the broader move towards comprehensive schooling.

The 1944 Act distinguished between those who were to be educated in special schools (the 'seriously handicapped') and those who might be educated in ordinary schools (the less seriously disabled). That distinction was to be blurred with time but, as we have noted, it was not until the Education (Handicapped Children) Act 1970 that the legal division between those who were educable in schools and those who were not was removed.

The Warnock Committee envisaged a 'continuum' of special educational provision from non-segregation to segregation:

   (i)   full-time education in an ordinary class with necessary help and support

  (ii)   education in an ordinary class with periods of withdrawal to a special class or unit or other supporting base

 (iii)   education in a special class or unit with periods of attendance at an ordinary class and full involvement in the general community life and extra-curricular activities of the ordinary school

 (iv)   full-time education in a special class or unit with social contact with the main school

  (v)   education in a special school, day or residential, with some shared lessons with a neighbouring ordinary school

 (vi)   full-time education in a day special school with social contact with an ordinary school

(vii)   full-time education in a residential special school with social contact with an ordinary school

(viii)  short-term education in hospitals or other establishments

 (ix)   long-term education in hospitals or other establishments

  (x)   home tuition.
        (Para. 6.11)

The Committee also distinguished between three main forms of integration — locational, social and functional:

> Each element of the triad has a separate validity, although the functional element is perhaps uppermost in most people's minds when they speak of integration. Together these elements provide a framework for the planning and organisation of new arrangements for the education of children with special educational needs jointly with other children, and for later judgement of how effectively it has been achieved.
> (Para. 7.10.)

Similarly, thinking about parents' rights conferred by the 1944 Act was extended by the Committee to include a right to participation in decision-making. That is, parents should be closely involved in the assessment of their children's needs, and their views should be sought.

The increasing emphasis on inter-service co-ordination and planning of services for children was outlined in the Circular which followed the report of the Court Committee on Child Health Services (Court Report, 1976).

The changes which have been detailed reflect an important evolution in the roles and relationships between professionals, administrators and politicians. No longer do they do 'good works', but rather carry out obligations to individuals using resources provided through taxation. This leads on to the final major principle arising from the need for all those to be accountable to the 'client'. Such a view produces the obligation to provide effective services for identifying, assessing and meeting special educational needs.

## Principles concerned with the effectiveness of identifying, assessing and meeting special educational needs

Principles concerned with effectiveness can be seen as originating from a number of different concerns, both with special needs and from the broader educational context.

The major principles appear to be those concerned with the following.

## The aims of education

The elimination of the concept of ineducability and the emphasis on the movement towards integration in all its various forms have demonstrated the growing importance attached to the principle of a uniform set of aims for all children. The Warnock Committee focused its attention on the need for common curricular aims for all children. These have also been reflected in the movement towards a comprehensive system of education and the recent replacement of 'O' level and CSE examinations by a single examination at the age of 16+. A growing interest in mixed-ability teaching could also be seen as part of this movement.

## The compensatory nature of education

The important elements here are the increasing emphasis on the supportive role of parents, the value of early intervention and the support to be gained from close interdisciplinary collaboration. Within schools, the focus has been turned to the role of the teacher in supporting the pupil's progress through the curriculum and to the school's accountability for achieving this. Parallel with this has been the emphasis on the role of advisory services to support those with day-to-day responsibility for the child.

## Education as preparation for life

Concern in this area has been related to curriculum content and balance and its effectiveness in enabling children to prepare for adult life. This includes both those children following the general curriculum and those following a 'modified' or 'developmental' curriculum. It has been accepted that, for many of those with special educational needs, adequate preparation for adult life involves the extension of education beyond the statutory school leaving age.

These concerns have implications for the effective organization and functioning of both ordinary and special schools. Indeed, as early as 1955 the Scottish Education Department declared that:

> Special educational treatment should . . . be regarded simply as a well-defined arrangement within the ordinary educational system to provide for the handicapped child the individual attention that he particularly needs . . .

There are also important implications for the way in which special and mainstream schools co-ordinate curriculum and organization to facilitate the transition of pupils between them. Similar transitional implications also arise for those providing primary, secondary and further education in the mainstream.

*The need for appropriate staff development*

Last (and these were also spelled out clearly by the Warnock Committee) are the implications of all that has gone before for training the education, health and social services staff professionally involved in meeting special educational needs effectively.

## THE ACT, REGULATIONS AND CIRCULARS

This section seeks to examine the content of the new legislation in relation to the principles set out in the previous section. As discussed earlier, the Act, Regulations and Circulars sought to reflect prevailing notions of 'good practice', as well as to provide a legal framework to encourage LEAs to improve practice. The difficulties in translating principles into legislation was acknowledged by the then Minister of State, Baroness Young, who, in a speech to a conference on the White Paper, anticipated possible criticisms that:

> somewhere on the long road leading from the Warnock Report towards legislation some of the spirit of the report appears to have been lost. . . . This is not the case. It is simply that in translating recommendations into law we move into the dispassionate world of the lawyers, who like builders have to construct secure foundations on which the building can rise. (1)

### The nature of special educational needs

The definition of 'special educational needs' in Section 1 of the Act is unquestionably a fundamental feature of the legislation. The meaning of the term is clarified through its interrelationship with two other concepts, 'learning difficulty' and 'special educational provision'.

As they appear in the Act, these three concepts are defined as follows.

1. For the purposes of this Act a child has 'special educational needs' if he has a learning difficulty which calls for special educational provision to be made for him.
2. Subject to subsection (4) below, a child has a 'learning difficulty' if:
   (a) he has a significantly greater difficulty in learning than the majority of children of his age;
   (b) he has a disability which either prevents or hinders him from making use of educational facilities of a kind generally provided in schools within the area of the local authority concerned, for children of his age; or
   (c) he is under the age of five years and is, or would be if special educational provision were not made for him, likely to fall within paragraph (a) or (b) when over that age.
3. 'Special educational provision' means:
   (a) in relation to a child who has attained the age of two years, educational provision which is additional to, or otherwise different from, the educational provision made generally for children of his age in schools maintained by the local education authority concerned;
   (b) in relation to any child under that age, educational provision of any kind.

There is, at this point, one specific exclusion:

4. A child is not to be taken as having a learning difficulty solely because the language (or

form of the language) in which he is, or will be, taught is different from a language (or form of a language) which has at any time been spoken in his home.

It is evident, therefore, that the Act marks a number of major changes incorporating the principles concerning the nature of special educational needs already outlined.

The Act refers to special educational needs as a subclass of the generality of special needs and rejects the categorical view of special educational needs, focusing instead upon the interactive, relative view.

The separation of special educational needs from the designation of handicap or disability can be linked directly to the recommendation of the Warnock Committee, and thus it represents a clear response to the majority of those giving evidence to the Committee who were critical of categories and wished them to be abandoned.

The term 'learning difficulties' was also the subject of a Warnock Committee recommendation. Its use was suggested to supersede the concept of 'educational sub-normality', which was a designation criticized for its stigma, imprecision and reliance on an assumption of 'agreement on what is educationally normal with regard to ability and attainment'.

By the very nature of their composition, committees such as the Warnock Committee are unlikely to produce recommendations which are at odds with the current consensus or take an opposing line to the prevailing trend of opinion. It is perhaps for this reason that what appeared to be quite fundamental changes, and their rationale, have proved to be remarkably resilient. Thus the DES press release accompanying the subsequent White Paper (*Special Needs in Education*, HMSO, 1980), reporting on the ten statutory categories, stated that 'it is now clearly recognised that a classification of this kind is not the best way of identifying the kind of education a child requires'. The White Paper itself, in endorsing the approach recommended by the Warnock Committee, gave the official view that:

> The present law relies too heavily on the identification of specific disabilities of mind or body, and its more general provisions do not ensure that the whole spectrum of special needs is adequately met . . . (Para. 21) . . . What is needed is a further legal framework which pays attention to the special educational needs of that minority of children and young people whose problems are greater or more persistent than those of the generality, and which include not only mental disability but also those which may be due to some other causes . . . (Para. 23) The application of this concept will help to break down the legal and psychological barrier which needlessly separates the handicapped child from his peers.
> (Para. 24)

When translated into the Education Bill in January 1981, the definitions emerged as they now stand in the Act. This was explained in the subsequent Circular (8/81) as establishing that a child has special educational needs if he has a learning difficulty that:

> is significantly greater than that of the majority of children of the same age.
> (Para. 4)

Such consistency might be taken as confirmation of the unproblematic nature of this notion of special educational needs. However, untangling the interrelated threads of the definition discloses problems which might be expected to give rise to difficulty in its operation.

One aspect is the circularity of the definition which, in seeking to clarify the concept of 'special educational needs', introduces two other concepts, 'special educational provision' and 'learning difficulty', without offering precise meanings for any of them. 'Learning difficulty' is clearly meant to indicate a state of affairs, rather than a diagnosis of a causal factor. The child demonstrates a 'difficulty in learning' within 'the educational provision made generally by the local education authority concerned'. Hence, this state of affairs 'calls for special educational provision to be made for him'. The definition thus asserts the interactive nature of special educational needs, in that it implies that the 'learning difficulty' is relative to the compensatory resources of the 'generally made' provision. The same applies to the 'disability' which 'prevents or hinders him from making use of educational facilities . . . generally provided in schools'. However, the Act does not offer any indication of the criteria on which the call for 'special educational provision' should be based, other than the criterion of a 'learning difficulty which is significantly greater . . . than the majority of children of his age'. It is hardly necessary to point out the unhelpfulness of such a criterion.

The Act does provide one further indication of a criterion of degree of special educational needs, in referring to those instances where the LEA has to 'determine' the provision, and Circulars 8/81 and 1/83 both attempt to provide pragmatic definitions for this. It is interesting to note how closely these formulations in the Act reflect the three types of criteria of degree of need mentioned in the previous section (p. 4).

There is another aspect of the concept which, while reflecting the interactive principle, also prompts some concern. The new terminology avoids attributing causality solely to within-child factors, but the Act's concept of 'special educational needs' still retains a focus on the special educational needs *of the child*, thus detracting from a wider conceptualization which takes account of the child, its relationship with others, home and school ethos and educational content and approach. Paradoxically, therefore, while the Act can be interpreted within the relativistic model in which any or all of these factors may require attention, it can also be read as directing attention primarily to interventions focused upon the individual.

Thus, the definition of the special educational needs of the child represents a legitimation of trends in existing professional ideas and practices and constitutes a step which falls short of acceptance of the principles or a major shift in paradigm. The term can thus be seen as a pragmatic recognition of the difficulty in accurately and consistently categorizing all those in need of some form of special educational intervention. It reflects a recognition of the potential risks of social and emotional damage and the economic dangers resulting from reduced life chances by allocating a semi-permanent label of difference to the individual. Thus there is a need for further development of the term to move the focus away from the individual towards 'outside factors', such as the resources and expertise available in the school. However, given the variability of educational provision between and within LEAs, and the differences in view about the content and progress of curricula offered by schools, it is hardly surprising that such an extension of the definition has not been attempted.

**The rights of those with special educational needs and their parents**

Sections 2, 3 and 4 of the Act specify the requirement placed upon LEAs to identify and meet needs in mainstream schools. Because it is an element of the definition of special educational needs, the concept of special educational provision was introduced in the previous section and explored in a limited way. Mainstreaming can be seen as either a pragmatic consequence of the removal of categories, with the necessary loss of linkage between disability and placement, or as a more flexible response to the new needs focus of the legislation.

The realization of integration under the Act is constrained by the way in which local authorities offer provision which is 'additional to' or 'otherwise different from' that 'made generally'. Local authorities are directed to secure that special educational provision is made in 'an ordinary school' (Section 2(2)). Section 2(3) of the Act subsequently directs that:

> The conditions are that account has been taken, in accordance with section 7, of the views of the child's parent and that educating the child in an ordinary school is compatible with:
>
> (a)   his receiving the special educational provision that he requires
> (b)   the provision of efficient education for the children with whom he will be educated
> (c)   the efficient use of resources.

These criteria reflect and extend the intention which was apparent within the 1944 Act that special educational provision should, wherever practicable, be made in ordinary schools. Although they have been variously identified as urging or constraining mainstream provision for special educational needs by local authorities, the criteria may also be identified as maintaining the *status quo*. A *status quo* which, in legal terms, if not in respect of the actual allocation of children with special educational needs to different types of placement, was already oriented towards mainstream provision. It is perhaps important to recognize that, in this respect, the 1944 Act marked a considerable contrast to the 1921 Education Act which had gone before. The fact that, even in the post-war period of massive social and economic rethinking, the 1944 Act did little to decrease the division between those with and those without disability also provides a salutary lesson to those expecting massive and immediate change as a result of the present Act. The relationship between policy, legislation and practice will be discussed in Chapter 2.

Each of the criteria which should be fulfilled prior to the mainstream placement of a child with special educational needs illustrates an important and basic feature of the Act, and also the difficulties inherent in such a system of safeguards. The precursor that emphasizes the importance of 'taking account' of the views of the parents fits well into a piece of consumerist legislation, assuming that the 'consumers' are indeed the parents. As is made clear elsewhere, little else within the Act indicates so explicitly that it is a piece of consumer-oriented legislation. The present formulation also fails to provide any place for the views of the real subject of the action, the child, apparently assuming that, no matter what his age, this aspect will not concern 'the child' or will be a matter of agreement between child and parents.

The three criteria which LEAs must meet before a child identified as having special educational needs may be placed in a mainstream school each conceal similar assumptions. The first condition, relating placement to the required educational provision, assumes that this can be defined precisely enough to allow such a distinction to be made and that agreement can be reached in this respect; the second, aimed at ensuring that the child's fellow pupils continue to receive an 'efficient education', assumes a consensus concerning such a concept; the third implies a similar consensus about what constitutes an 'efficient use of resources'.

Thus, while offering apparent criteria for determining where provision might be made, there is little within the Act to allow these to be operationalized in any systematic way. The Act does, however, clearly confirm the 1944 Act's lower age boundary of two years, with regard to the LEA's duty to provide. Thus local authorities cannot enforce parents' acceptance of special educational provision for a child under that age, nor can LEAs be forced to make educational provision available unless the child has a Statement. Interestingly, above the age of two years, the LEA's duty to provide is limited by the extent to which pre-school provision is generally available in the locality (Section 1(3)). However, the Act does ensure that an LEA's duty to make provision is extended beyond the minimum school leaving age by specifying a definition of 'child' which:

> includes any person who has not attained the age of 19 years and is registered as a pupil at a school.
> (Section 20(1))

As with the relativist elements in the definition of special educational needs, so the elements of 'additional to' and 'otherwise different from' in the description of provision offer a possibility for dispute as well as allowing local variation. In abstract philosophical terms, the concept has a certain elegance. Its practical application may not be quite so susceptible to interpretation. Again, the form of words can be clearly traced back to the Warnock Committee, which described children whose needs required:

> special educational provision not generally available in ordinary schools
> (Para. 3.3)

The exclusion of the words 'ordinary schools' in the Act must make the operationalization of the concept considerably more difficult for advising professionals and administrators.

The Warnock Committee identified ten discrete points on the continuum of special educational provision. These have been detailed previously (pp. 5 and 6). No specific recommendation with respect to any 'principle' of integration emerged from the Warnock Committee, and therefore the Act could be identified in Section 2(2) as not falling short of the recommendations nor going beyond them. The recommendation most concerned with integration focused on ensuring 'the maximum educational and social interaction' for those children given mainstream placement (Para. 7.21). This is also emphasized within the Act, which specifies that, where a child who has special educational needs is being educated in a maintained mainstream school, it is the duty of:

> those concerned with making special educational provision . . . to secure . . . that the child engages in the activities of the school together with children who do not have special educational needs.
> (Section 2(7))

The view that access to integrated provision is the right of every child is not a proposition which is discussed in the Warnock Report, suggesting, perhaps, the peripheral role allocated by professionals to the place of children's rights in the overall balance of power between themselves, parents and children. This is an issue which, while clearly identified as a principle, is not addressed explicitly in the Act, the Regulations or, we would suggest, in the Circular.

The Education (Special Educational Needs) Regulations, 1983, have nothing further to offer in terms of attempting to secure the adoption of particular provision practices by LEAs. As we discuss in Chapter 2, there are obvious difficulties in attempting to legislate, even in a weakly prescriptive way, in an area where LEAs vary so much in their policies and existing patterns of provision. The legal framework offered by the Act in respect of provision potentially allows different LEAs to respond differently to the same child because of their varying 'educational facilities'. It offers no threat to those making no provision for the under-twos, nor to those which have no nursery education. Similarly, LEAs' responsibilities to make provision for those aged between 16 and 19 years is legally enforced only for those who remain in school.

Guidance within Circular 1/83 is limited to the two aspects concerned with the *documentation* of provision:

> The LEA must specify . . . the special educational provision to be made for the child in terms of facilities and equipment, staffing arrangements, curriculum and other arrangements to be made . . .
> (Para. 44)

The LEA must describe the type of school they consider appropriate for the child, and name the particular school if known, or the provision to be made if he is to be educated somewhere other than at school (Para. 45). The legislation, therefore, formally marks the end of the conceptualization of meeting needs by allocating 'special educational treatment' and legitimates the distinction between provision and placement. However, it offers little in terms of legal definition, or indeed in identification of good practice and placement, which can ensure that change occurs where change may be needed.

As has already been indicated, the rights of those with special educational needs are protected by the requirement for LEAs to assess their special needs and, where the requirement for extra or alternative provision warrants it, to commit themselves to legally binding provision. The annual review and the statutory (13+) reassessment also represent a clear protection of the rights of the child to provision.

The new relationship which the Act posits for parents is, however, far-reaching in its implications. As a result of the legislation, parents are able to make representations about the initiation of statutory assessment (Section 5(4)); they can prevent it being carried out if the child is under the age of two years (Section 6); they may submit information and evidence provided by others about their child for consideration alongside that produced by professional advisers (Schedule 1, Part I, 2(3)/Regulation 8); they can attend examinations which are part of the statutory assessment process (Schedule 1, Part I, 2(3)); they can appeal (to the Secretary of State) if the LEA decides not to prepare a Statement of Special Educational Needs (Section 5 (6)) and can disagree with the content of any Statement (Section 7(4)), the proposed form of which must be sent to them (Section 7(3)); if they wish, they can have access to an officer of the LEA and/or those offering professional advice on their child to discuss 'any part of the assessment' (Section 7(5)); and, finally, parents can appeal against the special educational provision specified in the Statement (to a Local Appeals Committee and, if not satisfied with the outcome, to the Secretary of State) (Section 8).

Statutory waiting periods built into the procedures allow parents to make known to the LEA whether they wish their child to be assessed. They also give parents time to consider what evidence they wish to bring to the assessment. The opportunity and time given for parents to consider the content of the Statement marks a real change from the previous procedures, where parents had no access to the information upon which the LEA based its decisions. The waiting periods can be seen as introducing unnecessary delays into the procedures, but if they wish to take these opportunities, they allow parents to play a much greater role in the assessment.

The fact that parents are given a copy of the Statement and the advice upon which the decisions recorded in the Statement were made marks a significant move towards giving parents rights in the decision-making process about their child's education. Parallels can be seen in the move towards giving social work clients access to their records, and a more hesitant move on the part of the medical profession to allow patients to have more control over their medical records. The Warnock Committee had recommended that parents should have access to the proposed 'Record of Needs' prepared for a child with special educational needs, but the 1981 Education Act goes beyond this in its insistence that the parents be given a copy, not only of the Statement, but also of the written advice given by professionals to the LEA.

The introduction of a formal system of appeals can also be seen as changing the parent–authority relationship. Clearly power still resides with the LEA, particularly when one considers the array of professional and technical resources the authority can command. The LEA also retains powers to select the local appeals committee members; unlike appeals committees set up under the 1980 Act, their decisions are not binding on the LEA.

The introduction of a semi-judicial appeals process into what is a very complex interaction may produce a variety of outcomes. The extent to which families following the litigation path lose track of their educational objectives is uncertain. In certain areas at least, it will be the articulate and the determined who benefit most from such a process; thus the distribution of special needs resources could be distorted and resources deployed, not according to need, but in response to facility with the appeals process. It is possible to conceive, therefore, of a reallocation of resources from the large group of children with clearly identified needs, but no articulate advocate, to the smaller group also with needs, but more importantly whose access to social, emotional, financial and educational resources is able to achieve that end.

However, the appeals procedure does provide an opportunity for LEA decisions to be challenged, and for the evidence upon which decisions are made to be reviewed in a public process.

Despite such a clear extension of the rights and powers of parents, there are a number of aspects where the legislation falls short of the principles identified in the Warnock Committee's model of the ideal of parity:

> . . . the relationship between parents and members of the different professions who may be helping them at any time. It is a partnership, and ideally an equal one.
> (Para. 9.6)

For example, parents whose children are over two years of age can achieve only a brief delay should they disagree with the decision to initiate the statutory assessment process, since they must comply with a notice from the LEA requiring their child's attendance for examination (Schedule 1, Part I(2)).

In the Act's statutory procedures, parents lose the rights of school choice which were conferred by the 1980 Education Act. Also absent, despite attempts by MPs to introduce amendments during the passage of the Bill through Parliament, is the Warnock Committee's concept of the 'named person' to whom parents could turn for help and possibly through whom parents could respond to the LEA.

However, the curtailment of parents' rights could be seen as a safeguard for the rights of children to have their needs met in the way seen as most beneficial by the professionals concerned with the child. The centrality of the concept of the rights of children to have their needs met has been safeguarded in the Act by placing restrictions on the parents' rights to equal partnership in the decision-making process. However, any explicit mention of a place for the child in the decision-making process can only be found in Circular 1/83:

> The feelings and perceptions of the child concerned should be taken into account, and the concept of partnership should wherever possible be extended to older children and young persons.
> (Para. 6)

This does not allocate any rights of decision-making to children within the statutory procedures, which may, in the long term, prove to be of the greatest significance.

Subtle aspects of professional and administrative process and procedures, such as the relationships with parents, do not, of course, lend themselves easily to legislative intervention, and later chapters examine the extent to which the Act does represent an optimal legal support for the model of parent participation which is encouraged in Circular 1/83.

### Concern for effectiveness in identifying, assessing and meeting special educational needs

Much that has already been described confirms the incorporation into the Act of principles concerned with the effective education of children with learning difficulties. The emphasis on the principle that educational aims are the same for all children, and on the compensatory nature of education, has already been identified. It is at the point where the education offered to a child within generally available resources does not appear to achieve these curricular aims that the provisions of the Act come into force to secure extra resources for that child.

In general terms, the Act reiterates the duties of the LEA in respect of the provision of special education included in the 1944 Act, bringing the terminology in line with other aspects of the legislation. Thus, section 8(2) of the 1944 Act is substituted by:

> (i) the need for securing that special educational provision is made for pupils who have special educational needs.
> (Section 2(1))

The Act clearly allocates to LEAs the responsibility for determining provision. The Statement, by its format and through its completion, identifies the legal responsibility unambiguously. Wedell has, for example, taken the view that:

. . . the main function of the Statement is to ensure that the extra provision is made for a child on appropriate grounds — in other words, that the decision is made with accountability both to the child and to the community which bears the cost of the additional provision. (Wedell, 1983)

An alternative view of this process might see those seeking appropriate provision for the child to be using a Statement as a battering ram to release resources from the LEA. Those viewing it in this way question the morality, as well as the justification, of risking damage to the already vulnerable child and family.

The statutory assessment procedures, therefore, are simply a mechanism whereby already identified needs can be formulated in a summative assessment and a case be made for the allocation of extra resources. The main responsibility for meeting the special educational needs of children and all that this entails, in terms of monitoring their progress through the curriculum, remains with the school. As already mentioned, the responsibility for special educational provision in the mainstream school is transferred directly from the 1944 Act. There is, for example, a new (implied) flexibility in the duty to keep special educational arrangments under review (Section 2(4)). In conformity with other intended extensions of their role, school governors are given the specific duties in this respect:

It shall be the duty of the governors, in the case of a county or voluntary school, and of the local educational authority by whom the school is maintained, in the case of a maintained nursery school:

(a)  to use their best endeavours, in exercising their functions in relation to the school, to secure that if any registered pupil has special educational needs the special educational provision that is required for him is made
(b)  to secure that, where the responsible person has been informed by the local education authority that a registered pupil has special educational needs, those needs are made known to all who are likely to teach him
(c)  to secure that the teachers in the school are aware of the importance of identifying, and providing for, those registered pupils who have special educational needs. (Section 2(5))

In subsection (5) (b) above 'responsible person' means:

(a)  in the case of a county or voluntary school, the head teacher or the appropriate governor (that is to say the chairman of the governors or, where the governors have designated another governor for the purpose of this paragraph, the other governor)
(b)  in the case of nursery school, the head teacher. (Section 2(6))

The extent to which school governors have the skills and knowledge to allow them to fulfil these responsibilities is somewhat problematic, and LEAs who place emphasis on this aspect of accountability clearly need to offer them both an induction to the Act and training in how to perform their duties.

In the case of children with Statements, another element is added to the responsibilities of those charged with their education. This is the duty to review their progress 'at least annually'. However, there is no mention of the need for staff development and training in order that greater effectiveness in identifying, assessing and meeting children's special needs may be achieved.

## SUMMARY AND CONCLUSION

This review of the Act, the Regulations and Circular 1/83 has sought to show the extent to which the new legal framework is founded upon that which preceded it. While both content and intention clearly owe much to the deliberations and recommendations of the Warnock Committee, there are also obvious aspects which reflect the way in which priorities and beliefs have changed with the passage of time. Some aspects of special education which received a less than full coverage in the Committee's report still await clarification. Notable among these must be the very limited concern for the nature of the educational experience gained by children with special educational needs, the curriculum they are offered and its relationship to that encountered by their peers. General principles here can do little to focus the debate.

Underlying much of what has been included is the fundamental dilemma of an unfunded Act which set out to bring about changes in policy, practices and attitudes. Some authorities consider the need for change to be minimal, while for others, almost certainly the LEAs with the lowest levels of investment in education, the Act demands fundamental changes. Although the government case for funding the Act by reallocating resources has been made loud and clear, thus far central government has appeared unable to accept that 'pump-priming' or short-term 'top-up funding' is frequently necessary to allow the release of resources tied up in an inappropriate way.

The Act, the Regulations and the Circulars do, to a circumscribed extent, reflect principles in the three areas identified. However, a number of issues remain unclear. It is difficult for many to accept that the wording of the Act deserves the benefit of the doubt. Just how far can the wording be justifiably interpreted in the context of current ideas about the principles? Therefore, from the point of view of those seeking to evaluate practice, it is necessary to consider both the principles and the wording that the Act provides. It is also necessary to consider the practices which emerge in the context of post-Act developments in thinking.

No one group has emerged in this discussion as having gained or lost overall. Clearly the balance of gain or loss is a fine one for children, parents, professionals and administrators. What has become apparent is that the new legal framework encourages, and to some extent requires, the adoption of a new set of relationships between all these parties. While administrators are necessarily those who will, at this early stage of implementation, be most aware of the consequences of change, professionals to some extent having the protection of established practice, it is probably the parents and the children who will be the last to become aware of their new opportunities.

## NOTES

(1)  Minister of State, Baroness Young's address to the White Paper Conference at the University of London, Institute of Education, 28 November 1980.

# Chapter 2

## Policy Implementation and Change

### INTRODUCTION

The previous chapter outlined the development of the changes in thinking about the identification, assessment and education of children with special needs which culminated in the passage of the 1981 Education Act. A distinction was also made between the mandatory requirements of the new legislation and the model of 'good practice' put forward in the circulars which described the way in which these requirements should be carried out. Circulars do not have the force of law, but they are one method by which the government indicates to local authorities how they are expected to implement legislation. In fact, the previous amendments to the procedures by which children with special educational needs were assessed were enunciated in a circular (Circular 2/75).

The 1981 Education Act and its associated Regulations and Circulars might, therefore, be seen as the expression of the government's policies regarding the identification and education of a certain section of the pupil population of England and Wales, namely those children with special educational needs. In this sense, the Act could be seen as a starting point for a series of changes and innovations in special education. In Chapter 1 we described the origins of these policies and the practices which could be expected to follow the implementation of the 1981 Education Act by local authorities. However, to see the Act as a starting point for a series of changes in professional and administrative behaviour assumes that policies are implemented in a coherent and linear fashion, and that directives from the top, in the form of legislation, will be followed by actions at the local level which will be in line with the new policy. From this perspective, the extent to which local activity deviates from what is expected as a result of the legislation will be seen as a failure of the policy.

In order to understand the complexities of the process, and to indicate the context within which we planned our research, in this chapter we analyse the process of policy formulation and implementation.

## THE PROCESS OF POLICY IMPLEMENTATION

Elmore (1980) has criticized the 'forward mapping' approach to policy implementation. He calls it 'the "noble lie" of conventional public administration and policy analysis' that policy makers exercise or ought to exercise direct control over the policy implementation process. Instead he offers the concept of 'backward mapping' which starts at the last possible stage, at the level where administrative decisions influence individual behaviour. It is at this level where many, often conflicting, policies interact with individual perceptions, needs and pressures that the impact of policy making will be clearly visible.

Weatherley (1979) recognized this phenomenon in his study of the implementation of special education legislation in the state of Massachusetts, USA. He described the way in which the professionals and administrators in the school systems implementing the new law developed coping mechanisms to manage the demands of their jobs which 'in the aggregate constrain and distort the implementation of special education reform'. He called such personnel 'street level bureaucrats', since it was they, rather than the law-makers, who made policy as it was experienced by the consumers of the legislation, i.e. parents and children.

Implementation, then, is not a simple linear process whereby policy statements, in the form of legislation, emanate from the top of a hierarchical system and are implemented in a systematic way by organizations set up for the purpose. This is partly due to the fact that all policies are, in the end, implemented by individuals and those individuals will interpret them in their own idiosyncratic ways. This is particularly the case in the public services, such as education, health and social services, which are staffed by a number of professional groups each with its own priorities and conceptualizations of client needs.

Such organizations have been termed 'loosely-coupled' (Corwin, 1981). He defines a loosely-coupled organization as one 'characterized by a high degree of autonomy between its interdependent parts and isolation between strata'. It follows that policy implemented within such a structure will be subject to a high degree of 'slippage' because such organizations are, by their nature, difficult to standardize. The high degree of independence and autonomy of those working in the welfare services is ideologically underpinned by the notions of professional competence and judgement. Within such a context, there is the possibility of a wide range of responses to any change in policy.

This is also reflected in the nature of the relationship between central and local government in England and Wales which, until recently, allowed a great deal of autonomy to local authorities to pursue those policies which they felt were most suited to the needs and wishes of local communities. For this reason, as Welton (1983) has observed, British educational legislation tends to be broadly enabling rather than minutely prescriptive.

It would be misleading, therefore, to see the legislation as the starting point for a series of changes in local authority administrative and professional practice. Such changes were taking place before the legislation was enacted and were part of the evolving view of special needs which brought about the change in the law. At the same time, many other policy changes not directly connected to special education, or even to education, were influencing the way in which local authorities could respond to the 1981

Act. These included central government economic policies, MSC initiatives, moves towards 'care in the community' by health and social services and, more recently, the signalling by the government of certain priorities by the allocation of the Education Support Grant.

Thus, implementation of legislation is a very complex process. It involves the consideration, not only of the legislation itself, but of other government policies which will impinge upon the work of implementers. It also involves consideration of the structure of the implementing organizations, their relationships with one another and with central government. It is not a hierarchical process in which orders from the top are filtered down through the organization until they reach the level of the individual worker. Barrett and Hill (1984) describe policy implementation as:

> essentially a political process characterized by negotiation, bargaining and compromise between those groups seeking to influence (or change) the actions of others, and those upon whom influence is being brought to bear.

The present study and a previous project which was undertaken by Wedell, Welton and Vorhaus (Wedell *et al.*, 1981) indicate that very similar processes of negotiation, bargaining and compromise occur during the period leading to the design of new legislation, its passage through Parliament and its implementation. A new law may be seen as just one significant event in the general process of service and policy development. Barrett and Hill (op. cit.) add that:

> the political processes by which policy is mediated, negotiated and modified during its formulation and legitimation do not stop when initial policy decisions have been made: but continue to influence policy through the behaviour of those responsible for its implementation and those affected by policy seeking to protect or enhance their own interests.

As a starting point for understanding the development and implementation of policy, Barrett and Hill (op. cit.) suggest a study of the *policy process*, or as Hill (1981) describes it, '*a policy-implementation chain*' within which issues are increasingly 'solidified', but where there is no clear cut-off point when policy-making stops and implementation begins.

From the point of view of central government, all that occurs after the legislation has been passed and the Regulations and Circulars have been published appears to be implementation. From the perspective of the local agencies, they will still be in the stage of formulating policy as they consider how best to adapt and develop their existing arrangements to fit in with the demands of the new legislation. During this local policy-making process they will be negotiating not only with each other, but also with central government in an attempt to gain clarification about whether their proposed new procedures are in line with the requirements of the legislation.

Whitmore (1984) has developed a model for the study of policy formulation and implementation which acknowledges this complexity and the inherently interactive and dynamic nature of the relationship between policy-makers and implementers. He has distinguished six aspects of the process:

1.   The core dimension — in this case the problem of the education of children with special needs.
2.   The policy paradigm, i.e. the way in which the problem and solutions to the problem are defined.

3. The monitoring framework — the 'policy' in the sense of Acts of Parliament, Regulations and Circulars.
4. Inter-organizational resource dependencies, i.e. the statutory relationship between central and local government, relationships between education, health and social services departments, funding, personnel.
5. Administrative structures and processes — the channels through which policies are formulated and carried out.
6. The professional interface with the consumer, i.e. how the policy is carried out at the fieldworker/client level.

This is a much more complex formulation than the simple linear model of policy implementation discussed at the beginning of this chapter. It describes a fluid situation in which each of the aspects of policy implementation identified in the model can interact at any stage in the process.

For example, the policy paradigm, or the prevailing view of the best way to meet the needs of children with learning difficulties, is evolving constantly as knowledge increases about the learning process and about the capacity of people with handicapping conditions to benefit from different sorts of education. It is also influenced by current thinking about 'rights' and equal opportunities for all citizens.

The Act itself may be subject to amendments, or new circulars of guidance may be issued following feedback on the experience of those in local authorities who are involved in implementation or as a result of a successful challenge to the legislation in the courts.

Changes in the relationships, both formal and informal, of those organizations concerned in co-ordinating activities providing for children with special needs may occur. For example, the inclusion of education authorities in the joint funding arrangements with health authorities may lead the way for new developments in provision for such children.

Significant changes in the working practices and relationships of the professionals and administrators in health, education and social services may occur as a result of new administrative procedures set up for the assessment of children with special needs.

Most significantly, there may be a shift in the relationship between parents and professionals and administrators in the three services who will be constrained to interact in a different way following the new rights given to parents by the legislation.

## THE APPROACH ADOPTED FOR THE PROJECT

The focus of our work has been on policy formulation and implementation at the local level following the passage of the legislation. We recognize the variety of actors and agencies involved and the link between them — their value systems, interests, relative autonomies and power bases; and the interactions taking place between them, in particular their negotiating and bargaining behaviour. To understand what happened in local authorities and health authorities after the legislation was passed, it is useful to view them from four distinct, but related perspectives:

1. *as formal organizations* set up for specific purposes, accountable to the local community and to central government

2.   *as decision-making bodies* at all levels, from street level to political level, involving the exercise of political, administrative and professional power and authority
3.   *as collections of interest groups*: political, professional, administrative and consumer
4.   *as collections of individuals* seeking to fulfil their own as well as client needs.

There are, of course, distinct differences between the formal structures of education, health and social services at both the operational and political levels. Education and social services are both part of the local authority which is an elected body, directly accountable through the ballot box to the local community. The district health authorities are not directly elected bodies, though local authority nominees have a role to play within them. District health authorities are funded from central government through the regional health authorities and do not rely on contributions from local taxes for their income. These differences in structure, funding and accountability must be taken into account when assessing the impact of the 1981 Education Act on local policy-making.

Decision-making within these organizations, at any level, is the exercise of power and authority. Decisions can be political (that is about policies and the allocation of resources) or they can be professional (for example, about identifying and meeting the educational needs of a particular child). In practice, such a clear-cut distinction is rare, since the 1981 Education Act specifically links special educational needs to what is generally available within local authorities. This means that professional decisions about children's needs almost inevitably have resource implications.

Local education authorities and other public service agencies, such as social services departments and district health authorities, are staffed by a number of different professional groups, each with its own professional ideology and definition of client needs. Wilding (1982) maintains that professionals in the education, health and social services have played a crucial role in shaping the organizations within which they work and in maintaining their influence, sometimes at the expense of the needs of the consumer. He argues that these groups tend to compete for power and influence within the authority and seek to maintain their identity and autonomy within the hierarchy. Other groups, such as political and pressure groups, will also seek to influence the service provided by the local authorities. It is useful to distinguish the various types of groups in terms of their interests and definitions of the situation which structure their perception of their role within the system. It is also useful to look at them in terms of their power and status within the system.

In the last analysis, the actions of organizations are the actions of those individuals who work within them, the 'street level bureaucrats' to use Weatherley's (op. cit.) term. The focus of our research has been on individuals and their reactions to and perceptions of the changes brought about by the legislation. Those deliverers of a service who interact with parents and children directly will be the final arbiters of the policies generated by central government through the legislation. The actions of individuals will be constrained by their knowledge of and attitude towards the new working requirements, by their position within the organization, by their professional orientation and personal preferences. This individual focus appears to be especially relevant with respect to the 'consumers' of special education: parents and children. The 1981 Education Act has given parents a new role in the decision-making process concerning their children. It is from their experiences and those of their children that we can evaluate whether the intentions of the policy-makers in central government and in the local authorities have been achieved.

Thus there are two strands to our approach to the study of the implementation of the 1981 Education Act. One is the acknowledgement that policy implementation is not a simple linear process from the 'top down', but rather a complex series of negotiations between different interests, which precede and follow legislation. The second is that the organizations involved cannot be studied adequately from one perspective alone, whether it be a 'systems' or an individual perspective. One factor which will influence individual behaviour is the structure of the organization, but there will be other influences, including professional and personal interests.

## THE CONCEPTUAL FRAMEWORK

The conceptual framework which we adopted to guide our data collection and analysis is the synthesis of these two separate strands. It involved the study of:

1. *DES/DHSS policy formulation and dissemination with respect to children with special educational needs*: consultations prior to the framing of the Act; dissemination activities.
2. *Local and health authority organizational factors relevant to implementation*: central–local relations; inter-service relations; political complexion and style; geographical, historical and social context; administrative structure; pattern of provision.
3. *Policy formulation at the local level*: policy-making procedures; involvement of other services; involvement of other groups, including parents; response to the 1981 Act by elected members, service managers, professionals and 'consumers'; resource allocation policies; the influence of interest groups; individual actions at all levels which may have influenced policy-making.
4. *Policy and practice at the local level* (as an outcome of the interaction of 1, 2 and 3 above) regarding: special educational needs; special educational provision; allocation of resources; the statutory assessment; staff roles; parental involvement; working relationships between professionals.
5. *LEA, DHA, and SSD activities designed to facilitate implementation*: dissemination of information to all those involved; preparations and training/retraining of staff; resource allocation/reallocation.
6. *Implementation of procedures for identification, assessment and allocation of provision*.
7. *Evaluations of policies, procedures and provision by* 'consumers', professionals, administrators and politicians.

Using this framework, we have attempted to make sense of behaviour which occurred over a period of time, but did not occur in a single process of cause and effect, namely:

– the development in ideas and practices which led to changes in the dominant policy paradigm for special education.
– the consultations (bargains and negotiations) between the government and professional, local authority and parent/voluntary associations.

- the process of the design and the passage of the Act and associated Regulations and Circulars of Guidance through the civil service and Parliament.
- the dissemination of government information and the negotiated interpretation of the legislation with local authorities, professional associations and parent/voluntary groups.
- the way in which the local education authorities, social services departments and district health authorities and the professionals working within them responded to the new legislative framework.
- the dissemination by the local authority, of information about its response to the new legislation, to all those involved, professionals, administrators and parents.
- any adaptations in local education authority, social services and district health authority arrangements and procedures in response to the new framework of inter-organizational co-operation.
- any adaptations of working styles and communication processes between professionals in the three services concerned with co-operating to provide a service for children with special needs.
- changes in policies regarding the allocation of resources to special education and the arrangements for the provision of special education within local authorities.
- the working practices of 'street level' administrators and professionals interacting with children and parents.
- the way in which children and parents experience the special education service.

Table 2.1 illustrates the dimensions and stages involved as new policies emerge and are clarified, modified and implemented. What emerges from this process is a 'progressive focusing', whereby the issues involved in the implementation of policy become increasingly solidified (to use Hill's term), but where the distinction between policy-making and implementation remains unclear. The focus of activity moves back and forth from central to local government throughout the process and the interests involved change according to the focus. The evolution of policy places increasing constraints upon the actions of individuals as the policy becomes more clearly articulated. These constraints are not only those of the legislation, but also of the nature of the organizations involved, and the pressure of other policies, such as those from the Treasury.

## SUMMARY AND CONCLUSION

The changes in the policies and practices of local education authorities and health authorities with regard to children with special educational needs will have been brought about by a complex interaction of factors. The 1981 Education Act will have been only one factor, albeit a major and catalytic one. The directions of change will not necessarily have been those envisaged by the legislators and their advisers, but as stressed earlier in this chapter, such adaptations of policy in the local context are to be expected given the loosely-coupled relationships between central and local government and between the local implementing agencies. These policy adaptations should not be viewed as 'failures', but as part of the political process of negotiation which takes place as local authorities endeavour to reconcile competing policy objectives at a time of limited resources and growing expectations.

**Table 2.1.** *Progressive focusing and the development of special education policy — 1970 to 1985*

| Stages of policy development | Focus of activity | Interests involved | Constraints on action | Action |
|---|---|---|---|---|
| Changes in policy paradigm | Local | Professionals, administrators, voluntary organizations | Present practice, ideas and provision | Warnock Committee set up |
| Consultation pre-legislation | Local to central | Professionals, administrators, voluntary organizations, DES, DHSS | Present practice, LEA structures, professionals | Warnock Report; White Paper |
| Enactment of legislation | Central | Civil service, government, pressure groups | Other government policies, LEA/SSD/DHA structures, Warnock Report/ 'public' opinion | 1981 Act |
| Interpretation | Central to local | Ministers, civil servants, administrators, professionals | Legislation, other government policies, LEA/DHA/SSD structures and funding; professional and public opinion | Draft Circulars and Regulations |
| Presentation of statutory instruments, circulars of guidance | Central to local | DES, DHSS, LEA/SSD/DHA | Legislation, other government policies, local government practice and funding; professional and public opinion | Issue Regulations and Circulars |
| Dissemination and interpretation, negotiation | Central and local | DES/HMI/DHSS, LEA/DHA/SSD, voluntary organizations | 1981 Act, Regulations Circulars; Local government structures professional and public opinion | Seminars, conferences, letters, media coverage |
| LEA/SSD/DHA policy appraisal and formulation | Local | LEA/SSD/DHA, professions, 'members', voluntary organizations | Legislation, local service-structures, professions, public opinion | Policy adaptation |
| Local authority dissemination, interpretation, negotiation | Local | 'Members', 'officers', professions, voluntary organizations, schools, parents | Legislation, local service structures and policies | Directives, INSET |
| Structural and procedural change | Local | 'Officers', professions, clients | Legislation, other government policies | Adaptation of structures procedures |
| Professional/ client interface | 'Street' | Professionals/ administrators, clients | Legislation/local, procedures/resources | Service delivery |

# Chapter 3

# Research Methodology

## INTRODUCTION

The aims of the research project are set out in the previous chapters. The conceptual framework for the investigation of policy and practice has been presented in Chapter 2. This chapter outlines the research methodology selected to carry out our investigation.

## PRELIMINARY INVESTIGATIONS

A pilot study of the way in which the special education procedures of Circular 2/75 were implemented, based at the University of London Institute of Education, had already been carried out by Wedell *et al.* (1981). This study consisted of an investigation of the application of the Circular 2/75 procedures in four LEAs. Data were collected by means of semi-structured interviews with professional and administrative personnel and individual parents. Group interviews with parents were also carried out.

This pilot study, and other relevant reports on policy and practice concerning provision for children and young people with special educational needs, formed the starting point of the project reported in this book.

Preliminary investigations for the project included:

(a)  An examination of documentary material produced by LEAs in response to the enactment of the 1981 Act. All LEAs were sent letters requesting any documentation they had produced, which set out their policies and recommendations for practice. Such documents consisted mainly of dissemination materials to professionals, administrators and parents as detailed in Chapter 6, Table 6.16.

(b)  Group and individual interviews and discussions with personnel from the education, health and social services in 37 LEA areas. These focused on the way in which the Act was being implemented and the procedures and practices adopted. Individual and group discussions were also held with parents and members of voluntary organizations. The aim of these interviews and discussions was to establish a basis for our main investigation.

## RESEARCH RESOURCES

The project was one of three funded as part of the DES programme of research relating to the 1981 Act. In addition, an ESRC-funded project, 'Screening and Special Educational Provision in Schools', was carried out at the University of London Institute of Education during a period overlapping with the three DES-funded projects. Meetings between the researchers involved in the four projects were arranged at intervals, to consider the subject matter of the projects and particularly the research methodologies used. The discussions also helped to define the scope of the individual projects, with the aim of avoiding overlap and ensuring complementarity of content.

In addition to the Joint Steering Committee for the three DES-funded projects, an Advisory Committee was set up for the present project. The members of this group were selected to represent the main service and professional groupings involved in the implementation of the Act. The members of both the Steering and Advisory Groups are set out in Appendix A.

The Advisory Committee met at intervals during the project to consider the outcome of the various stages of work, and also received preliminary reports for comment.

A conference of invited individuals from the main service and professional groupings, and of researchers in the field of policy implementation, was held at the end of the preliminary investigation phase of the project. The main purpose of this conference was to consider the conceptual framework for the study of policy-making, implementation and provision which had been built up during this phase, as the basis for the main investigation. This is the framework outlined in Chapter 2.

## THE MAIN INVESTIGATION

The main investigation consisted of detailed studies of policy and practice in five LEAs, a questionnaire survey of administrative practice in all English LEAs, and limited investigations on particular topics: the implementation of the Act in sparsely populated areas; the role of administrators in carrying out the 1981 Education Act; and the role of voluntary agencies.

In addition to these investigations, the research included:

– an analysis of Form SEN 2 returns to the DES
– analysis of publicly available statistics on relevant local authority and other services
– study of findings from relevant surveys carried out by other agencies
– a survey of literature appearing before and during the research period.

### The detailed studies of LEAs

The decision to devote a major part of the project to a detailed study of a small number of LEAs derives from the research aim to investigate the *process* of the implementation of the Act. The duration of the project was too short to collect data for a longitudinal study and it was decided to adopt a qualitative, 'case study' approach for this aspect of the project, focusing on the nature of the interactions which determined the implementation of the Act. In each area, semi-structured interviews were conducted with professionals and administrators in the local education and social services departments and health authorities concerned with implementing the Act. Individual and group interviews were also conducted with parents and members of voluntary organizations. The enquiries were carried out by means of semi-structured interviews, the content of which was based on the conceptual framework of implementation built up in the preliminary phase of the project. In addition, published documents and other documentary information sources made available to us were studied. These came from a wide variety of sources, from committee minutes to Statements provided for individual children.

### Sample of LEAs used for detailed study

The number of LEAs sampled was determined by the time available and by the combination of variables hypothesized as likely to be relevant to the process of implementation. It was decided that it would be possible to make sufficiently detailed enquiries in five LEAs. Relevant variables chosen to select the areas included:

–  geographical location within England (e.g. north/south)
–  urban/rural differences
–  social, economic, political, cultural and demographic factors
–  differences in patterns of provision for children with special educational needs
–  coincidence of LEA and DHA area boundaries ('coterminosity').

Since these variables had also been used to determine the selection of the four LEAs investigated in the pilot study, it was decided to include these and one additional area. The five authorities were distributed across the North-West, the Midlands, the South-East and South of England:

*A-shire*: a rural shire with widely scattered, but intensively populated suburban areas. Size and population scatter had led to the adoption of a regionally based administrative structure. Although it was centrally co-ordinated in a number of ways, day-to-day responsibility for special needs administration was added to the existing workload of regional administrators. Regional variation in provision still reflected developments which had taken place prior to local government reorganization. Children with Statements were placed in special schools.

*B-Borough*: a multi-ethnic outer London Borough, geographically close-knit and centrally administered. Response to the 1981 Act had been developed by a multi-professional group after the Act was placed upon the statute book and the authority did not implement it for 16 months. This late implementation resulted in a less clear-cut picture of practice emerging. While there were children with Statements in mainstream schools, the majority were placed in the many special schools and units.

*C-Shire*: a rural shire with small town and semi-industrialized county-town centres of population. Although post titles appeared to indicate a regional administrative structure, all administrators were centrally based. Various aspects of special needs administration were split between 16 officers. Few children with special needs moved on from the local 'informal' procedures to the 'formal' procedures introduced by the Act. A variety of approaches to integration was apparent.

*D-Shire*: an industrialized county authority with a widespread suburban and semi-rural distribution of population. It had a unitary administration and the special needs service was organized by a small, powerful central group. Children with special needs received the 'protection of a Statement' wherever their needs were met.

*E-Borough*: a small, but populous metropolitan borough, coterminous with its district health authority, displaying many of the socio-economic features associated with the decline of the textile industry upon which its nineteenth-century growth was founded: unemployment, poor housing stock, derelict industrial sites and concentrations of ethnic minority populations. It had a special needs service administered by a small, tight-knit central group working closely with other officers and elected members. While children with a Statement were most commonly placed in special schools, there were some mainstream placements. However, in a low-spending authority this did not necessarily provide the child with extra resources.

In each of the authorities, detailed enquiry into practice was focused on districts and aspects of the services which they identified as characteristic of their style of policy and practice.

## Interviews

In each LEA, interviews were carried out with relevant individuals from the education, health and social services, as well as with parents. Social services staff were chosen from the authorities' social services department, and in the larger local authorities, local staff were chosen from the sub-areas studied within the LEAs. National Health Service staff were similarly chosen from DHAs serving the relevant LEA areas.

The range of individuals and the numbers interviewed are listed below:

| *Those contributing information in the detailed studies* | |
| --- | --- |
| Parents (including individuals and groups) | 66 |
| Elected members | 4 |
| Education service | |
| administrative staff (including senior, assistant and administrative officers) | 24 |
| educational psychology staff (including chief/principal educational psychologists) | 15 |
| advisory staff (including inspectors/advisers and advisory teachers) | 26 |
| careers staff (specialist advisers) | 5 |
| education welfare staff (EWOs/ESWs) | 10 |
| staff in schools/units (including headteachers and teachers in mainstream, specialist and special school provision) | 70 |
| Health | |
| administrative staff | 11 |
| clinical staff (including consultants, CMOs, nurses, health visitors and speech therapists and physiotherapists) | 21 |
| Social Services | |
| administrative staff | 5 |
| fieldwork social workers | 9 |

In each LEA, a random sample of ordinary and special schools was selected. In ordinary schools, the sample of teachers always included the teachers with responsibility for children with special educational needs.

Parents selected for interview were from among those whose children had most recently been given a Statement, irrespective of the nature of their child's special need. Parents were invited to meet a member of the project team, and approximately half of those invited accepted. Three group discussions were also held with parents. One group consisted of parents whose children attended a primary school for children with moderate learning difficulties and another of parents whose children were receiving help from a special needs advisory teacher, but had not been given Statements. The third group of parents were members of a voluntary support group.

*Detailed studies report*

A draft composite report on the five studies was drawn up based on the interviews and other information collected. The content of the report covered the topics outlined in the conceptual framework. This report was passed to the LEAs concerned for comment. Each LEA was given an opportunity to discuss the draft report and three of the five LEAs took part. The aim of this report-back to the LEAs was to check for factual accuracy and correctness of interpretation about their respective policies and practices.

A final report incorporating the findings from the five individual LEAs was then produced. The implications of these findings were reviewed at two workshops attended by a national sample of individuals from the education, health and social services, and from voluntary agencies. A further breadth of view was obtained by inviting professionals and administrators, particularly from those LEA areas which had not been included in the five detailed studies, or the preliminary stage of the project.

*Cross referencing of research findings*

It is apparent from the above that the qualitative findings from the detailed studies of implementation in the five LEA areas were subjected to a sequence of consistency and accuracy checks. Within each detailed study, the reports and comments from the individual respondents could be compared in the context of the framework of the semi-structured interviews. The formulations based on these were then checked, through the feedback to the LEA areas. The main issues arising from the composite report on the five LEA areas were then checked at the two national study workshops. The study of implementation processes did not, of course, lead inevitably to single generalizations. More frequently, a variety of contrasting processes emerged. In validating the reported findings it was, therefore, necessary to check the ranges of variation and the salience of individual items of information, as well as the justification of any inferences leading to generalizations. Where relevant, the findings from the questionnaire survey also provided a framework of reference.

The composite report on the five detailed study areas is presented in a paper available for reference from the library of the University of London Institute of Education (1).

**The survey of all English LEAs**

It had originally been intended to carry out a questionnaire survey of policy and practice in English LEAs at the start and end of the project. The initial survey had to be withdrawn from the research proposal as a result of a DES request to reduce total cost.

As a result, the purpose of the final survey was limited to obtaining an overview of practice, which would also provide a normative context in which the findings of the five detailed studies could be considered. When the time came to carry out the survey, it was apparent that pressures on staff within the education, health and social services were such that it would not be sensible to make any significant demands on the time of the officers asked to complete the questionnaires. It was decided, therefore, to limit the coverage of the questionnaire content to information about the changes in policy and provision following the starting date for implementing the Act, and about the implementation of the statutory procedures.

The questionnaires were addressed to the special needs service administrators in each LEA, and covered the following main sections:

(a)   Changes in special educational needs staffing since 1 April 1983.
(b)   Funding for special educational needs since 1 April 1983.
(c)   Changes in special educational needs provision since 1 April 1983:
    (a)   for children aged 0–2 years.
    (b)   for children aged 2–5 years.
    (c)   for primary and middle school aged children.
    (d)   for secondary school aged children.
(d)   Training to implement the 1981 Act.
(e)   Statement procedures under the 1981 Act.
(f)   Annual Review.
(g)   Mandatory 13+ reassessment.
(h)   Ceasing to maintain a Statement.
(i)   Local appeals.

The response format was mainly multiple choice, but opportunities for open-ended comment were also provided.

Questionnaires were returned by 79 per cent of the LEAs, and there did not appear to be any significant selective features characterizing the non-responding LEAs, except that those metropolitan authorities in the Midlands were slightly underrepresented.

A detailed analysis of the questionnaire survey data is provided in a paper available for reference from the library of the University of London Institute of Education (1). Survey data are included where relevant in this report.

**The collection of relevant documents produced by LEAs**

As noted above, during the autumn of 1983, all LEAs were contacted with a request for information about documents produced in relation to the Act. LEAs were also asked to provide copies of the following types of document:

(a)    public documents intended to provide information about the Act, and/or advice about implementation
(b)    'internal' memoranda as for (a)
(c)    documents concerned specifically to facilitate the implementation of some particular aspect of the statutory procedures.

A request was also made for LEAs to provide details about the dissemination of information on the Act through in-service training.

Responses were received from 74 per cent of LEAs. A similar request was sent out to all English LEAs in the autumn of 1985, so that new documents or alterations to previous documents could be noted. On this occasion, 68 per cent of LEAs responded.

The contents of the documents received were used as a further basis of information for the study, for example, to provide indications about the way in which the principles of the Act were interpreted (Chapter 5).

## THE FOCUSED STUDIES

Discussions with the DES members of the Steering Committee in the later stages of the study indicated that it would be helpful to attempt to obtain information more specifically focused on certain topics. Since time was limited, three topics were selected:

(i)    the role of administrators concerned with implementing the Act in education, health and social services
(ii)    the involvement of voluntary organizations as a consequence of the Act
(iii)    the implications for service delivery of implementing the Act in sparsely populated areas.

### The administrators' role

Information on the administrators' role was obtained by means of six focused discussions conducted with small, interdisciplinary groups of administrators from the education, health and social services, and educational psychologists responsible for school psychological services drawn from all parts of the country. The discussions covered the role of the administrator, the nature of within and inter-service collaboration, links with the voluntary sector, the implementation of the statutory procedures in the Act and contacts with parents.

The analysis of these discussions was derived from tape recordings (taken with the permission of the groups) and from notes made of the discussions by volunteer students from the University of London Institute of Education Special Needs Masters' course. At the conclusion of each set of discussions, a summary of the main points arising was agreed with the participants, including suggestions for modifications of the legislation.

### The involvement of voluntary organizations

This focused study was carried out through semi-structured interviews held with the education officers, or their equivalent, of eight voluntary organizations. The interviews covered the organizations' involvement in informing, supporting and counselling the parents of children with special educational needs; the provision of services for children; and the organizations' activities in lobbying and influencing public opinion.

### Service delivery in sparsely populated areas

Pairs of adjacent rural LEAs were selected to take into account different population sizes and distributions, and different approaches to the administration and delivery of services. Group discussions were held with those concerned in administering education, health and social services involved in the 1981 Act. The discussions were held in locations convenient to those from each pair of LEAs. Topics of particular relevance to service provision in rural areas were covered, and these included: local patterns of special educational needs; regional planning; inter-service collaboration; the provision of services to small or scattered populations and in-service training of teachers in such areas; mainstream placement of children with special needs; and the administration and monitoring of the delivery of special needs services.

The discussions were tape-recorded, with the permission of participants, and the draft report covering all the discussions was circulated for comment.

### COMMENTS ON THE METHODOLOGY AND DATA USED

The data on statementing rates from the Form SEN 2 returns for 1985 had to be treated with caution, since LEAs apparently interpreted the DES requests for information in different ways. Some LEAs, for instance, included children with 'provisional' Statements, while some did not. Where the returns indicated such differences, the project team attempted to obtain the correct data from the LEAs by direct communication.

In this chapter we have described the variety of methods used to collect information in this project, ranging from content analysis of documentation, interviews, group discussions with fixed agenda, to a multiple-choice questionnaire survey. We have indicated the procedures used to check the validity of the findings. The qualitative methods enabled us to investigate the processes of implementation, and from this has emerged an indication of the variety of ways in which implementation has occurred. The quantitative data from the questionnaire survey have provided us with a context for evaluating the range of variation found.

### NOTES

(1) A full list of the data papers supporting this study may be found in Appendix B.

# Chapter 4

# The Context of Implementation

## INTRODUCTION

Chapter 2 described the way in which we view the process of policy implementation and change. We emphasized the importance of including some consideration of the social, economic and political climate into which the Act was delivered in April 1983. This includes:

1.  The structural relationships of health, education and social service departments at both the central and local levels, and the relationship of the statutory to the voluntary sector.
2.  The relationship between central and local government, especially with respect to spending policies.
3.  The local context. The great variability between local areas in their social, demographic and economic environments has led to the development of differing policies and types of provision in local authorities and health authorities and these must be taken into account when assessing any authority's response to the legislation.

This chapter will attempt to describe these contextual factors which may have influenced the way in which local authorities set about implementing the provisions of the 1981 Education Act.

The first section will examine the relationships between health, education and social services departments at the local level, and the way in which these have been determined by the development of these services as separate elements of the Welfare State. The role of the voluntary organizations will also be considered. It will include some analysis of the part played by central government in formulating policies about the organization and funding of these services, and of the role of professionals in influencing government policies. The second section will examine the relationship between central and local government, and the way in which government policies have influenced the reactions of local authorities and health authorities to the demands of the 1981 Education Act. The final section will draw on research findings to examine in detail the ways in which individual circumstances have led to variations in the way in which the legislation has been implemented in local authorities and health authorities throughout England.

## RELATIONSHIPS BETWEEN HEALTH, EDUCATION AND SOCIAL SERVICES

The responsibility for the identification, assessment and provision for children with special needs has historically been a subject for co-operation between the health and education authorities. The emphasis on their respective roles has changed over time, and the 1981 Act clearly gave the primary responsibility to the education authorities. The Act also gave social services departments a statutory role within the new procedures, which they had not had before. The Act has redefined the roles and responsibilities of the statutory agencies concerned with children with special needs and has also given a role to the voluntary agencies.

The statutory assessment procedures require the co-operation of professionals in health, education and, to a more limited extent, social services to produce a multiprofessional assessment of children with special needs. They also require co-operation on the part of the three services to ensure that children receive provision to meet those needs.

Many writers have pointed out the difficulties involved in inter-agency and interprofessional co-operation of this kind. Welton (1983) sees one of the major obstacles to co-ordinated planning and delivery of welfare services of any kind as the:

> inherited division of welfare which (1) establishes and maintains the statutory and administrative framework and (2) creates, justifies and protects competing definitions of professional processes and client needs.

The two main agencies involved with implementing the 1981 Act, the education and health services, have completely separate resourcing, accountability and organizational structures. As noted in Chapter 2, the health service is organized on a regional and district basis. Regional and district health authorities are not directly elected bodies and are therefore shielded, to a certain extent, from the local political process. That is to say, they are not directly answerable to the local electorate for their policies and allocation of resources. Community Health Councils play some part in giving the local community a voice in decision-making, but they have no real power (Charnley, 1983). There are local authority elected members on the district health authorities, but they are in a minority.

### Health service policy-making

Health service policy-making has become increasingly centralized in recent years, especially as far as spending and manpower limits have been concerned. The thrust of government policy, which has been to reallocate resources out of London and the South-East into the provinces, has led to difficulties for some health authorities in responding quickly to pressures generated as a result of the 1981 Education Act. Most of the resources reallocated in this way have been used to improve hospital services, whereas the extra burdens imposed by the 1981 Education Act have fallen on the community health services. These burdens include a greater amount of clerical work resulting from participation in the new procedures; greater demand for speech therapy, as the importance of language development for other forms of learning becomes more widely recognized; and the greater demands made on the time of therapists, who are being asked to deliver a service to children integrated in mainstream schools, rather than placed together in one special school. Pressures on the community health services have also been increased by the policy of 'care in the community' which has meant that many patients in long-stay hospitals have been discharged and are now the responsibility of the community services.

In addition to changes in the funding levels for different regions of the National Health Service, there have also been two major reorganizations of the NHS in recent years. The first took place in 1974, and seems to be part of a tendency which Self (1972) has termed 'the Balkanisation of public programmes and policies'. In other words, professional groups such as doctors, nurses, therapists and teachers tend now to be employed by a single organization, irrespective of where their services are to be delivered. Prior to this reorganization, the community health services, of which the school health service is a part, was a local authority responsibility, and school doctors, nurses and speech therapists were employees of the local authority. Upon reorganization, this service was brought under the control of the health authorities.

To facilitate co-operation between health, social services and education departments, an attempt was made to preserve co-terminosity between health and local authorities, by the creation of area health authorities in which community health services were located. This tier of the health service was disbanded in 1982, following the recommendations of the Griffiths Report. The Report's implementation reorganized the management structure within the NHS in line with the government's policy of introducing the management practices of 'big business' into the organization of the public services.

The fact that this major upheaval was taking place at the same time as the Act was being implemented indicates the problems that education and health faced in trying to achieve some measure of co-ordination of approach. For example, the post of Specialist in Community Medicine (Child Health) had been an area health authority responsibility. Many of the new district health authorities had not appointed anyone in this co-ordinating role in 1983, resulting in difficulties for education authorities who wanted to negotiate with health authorities to arrange new procedures in line with the 1981 Act.

These difficulties were greatest for those local education authorities which had to co-ordinate with several district health authorities. In one of our detailed study areas, the LEA was dealing with six DHAs, one of which was not even in the same regional health authority. It was also dealing with 29 social services departments. As the medical administrator put it:

> There are so many different practices that proper co-ordination is impossible. How do you co-ordinate six district health authorities, eight education areas and 29 social services areas? It's not a nightmare, but there are different practices and we have to be flexible.

## The relationship between education authorities and social services departments

The relationship between education authorities and social services departments is scarcely less problematic than that between education and health. Although education and social services are both the responsibility of the local authority, and therefore the opportunities for co-ordinated planning and shared responsibility are arguably greater, it is competition for resources rather than co-operation which frequently appears to characterize the relationship between these two departments. This may be a result of the government's policies concerning local authority spending. In a period of 'no growth', competition for resources within local authorities becomes more intense. Social services departments, like education authorities, have had new demands placed upon them, but have been given very few extra resources to implement them. For example, the 'care in the community' policy, mentioned above, has meant that social services departments have had to take on responsibility for many of those discharged from long-stay hospitals. Social services themselves have a policy of attempting to keep children within their local community, rather than sending them into residential placements. All of these changes place extra demands on social services for resources.

Social services seem to have been marginalized, or to have marginalized themselves, as far as the 1981 Act is concerned. There does not appear to be a very clear idea within social services departments of the role they should play in the assessment procedures, and there have been differences in perceptions of responsibility for financing resources for children with special needs. There appears to have been little direction from management to field social workers about their new responsibilities under the Act. These uncertainties about role are illustrated by responses of social services departments to invitations to a series of conferences held by the project to discuss the effects of the Act on the work of administrators in the education, health and social services. A total of 120 social services departments were approached, but only four social workers attended the conferences. They reported that there had been some confusion in their departments about who should come to the conferences. This finding is confirmed by some recent research in two local authorities (Wingham, 1986). Like the health authorities, social services departments have other priorities and demands upon their time and resources, and unless education authorities have taken positive steps to involve them in policy-making and planning for implementation, special needs issues are unlikely to be given due weight.

This is unfortunate, since, as the Fish Committee reported (ILEA, 1985), when there is good co-operation between departments to provide a co-ordinated service, the benefits more than repay the extra effort involved. Those authorities in our study who have set up procedures for co-ordinated planning for health, education and social services provision for children with special needs have been able to avoid duplication of effort and make the most efficient use of limited resources. The different organizational bases of health and local authorities can cause difficulties in co-ordination, but, as we describe in Chapter 7, our research evidence has shown that these difficulties can be overcome.

**Establishing a common approach**

Within each service, there were also difficulties of establishing a common approach among professionals dealing with the same children. This was especially noticeable in the district health authorities, where there were debates about the way in which the advice for Statements about particular children from, for example, speech therapists or school nurses should be co-ordinated and forwarded to the education authority. There was a feeling among these health professionals that a designated medical officer did not necessarily have the expertise to summarize advice from other professionals, and that such advice should be sent verbatim to the education authority or, if a summary was required, it should be provided by the advising professional.

This illustrates the point that the interests of professionals have been a very powerful factor in influencing the way in which the 1981 Act has been implemented. Professionalism has been defined as 'a strategy of job control in which one of the main prizes is the right to define and determine situations in a given sphere of work.' (Whittington, 1983). It seems that such expectations by professionals of the right to autonomy in decision-making about clients' needs can cause difficulties when there is a necessity to re-negotiate the boundaries of professionals' responsibility. For example, one of the recurring complaints of doctors involved with parents of children who were being assessed was that they were no longer 'allowed' to mention to parents their views about which particular school placements were appropriate for their child. They saw this as cutting across their freedom to carry out their responsibilities in the way that they saw as most appropriate for their 'patients'.

An extreme example of the difficulties posed by the power of professionals acting as an interest group was seen in one of our detailed study authorities, where implementation of the Act was delayed by 16 months, apparently because the first attempt to get a co-ordinated approach between education, health and social services became so acrimonious that it was felt necessary to postpone any future attempt until certain key figures had retired. These initial difficulties led to the setting up of a two-tiered system for negotiation between the three services. It comprised a 'board' which decided on matters of policy and played a monitoring role once the new procedures were under way and a 'panel' which was a multi-disciplinary group which considered each child's case at the draft Statement stage.

Such co-ordinating groups may be easier to arrange in small metropolitan authorities, but the need for some forum for discussion appears to be even more acute in larger authorities with problems of lack of co-terminosity. However, the setting up of these groups is inhibited by the greater travelling distances involved and the greater number of people who would have to be included in such a forum. One of our detailed study authorities, a large shire county, had set up a multi-service working party to consider the implications of the Act for the three services, but the six health authorities involved were represented by only one person, and feedback from the group to all professional groups in the health authorities was difficult to achieve. Once the new procedures for assessment were judged to be working effectively, the working party was wound up and did not perform a monitoring or further strategic planning role.

The absolute necessity of, and the difficulties inherent in, monitoring demands for services in a multi-disciplinary way is highlighted by the concept of shared responsibility enshrined in the 1981 Act.

### The role of the voluntary organizations

The voluntary organizations have played a vital role in shaping policy for children with special needs and in making provision for particular sorts of needs. They were actively involved in lobbying Parliament to set up a committee of enquiry into special education, and made a substantial contribution of evidence to the Warnock Comittee.

The 1981 Act gives a role to voluntary organizations as sources of advice and support for parents of children with special needs. When health authorities identify a child with special needs, they are obliged to give parents the name of a voluntary organization, if they feel it would be appropriate.

The government has emphasized its commitment to extending the role of the voluntary sector in making provision of welfare services and indeed, in some local authorities, voluntary organizations do make a significant contribution to providing services for children with special needs, especially the under-fives.

It was surprising, therefore, that we did not find much evidence of involvement of voluntary organizations in the discussions surrounding the implementation of the 1981 Education Act. Only 17 per cent of authorities responding to our questionnaire had any form of regular planning meeting with voluntary organizations and only 11 per cent provided training for voluntary organizations about their new policies for special education following the Act. Many voluntary organizations appear to be being forced into conflict situations with local authorities because they are contacted by parents at too late a stage in the statutory assessment procedures, when relationships between parents and the LEA have become strained. The dual functions of voluntary organizations, as pressure groups and providers of services, put them in a difficult position, as far as negotiating with local authorities is concerned. These issues of the involvement of voluntary organizations with LEAs and parents of children with special educational needs will be covered in more detail in the following chapters.

## THE RELATIONSHIP BETWEEN CENTRAL AND LOCAL GOVERNMENT

In recent years, there has been a tendency for central government to play a greater role in controlling the activities of local government. This stems from the perception of central government that the control of local authority spending is a crucial element in its attempts to curb inflation. The Layfield Committee (1976) was told that local authority expenditure was the 'Achilles heel' of public expenditure control, since local decisions about the level of expenditure on public services, such as education and housing, effectively controlled the amount of grant given to local authorities by central government. Governments since the 1970s have adopted several strategies to control local government spending and to exert some influence on the direction of that spending. The government's view was that, as far as education was concerned, falling numbers of pupils would leave some room for the reallocation of resources within the education system. Commenting on the government's decision not to provide extra resources to help with the implementation of the 1981 Education Act, Baroness Young said:

> I readily acknowledge that additional resources for certain aspects of special education would help in achieving some of the Warnock Committee's goals, but I must say that I am a little horrified by the way in which a few people, who should know better, have read the White Paper and said that nothing can be changed without extra resources. This is simply not true. There is scope for some redeployment of existing resources within the new statutory framework and over the next five years the total school population will fall dramatically. This demographic trend must be reflected in the number of children with

special educational needs. I suggest to you, that those who say that now is not the time to make changes run the risk that change will never be made.
(Address to the White Paper Conference held at London University Institute of Education, 28 November 1980)

This indicates that the government's view was that the number of children with special educational needs was likely to be a static proportion of the total school population, and that significant changes in the way in which children's needs were to be assessed and provided for could be achieved within the local authorities' existing budgets. Our research indicates that this was a mistaken view. The relative definition of special educational needs has led to changes in perceptions of those working in local authorities about the numbers of children with special needs who require extra resources. Recent figures published by the Department of Education and Science (*Education*, 1985) indicate that, though the Circular 8/81 suggested that the proportion of children requiring Statements would be roughly the same as those ascertained under the SE procedures (i.e. 1.8 per cent), some authorities are giving Statements to up to 5 per cent of their school population. The High Court decision in the case of *R.* v. *Hampshire ex parte J.*, which was interpreted by some commentators to indicate that any extra resource given to a child with learning difficulties should be protected by a Statement, may lead to a far greater proportion of children being given Statements than was originally envisaged.

Even if this change in the numbers of children given Statements does not take place, the implementation of the 1981 Act would appear to have resource implications. Responses to our questionnaire of English local authorities show that in 72 per cent of those authorities that responded the proportion of the total education budget directed to special educational needs had increased. Gross spending on special educational needs had increased in 91 per cent of the authorities, and in 53 per cent of cases the spending had exceeded the rate of inflation. Where staff had been increased, it appears that most of these increases were *not* achieved by redeploying staff from other areas of work. It is not surprising, therefore, that we came across a marked degree of dissension in local authorities from the government's view that the Act did not have resource implications, and considerable resentment that extra resources were not available from central government to help implementation.

This perhaps illustrates the point made in Chapter 2, that local authorities are subject to a number of potentially conflicting policy requirements from central government. The way in which local authorities can adapt and reconcile these objectives will depend upon several factors, including their own local circumstances, the way in which they decide to allocate resources, and the history of previous policies with regard to the education of children with special educational needs.


## THE LOCAL SITUATION

Local authorities and health authorities in different areas of the country differ widely in the way in which they organize their services. This is a historical phenomenon related to the way in which these services developed, and attempts to standardize services have been strongly resisted by both professionals and local politicians (Wilding, 1982; Levitt, 1976).

Legislation enacted at the national level may be subjected to widely differing interpretations and styles of implementation at the local level. The education system of England and Wales has developed in such a way that local education authorities have evolved systems of education to suit local needs and requirements; there is no uniform national pattern of educational provision. This applies equally to both special education and mainstream education.

Educational legislation reflects this diversity, in that it tends to be enabling rather than minutely prescriptive. It encourages the local authorities to implement the government's perception of 'good practice', while recognizing that local authorities will adapt the legislation to fit into the framework of their existing arrangements.

The 1981 Education Act is an acknowledgement of the fact that local authorities differ in their arrangements for educational provision. It embodies a 'relative' definition of special educational needs and special educational provision:

> . . . a child has special educational needs if he has a learning difficulty which calls for special educational provision to be made for him.
>
> Special educational provision means provision which is additional to, or otherwise different from the educational provision made generally for children of his age in schools maintained by the local education authority concerned.
> (Section 1, Education Act 1981)

This relates special educational provision to what is *generally available* in schools maintained by the local authority, so what is 'special' in one LEA might not necessarily be so in another. Even the clear recommendation for integration — that, subject to parental agreement, children with special educational needs should be educated in ordinary schools — has three provisos. These are that it is compatible with:

(a)   his receiving the special educational provision he requires
(b)   the provision of efficient education for the children with whom he will be educated
(c)   the efficient use of resources.

These provisos allow local authorities to take local factors into account when deciding whether or not a child with special educational needs should be educated in the mainstream.

The variation in provision by local authorities is due to a number of factors, including population density, economic resources, political ideology, cultural and ethnic mix, interest group influence and the past history of provision.

## Patterns of provision and administration

It was a surprise to hear that, in many areas, the pattern of provision within authorities was still very much influenced by the situation which obtained *before* local government reorganization in 1974. Local education authorities which combined in 1974 still kept their old patterns of provision. For example, in the three shire counties in which we undertook detailed studies, certain areas had many more special schools than other areas. This was due to the fact that large urban concentrations which had been separate education authorities pre-1974 had been absorbed into rural shires which had very little provision. This meant that in some counties there were different patterns of provision within one LEA. In such situations, a co-ordinated approach to implementation appeared to be very difficult to achieve.

This lack of standardization of approach led to anomalies. For example, at one end of one county, it was claimed that 5 per cent of the school population were being given Statements to entitle them to remedial provision which otherwise would be lacking within mainstream school, whereas the overall figure for the county was nearer 2 per cent. This suggests that at the other, more urbanized end of the county, where more schools had remedial departments, fewer than 2 per cent of children were being given Statements. Such discrepancies of approach within authorities, especially rural authorities, were noted in our special study of eight sparsely populated local authorities. These areas were also characterized by low levels of provision for children with special educational needs, low spending on education and difficulties of communication and co-ordination, both within the education authority and between education and health and social services.

It seemed that changes were difficult to achieve within such organizations, not least because there was very little 'political' pressure for change. The dispersed population made it difficult for pressure groups to arise or to take collective action. The relationship between officers and elected members was characterized by a clear split between their functions. Elected members provided very broad guidelines and left the details of policy to officers.

The difference in approach between these rural authorities and the smaller, urban authorities is quite marked. In metropolitan authorities there appears to be a much greater involvement of members in the detail of policy-making. There are frequent meetings between officers and members to discuss policy, and the members take an almost 'professional' role in policy-making. In one of our detailed study areas, a metropolitan borough, members and officers were meeting on a weekly basis to discuss all aspects of education policy, and the council's cycle of meetings was monthly. By contrast, in some rural areas, council meetings took place every three months, and reports from officers to members were made formally, in writing. This professionalization of the role of members in urban authorities was noted by Houlihan (1984) in his study of the regional offices of the Department of the Environment.

In such circumstances, it could be expected that urban authorities would be likely to make adaptations to their arrangements and services more rapidly than rural authorities. However, there were other factors which made rapid change within authorities difficult, including the attitudes of professionals within services, which, as noted earlier, could have an inhibiting effect.

There was also the fact that many urban authorities had invested heavily in separate special schools and units at a time when this had been thought to be the best way to meet children's special educational needs. There was rapid expansion in the building of special schools in the late 1960s and early 1970s, which resulted in a great increase in the numbers of children being educated in segregated provision. This trend has been documented by Swann (1985). Although the thrust of professional and pressure group opinion was turning away from the idea that children with special needs should be educated separately, the momentum of the building programme was such that more children were being sent to segregated schools. Thus the anomaly arose, noted by Swann, of a change of philosophy which indicated that more children with special needs should receive their education in mainstream schools, coinciding with a trend of placement which was segregating more children, in particular those with moderate learning difficulties and behaviour problems.

For the reasons outlined above, any changes in policies concerning the provision of special education which have involved a major shift of resources from special to mainstream schools will have necessitated local authorities undertaking complicated negotiations with the interests involved: parents, teachers, professionals and pressure groups. We have not studied such major changes in detail, but have noted that a number of authorities have conducted major reviews of their approach to special education following the 1981 Act. The most notable of these has been the ILEA's review conducted by a committee chaired by John Fish. The setting up of this Committee illustrates the point that those authorities with a great range of separate special educational provision face a daunting task in attempting to reallocate those resources. Those working in the administration of special education report that their time is so taken up with administering the new procedures that it is very difficult to make time for evaluation of the service as a whole or to undertake a large-scale review of special education provision.

## Funding education services

The responses to our questionnaire survey indicate that there have been some changes in the balance of priorities for special education funding. Some 29 per cent of authorities reported a decrease in the proportion of the special education budget going to special schools; 34 per cent reported a decrease in spending on provision in other LEAs; and 42 per cent reported a decrease in spending on provision in independent schools. Between 60 and 65 per cent of authorities reported an increase in funding for the schools psychological service, peripatetic advisory/support teachers and welfare assistants or non-teaching auxiliaries. There were also increases in the proportion of funding going to special units (49 per cent of authorities), mainstream-based SEN teachers (37 per cent of authorities), special school teachers providing mainstream support (37 per cent of authorities), special needs advisers (25 per cent of authorities) and special education-al provision in FE colleges (51 per cent of authorities). We did not ask authorities to quantify the extent of these changes, so have no way of assessing their significance. They do, however, indicate a trend away from putting resources into separate special schools.

Increases in funding seem to have been more common in the shire rather than metropolitan authorities. This may be a reflection of the fact that, on the whole, they were lower spenders on education; thus, in order to meet the demands of the new legislation, they were obliged to increase their resourcing of special education to a greater extent than the more urban authorities who had been higher spenders on education services in the past. For example, in the past, shire counties have been net consumers of special education, spending more on sending children into schools in other LEAs than they received in revenue from other authorities using their provision. They also tended to make greater use of non-LEA provision than metropolitan authorities. Many shire authorities have now adopted an 'Out to In' policy, either explicitly or implicitly, where they have attempted to reduce the amount of funding on 'out-county' placements. Two of the three shire counties that we studied in detail had such a policy, which was being pursued with some vigour in one of them, to the extent that all out-county placements had to be approved by the Chief Education Officer. Money saved in this way was to be used to improve special education facilities within the authority. Urban authorities did not have this leeway to make savings and transfer funds, since, on the whole, they were net providers of special education.

The differences between shire counties and metropolitan boroughs in their social, economic, cultural and ethnic environments are reflected in the size of their special needs population and in their responses to meeting those needs. This was recognized in the report of the Warnock Committee, which noted that, in any area, the proportion of children with special needs would be a result of the interaction between children and their environment and the provision available to meet those needs. There appears to be a very complex relationship between needs, provision and the proportion of children being given Statements within LEAs. There is no direct relationship between the amount of provision available in local authorities and the proportion of children given Statements. The example given earlier, of 5 per cent of children in one area of an authority being given Statements to entitle them to provision which, in other areas, would ordinarily be available in mainstream schools, has been reflected elsewhere, but there are examples of an opposite trend. In one of our detailed study areas, the education authority had adopted a policy of 'minimal statementing', which meant that only children receiving education in separate special schools would receive Statements. The authority had very few separate special schools. Therefore, a large proportion of children with special needs were being educated in mainstream schools, with extra resources, such as non-teaching assistants, but these children did not have Statements.

Using the Warnock Report's formulation that learning difficulties arise because children's needs are not being met, it might be expected that authorities with a comparatively large amount of provision would issue Statements for fewer children. However, some authorities have taken the view that Statements are necessary to protect resources, and therefore they provide Statements for all children who receive extra resources of any sort. For example, one of our detailed study authorities had decided to give Statements to children placed in tutorial units and those receiving help from the peripatetic remedial service, even though these were excluded by Circular 8/81.

These are policy decisions based on political, as well as educational, considerations. Some authorities wishing to curb expenditure will limit the cases to which Statements apply. Others, wishing to maintain or expand expenditure, will issue Statements for children in order to gain extra resources, or to protect resources from expenditure cuts. Respondents to our questionnaire noted that special education budgets had, on the whole, been protected at a time when other education spending had been cut.

**Funding health services**

Such pressures are found in the health authorities also. We have already noted the changes in health authority organization and the attempts to reallocate resources within the health service. Another crucial factor in influencing the extent to which health and education are able to meet special educational needs is the level of funding of district health authorities and the apportionment of funds between acute services and community health.

Health authorities vary considerably in the levels of funding they receive and in the services they provide. These variations have been documented in the Black Report (Townsend and Davidson, 1982), which showed that a disproportionate amount of health resources were concentrated in London and the home counties to the detriment of the provinces. Several areas were singled out as targets for extra resourcing since their standardized death rates were exceptionally high. One of our detailed study authorities came into this category, but in the five years since publication of the Report there had been very little change, and research by Holland *et al.* (1983) indicated that the problems for these deprived areas were still acute. These problems apply to both community health services and hospital-based services. The two are in competition for resources from the regional health authorities, and decisions to spend money on a new hospital, for example, can mean that there is very little room for growth in the community health services. This leads to difficulties for both education and health services when trying to implement the 1981 Education Act. The Statement of special educational needs should have appended to it the advice from medical, educational and psychological professionals. It should also state what provision is to be made to meet the needs that have been identified. Local education and health authorities run into difficulties when the health authority does not have the resources to provide what may be clearly indicated in the advice.

One example of the problems caused by lack of resources in a health authority is the shortage of speech therapy time, which has been reported by many LEAs. If speech therapy is clearly specified on the Statement and is not made available by the health authority, then the education authority is obliged to provide it. This leads to difficulties, because speech therapists are usually employed by the health service and not directly by LEAs. We have come across an example of an education authority which had built a new speech and language unit, but could not open it because there were no speech therapists available from the health authority to work in it. Thus, policy-making for inter-service collaboration is very much dependent upon the abilities of health and education authorities to respond to the demands made upon their services by local circumstances.

## The administration of special education

Another local factor which determined the way in which local education authorities responded to the 1981 Act was the different administrative structures which they had adopted. There is some debate in education circles about whether a segregated special needs administration reinforces the separateness of special education and works against the integration principles enshrined in the Act. Responses to our questionnaire indicate that 45 per cent of special education officers had other responsibilities besides special education attached to their work. However, the range of other responsibilities was not necessarily within mainstream education, often concerning services such as education welfare, transport, home tuition, grants, ethnic minority children and travellers' children. In only 10 per cent of the authorities responding to the questionnaire did the administration of special education appear to be integrated with that of mainstream education.

In the detailed study authorities, we had examples of a range of different administrative responses. In one authority, the administration of special needs was dispersed among 16 different officers, whose duties included area and age group responsibilities as well as advisory and clerical functions. First attempts at implementation, using this model, had been problematic. Different and conflicting sets of instructions about the procedures had been issued and then withdrawn. Officers found that more and more of their time was taken up with special, rather than mainstream, education.

In another authority, day-to-day responsibility for special and ordinary schools was in the hands of area officers, who also had the capability to 'vire' funds from 'out-county' placements to support children in mainstream education. Administrative responses to the 1981 Education Act were co-ordinated by close monitoring of what was happening by a working party set up for the purpose. Regular meetings between area officers were arranged to ensure consistency of response throughout the authority. Nevertheless, it was felt that there were significant differences between areas in the way that they approached the implementation of the Act.

We have already described the 'board' and 'panel' system adopted by one authority. This mechanism, originally designed to defuse professional conflicts, enabled the education department to keep special education as a high priority. Additionally, a rotation of senior education officers every four years meant that those working within special education did not become separate from other education administration.

An example of a separate, high-status group involved in the administration of special education was found in another of our authorities. This group consisted of a principal education officer, his assistant education officer, three advisers and the principal educational psychologist, plus a number of clerical assistants. The group worked extremely closely: the three advisers and the assistant education officer shared one office, and the other officers were located close by, so communication was easy and frequent. The administration of the statutory assessment procedures was in the process of being computerized, and the impression given was of a highly organized and tightly-knit administrative team. This, of course, begs the question of whether such a system tends to reinforce the separateness of special educational services and whether special efforts are needed to ensure communication across boundaries.

In another of our detailed study authorities, the administration of special needs was in the hands of a team of three: the adviser who counted special needs as just one of 11 areas of curriculum responsibility (including English), the senior educational psychologist (there was no principal) and an assistant education officer. The AEO was responsible for special schools, for the special needs departments in mainstream schools and for the peripatetic remedial service. There was close co-operation and involvement between these three in all aspects of implementation, but education spending in this authority was among the lowest in the country, and so it was inevitable that difficulties and delays would be experienced in the implementation of the procedures.

In the small sample of five authorities which we studied in detail, we found a wide range of response to the 1981 Education Act. In our contacts with other authorities, this impression of variety is confirmed. The aim of the 1981 Act was to bring some measure of consistency to the service provided by local authorities. Baroness Young, Minister of State at the time of the passage of the bill, described it as:

> Government policy intended to achieve a new legal framework . . . to cause everyone with responsibility for children with special educational needs to look again at their practices

. . . and to be a starting point for all LEAs to match the practice of the best.

This chapter has described some of the difficulties inherent in achieving this aim.

## SUMMARY AND CONCLUSION

Special education assessment and provision involves a minimum of three separate organizations: the local education authority, the district health authority and the social services department, not counting the contribution of voluntary organizations. Each has its own history, paradigms, policies, structures and procedures. District health authorities are funded directly by central government and have no direct accountability to the public through the local ballot. Local education authorities and social services departments, on the other hand, are parts of the same local authority competing for revenue which is, in part, raised locally from an electorate to whom it is directly accountable for spending and service provision. District health authorities and local authorities are not necessarily geographically co-terminous, a fact which complicates co-ordination of practice and provision. These different structures of accountability, funding and administration cause difficulty in co-ordinating the system of assessment and provision for children with special educational needs envisaged in the Act.

The structural constraints outlined above provide the context within which negotiation between local implementers takes place in order to provide a framework for policy delivery, including the co-ordination of action across welfare sectors to provide education for children with special needs. The distinction between policy and action becomes blurred here, since it is often unclear to what extent policies evolve through an incremental adaptation of existing practices or as a considered response to the new legislation. Our study suggests a range of behaviours from rationally considered change, through incremental reactive coping, to rejecting or ignoring the demands for change.

Attempts by administrators to alter the framework and to impose new working practices upon personnel both in education and in other agencies are part of the process of adaptation where local arrangements are not in accord with the requirements of the new legislation. Within the education system there may be a tension between administrators and professionals and between different professional groups as roles are redefined and new areas of responsibility delineated. From the point of view of central government, all this activity may be seen as 'implementation', but from the local authority perspective, such activities represent another level of policy-making and the outcomes, in terms of matching service delivery to government policy, are problematic.

LEAs have adopted several approaches to policy-making for the 1981 Act. These may be described as:

(i) *Collaborative* — that is, a genuine multi-disciplinary discussion between health, education and social services personnel to achieve a consensus of approach and to co-ordinate structure.

(ii) *Consultative* — where, for example, the LEA has invited representatives of services on to a working party which is, in essence, a forum for education to promote its proposals for a new approach.

(iii) *Coercive* — where the LEA decides the new procedures it requires and then informs the health authority and social services department of its requirements.

The effectiveness of different methods of policy-making for implementing the 1981 Act depends as much upon previous relationships and policies as on subsequent policy-making activities. A collaborative approach in one LEA might have been designed to defuse previous conflicts, while a coercive approach in another may be the result of reliance on informal 'old boy' networks of communication. However, given the complicated nature of the relationships between education, health and social services described above, it would appear necessary to provide some regular forum for debate and discussion of mutual problems and interests. From our study, it appeared that it was in authorities where no such forum was available that the highest levels of conflict and confusion existed. Ultimately, all such co-operation will depend on the behaviour of individuals. If personnel in the three services see each other as the 'opposition' (as was described to us in one of our multi-disciplinary research exercises), then satisfactory collaboration will be difficult to achieve.

Whatever the conflicts of interest and differences in working patterns between the agencies involved with children with special needs, in the end, a service of some kind is delivered. Whittington (1983) has called this 'the negotiation of daily practice'. Service delivery agents — doctors, teachers, psychologists, social workers — have to evolve some kind of working relationship in order to fulfil their obligations to their clients. They will evolve ways of working with each other which will be constrained by the 1981 Act and by the policies that particular authorities have evolved to implement it. However, they will have a fair degree of discretion about the way in which they approach their task. The 'street level bureaucrats', to use Weatherley's (1979) term, adjust their response in line with their perceptions of clients' needs and their knowledge of resources available to meet those needs.

Given the financial, structural and ideological constraints built into policy-making which we have described above, the adaptation of policy by individual workers at 'street level' may be tolerated because it plays an important role in reconciling conflicting policies. For instance, a shortage of resources will mean that decisions about limiting access to resources will have to be taken, if the over-arching government policy of restricting local government spending is not to be breached. Decisions on resource allocation taken at the level of field workers are hidden or unofficial. They may be used to mask the fact that an authority is not able to make adequate provision to meet children's needs. Circular 1/83 demands that assessment and Statement of need for individual children is to be made without reference to resource implications. However, writers of Statements may, to some extent, be tempted to frame them to coincide with the resources available, either from health, education or social services. Professionals may tailor their advice to coincide with what they know is available. In a period of no-growth this would not be surprising. It has been suggested to us by professionals and administrators that it is foolish, even cruel, to raise parents' expectations of resources for their children, when such resources are unlikely to be available.

When assessing the impact of the 1981 Act on policy and provision for special needs in local authorities, a large number of factors have to be borne in mind. The circumstances of local authorities and their relationships with one another and with the government are crucial issues, as are the government's other policies concerning allocation of resources. Individual actions and decisions on the part of field workers will be the visible result of those policies and will form the experience of the individual parents and children of the working of the new legislation. Our research has indicated that these experiences vary widely from authority to authority, and within authorities, depending on the level and pattern of resources available to meet needs. The core of this report is an attempt to describe the range of policies within local authorities and the perceptions of those involved of the effects of those policies.

# Chapter 5

# Ideas of Special Education

## INTRODUCTION

In Chapter 1, the way in which the new legislation incorporates a number of principles, promotes a number of new concepts and produces new nuances in the interpretation of others was considered. As was further discussed in Chapter 2, the Act, in common with all other British educational legislation, depends for its intended outcomes on negotiation to achieve agreement with and a common understanding of its purpose.

This chapter will explore local authorities' understanding and interpretation of the Act and the extent to which the new and altered concepts have affected practice. In it, we will consider the incorporation of the new thinking in the crucial areas of:

(a)  the definition of special educational needs
(b)  the rights of children with special needs and those of their parents
(c)  the effectiveness of identification, assessment and approaches to meeting the requirements of those with special educational needs.

The chapter draws upon interview material, questionnaire data and the documentary material produced by LEAs.

## THE NEW DEFINITION OF SPECIAL EDUCATIONAL NEEDS

### Acceptance of the definition

The new definition of special educational needs was described at one meeting of administrators held as part of our research as 'the heart of the matter'. In its elimination of categories of handicap, its relativity, and its consequent openness to local interpretation, it is the most radical aspect of the legislation. In its definition of what constitutes special educational need, its attribution of what causes need, in the way in which such a need should be identified and responded to and in the nature of resulting provision, it marks a clear break with what went before. It is hardly possible that such a marked change from previous legislation could fail to have a major impact on local authorities, no matter how far they had kept pace with current changes in special educational thinking, nor how great an impact this thinking had on local policy and practice.

It was abundantly clear from all aspects of our research that while the new relativity did permit local authorities, in health as well as education, to respond pragmatically to the local availability of resources, particularly to local pattern of special needs services both institutional and individual, the very tractability of the concept also posed considerable problems. It was also apparent that the DES was not immune to these problems.

The Warnock Committee recognized some of the likely consequences of eliminating a category-based system, particularly for the administration of services. One issue singled out for attention was the issue of how to facilitate the collecting of statistical information without the structure of categories to frame local responses. The form and content of Form 7 M (the major annual DES statistical return) was, for example, the subject of criticism given to the team on a number of occasions. Quite apart from the 'what goes where' difficulties which the form gave rise to (and these were sufficient to cast doubts upon the value of much of the information made available by this means), within the detailed study authorities and in discussions and interviews with administrators, the format was widely seen as a confirmation of a perceived continued administrative necessity for categorization. The adopted framework, which requires schools to list pupils with special educational needs in terms of their disabilities, as well as the type of curriculum requirements they have, certainly gave rise to the possible emergence of a new set of categories.

Difficulties in coming to terms with the relative nature of the concept of need was also made evident in other ways. Some local authorities recorded that they had been condemned by HMI for the unevenness in their response to the Act. In A-Shire, one of the detailed study authorities, at least some of this 'unevenness' was a reflection of local differences in provision. Similarly, variability in other LEAs appeared to result not necessarily from any misinterpretation of the legislation, or of the principles inherent in it, but more from the difficulties of co-ordinating services for children living near the boundaries of all types of authority or in areas with a particularly low population density relative to other parts of the LEA.

It was possible to find a clear recognition of the new definition in LEA documents. Indeed, some repeated clearly the injunctions in the legislation:

> The emphasis is now upon deciding the special educational needs of an individual child and the appropriate provision for these needs without labelling them. It has long been recognized that the category labels inadequately described children's needs.
> (School Guidance Document, D-Shire)

An unequivocal rejection of labelling was not, however, universal and some professionals and administrators found obvious difficulty in accepting that labelling was an issue worthy of concern. A doctor, speaking about the Act at a DHSS training day, asserted the importance of reintroducing categories of handicap as the major requirement for determining the delivery of services and received a ripple of applause from some sections of the audience. For others, the matter was not clear cut. Thus, a special needs adviser from one authority reported, at one stage in an interview, that 'We no longer use categories'. At a later stage this was modified to, 'We have changed the terminology'.

There were also examples of the continued systematic employment of categories:

| *Former category* | *New description* |
|---|---|
| Blind/partially sighted | Visually impaired |
| Deaf/partially hearing | Hearing impaired |
| ESN (M) | Moderate learning difficulties |
| ESN (S) | Severe learning difficulties |
| Epileptic | Epileptic |
| Maladjusted | Emotional/behavioural problems |
| Physically handicapped | Physically handicapped |
| Speech defect | Language impairment |

(Report to A-Shire Schools Sub-Committee, September 1983)

Such new sets of descriptors were also in evidence in other documents such as LEA internal lists of schools.

We suggest that abandoning categories, while thoroughly laudable both in intention and many outcomes, also emphasized a number of crucial issues for those involved in special needs services. Included among these were the issues of forward planning, routine administration and the nature of service which can be offered. Such issues will be explored in Chapter 9.

## The use made of the definition of special educational needs

The detailed study authorities varied in their public use of the relative definition of special educational needs. C-Shire circulated to all its schools the definitions provided in the 1981 Education Act handbook published by the Advisory Centre for Education (Newell, 1983). In the other LEAs, guidance on the meaning of 'special educational needs' and what constituted the interrelated concept of a 'learning difficulty' largely repeated the form of words provided by Section 1 of the Act. While in one LEA there was little variation in the wording of documents produced for the different audiences (parents, teachers, heads of schools and professionals in other services), another LEA offered parents a document that differed greatly from that produced for professionals. In that LEA, parents 'of children who may require a full assessment and Statement of educational needs' were given the description:

Special needs may be of the following kinds: needs for

1.  Special equipment — physical aids, hearing aids, visual aids, etc.
2.  Special facilities and services — for medical examination, medicine, etc.
3.  Special educational resources — specialist teaching for various difficulties, etc.
4.  Other special resources — social work, occupational therapy, physiotherapy, etc.
5.  Special physical environment — facilities for pupils who are unable to walk, attention to lighting, etc.
6.  Special school organization and attendance — day attendance, weekly boarding, termly boarding, etc.
7.  Special transport — taxi or special bus service, etc.

[Notes on 1981 Act for Parents of children who may have Special Educational Needs: A-Shire]

This explanation of the nature of special educational needs is taken from the description of types of provision in Annexe 1 of Circular 1/83.

This scheme focused upon a catalogue of provision, rather than providing a specification of the needs which the provision was intended to meet. However, such a catalogue provided a helpful analysis for parents. Thus the scheme did not represent a local reconceptualization, but indicated the extent of the 'local resources' which could be called upon by the administrator when seeking to make provision for a child's special educational needs.

Interwoven with the ideas of what constituted the nature of 'special educational needs' and 'learning difficulty' was the issue of the degree of need as indicated by the size of the population with which the Act was concerned. The division between the Act's formal procedures for the few and the exemplars of good practice for a much wider population in the Circular produced a clouding of the issue for some professionals and administrators. Thus, the 1.8 per cent of the population identified by the Warnock Committee as requiring 'recording' and subsequently equated with the ascertained population in Circular 8/81 was seen by some LEA administrators as an unrealistic estimate of those who required special educational provision as defined in the Act. Administrators in some LEAs spoke of 5 per cent as their target population for Statements, while in others it was considered that 18 per cent could require a Statement. Such figures contrasted greatly with a detailed study authority which included much of their range of special needs support services as part of their 'generally made' provision and pursued a policy of 'minimal Statementing'.

These differences did not, therefore, reflect a misunderstanding of the concept of special educational needs in the Act, but were due more to a disagreement over what constituted the range of educational provision 'generally provided in schools, within the area of the local authority concerned' (Section 1(2) of the Act). Further confusion was introduced in this area by the judgement of Mr Justice Taylor in the case of *R.* v. *Hampshire ex parte J.* which, to some, appeared to indicate the necessity of producing a Statement in response to the existence of learning difficulty of any degree, no matter what the extent of the available compensatory resources or the local provision to meet the difficulty. As no appeal was made in that case, the legal interpretation of the Act will require further clarification, though it has been the cause of a restatement of the DES position.

The distinction between those children whose special educational needs were the subject of a Statement and other children showed the extent of the differences between local education authorities. The most recent publicly available information indicated that while 11 per cent of authorities were providing statements for 2.1 per cent or more of their school population (one shire providing the extreme at 2.7 per cent), 21 per cent were including 1.3 per cent or less in this group (see Table 5.1), confirming clear differences between authorities. There were also some shire–metropolitan differences, with twice as many metropolitan authorities appearing in the group providing Statements for the smallest fraction of children (1.3 per cent or less of the school population). There are a number of possible explanations for the apparent discrepancy between the figures and the claims, recorded earlier, of a need to provide Statements for 18 per cent of the population. These include:

(i)   localized variation in proportions of children being given Statements within LEAs

(ii)   accelerating use of Statements as the procedures become more commonplace
(iii)  a hitherto unidentified discrepancy between the number of children for whom statutory assessment was initiated and the number subsequently provided with a Statement
(iv)   differences in local interpretations of the nature of special educational need.

The relative nature of the definition introduced by the Act was also, in the view of both professionals and administrators, at least partly to blame for competing definitions of special educational need used by different professional groups, parents, voluntary organizations and pressure groups and local politicians. It was also seen as being at least partly responsible for the application of different criteria from LEA to LEA, as well as for those differences apparent between different areas within LEAs. The perceived vagueness of the definition did not in any way relieve the tension between the need to allocate resources to facilities catering for groups of children with similar special educational needs and the allocation of resources to meet the individual needs of children. This was despite the fact that the Act was designed to overcome this dilemma.

## THE RIGHTS OF CHILDREN WITH SPECIAL EDUCATIONAL NEEDS AND THOSE OF THEIR PARENTS

### The right to mainstream placement

The distinction in the Act between children for whom a Statement is considered necessary and children whose special educational needs do not require a local authority to provide that protection has been seen by some as perpetuating segregation. Others have suggested that it throws the whole concept of a continuum of special educational needs, which is a necessary adjunct to the idea of relativity, into doubt. Within the context of our research, the extent to which local authorities used the maintenance of a Statement to delineate a boundary between separate educational 'sectors', mainstream and special, can be used as an indicator of the extent of local acceptance of the rights of children with special educational needs.

In Chapter 1 we suggested that the Act does not contain a strong statement of the principles of children's rights. It does, however, offer conditional rights to placement in mainstream schools. In seeking to evaluate the extent to which the limited acceptance even of principles is reflected in thinking at local level, 'integration' becomes a crucial indicator.

During the preliminary investigations for this research, it was apparent that professionals and administrators in education, health and social services held a wide range of views concerning what constituted 'integration'. It also became clear that diametrically opposed opinions of, and attitudes towards, integration could easily be found within a local authority, and were also demonstrable among those working in different authorities. Few appeared to see integration as a 'right'.

It was not a surprise, therefore, to find that within four of the detailed study authorities, the provision of a Statement appeared to coincide with a decision to transfer a child to special school. The fifth authority had adopted a policy of 'minimal statementing', which, in effect, achieved a similar outcome.

**Table 5.1.**   *The proportion of the school population with a Statement of educational need/placed in special school by type of authority*

| Proportion of school population with a Statement | % LEAs | | |
|---|---|---|---|
| | Metropolitan (n = 41) | Shire (n = 32) | All LEAs† (n = 73) |
| 1.3% and below | 27 | 13 | 21 (18) |
| 1.4–1.7% | 32 | 38 | 34 (35) |
| 1.8–2.0% | 31 | 38 | 34 (35) |
| 2.1% and above | 10 | 11 | 11 (11) |
| Total | 100 | 100 | 100 (99)* |
| Missing cases | 2 | 1 | 3 |

† The number in brackets indicates the proportion of all English LEAs falling into each category including those not responding on the questionnaire
* Rounding error

Source: LEA returns on Form 7M for January 1985, updated by personal communication.

Responses to the questionnaire indicated that this pattern is reflected nationally and it is clear that in most authorities it is still true that a Statement can be equated largely with a decision to make a special school placement. Thus, as Table 5.2 shows, 24 per cent of LEAs placed 22.9 per cent or more of their children with Statements in mainstream schools. As might have been predicted from their different use of Statements (described in the previous section (p. 53), higher proportions of shire counties placed larger proportions of their children with Statements in mainstream schools. Among the authorities placing 22.9 per cent or more of children with Statements in mainstream, shire counties outnumbered boroughs by more than 3 to 1. At the lowest level of integration, 9.1 per cent of those with Statements and below, there were two metropolitan authorities for every shire county. Swann (1985), using data from the year prior to the Act's implementation, noted a trend towards the increased use of segregated provision. While our survey confirms the relationship between statutory assessment and segregated provision, further longitudinal studies are needed to see whether the Act is eventually followed by a reversal of this trend.

This aspect will be further explored in the next chapter. It is important to recognize here that children for whom a Statement is maintained appear more likely to have their needs met in a mainstream placement than was the case for children assessed under the SE procedures. This appears to be particularly true for those living in shire authorities.

The continued existence of the boundary between special and mainstream schools was also confirmed by the 38 per cent of LEAs where Statements were withdrawn if a child was moved from a special to a mainstream school. This aspect will be explored further in Chapter 7. While it would be naive to suggest that the survival of the mainstream/special divide emanates from a misunderstanding or rejection of the principles of the Act, the distinction is important. Where the 'sectors' remain, it cannot be claimed that the rights of those with special educational needs are fully recognized.

### The Statement as a record of rights

Chapter 7 will include an account of the preparation and content of Statements. Certain aspects of the Statement do, however, provide local authorities with opportunities to demonstrate their implementation of the spirit of the Act. Among those most readily susceptible to verification are:

### (i)  *The individual nature of the Statement*

The processes of assessment and the production of advice, described in Circular 1/83 and defined by the Act and Regulations, are clearly intended to respond to individual and contextual differences. The aim is to produce a rounded picture of a child, a view which is distinctive and includes both strengths and weaknesses.

The Statements produced by the five detailed study authorities seldom included any material which 'brought the child to life'. The advice, medical, psychological and educational, seldom included positive achievements and the descriptions of need were usually presented as a vague stereotype.

### (ii)  *The origin of special educational needs*

Because of their non-specificity, Statements did little to provide an individualized description of the child. Yet they were focused entirely on within-child factors. None of the Statements seen included any analysis of contextual factors, either curricular or pedagogic. The only references to curriculum consisted of statements of the child's need for 'structure'.

### (iii)  *The protection of the resources provided for the child*

The vagueness which permeated the Statements extended to the descriptions of the necessary provision. In some cases 'provision' was identified only in terms of the name of the school. In one detailed study authority the description of the provision was limited to a recommendation as to the type of school provision needed, without naming the school on the Statement.

In such circumstances, it is difficult to accept that local authorities had responded to the right of the child to resources which were protected by law.

### The rights of parents

In Chapter 1 it was made clear that the principles of parent rights incorporated into the Act, Regulations and Circulars, while much more evident than those of children, were still subject to various conditions. While aspects of policies concerned with parental involvement are considered in Chapter 6 and the parents' experiences of the new procedures are discussed in Chapter 8, the concept of a partnership with parents is so central to the view of rights presented in the Act, and so essential a component of many current ideas of special education, that it also demands some attention here.

Local authorities were obliged by the 1980 Education Act to provide parents with

**Table 5.2.**   *The proportion of children with Statements placed in mainstream schools*

| Proportions of Statemented children in mainstream | % LEAs | | |
|---|---|---|---|
| | Metropolitan (n = 42) | Shire (n = 33) | All LEAs† (n = 75) |
| 9.1% and below | 31 | 15 | 24 (23) |
| 9.2–14.5% | 29 | 21 | 25 (26) |
| 14.6–22.8% | 29 | 24 | 27 (26) |
| 22.9% and above | 12 | 39 | 24 (24) |
| Totals | 100* | 99* | 100 (99)* |
| Missing cases | 1 | 0 | 0 |

† The figure in brackets shows the proportion of all English LEAs falling into each category including those not responding on the questionnaire
* Rounding error

Source: LEA returns for January 1985, on Form 7M updated by personal communication.

information about their range of provision, and by the 1981 Education Act to provide information about the statutory assessment procedures. A recent CSIE study (Rogers, 1986) has indicated that parents cannot exercise their rights to the full, nor play a full part in their child's statutory assessment, because many LEAs fail to provide them with adequate information. The project's own detailed study of LEAs also indicated that there were marked differences in local policies about the role allowed to parents and about how these policies were applied.

In one shire authority, where the officers were proud of a long-standing policy of informing and involving parents, the approach was typified by the administrator who told us:

> We have said that all parental requests for assessment are reasonable, even within 12 months of the previous assessment.

However, the Act specified six months as a reasonable period of time after which parents could seek reassessment. Such a response was the most common one adopted by LEAs, with 53 per cent of respondents recording that they would always carry out a statutory assessment where this was requested by the parents (see also Chapter 7).

Documents for parents from the five detailed study authorities provided examples across the range of informing and involving parents. For most parents, the documentary material produced by the LEA was the only information they had about the Act. The content and presentation of booklets for parents is important, as a review of approaches made by these authorities at the time of the study illustrates.

Three booklets were available in D-Shire. One had the title 'Parents as Partners, Helping Children with Special Educational Needs', the second provided the detail of the special educational provision (as required by the 1980 Education Act), and the third was focused upon 'Specific Learning Difficulties' and set out to undermine acceptance of the concept of 'dyslexia'. The first document, the most important in order to identify local policy towards parents, gave a clear account of the statutory assessment procedures, confirming that 'parents are always fully involved'. However, it gave the impression that the decision to assess would be made before parents had any (formal) chance to express their views. While underlining the importance attached to parental views, including that they would form a part of any Statement, there was also an illustration of the fine line which exists between what D-Shire's guidelines for schools called the 'efficient and sensitive handling of parents' and a more authoritarian approach. The document admonished:

> But the 'D-Shire' authority regard parents as partners and almost always find parents and officers can agree on the best way to help a child in difficulties
> [Guidelines for Parents: D-Shire, emphasis in original text]

Elsewhere, the research team interviewed parents who stated that not only had the decision to assess been taken before any formal communication had been made to parents, but also in some cases the Section 5 examination itself had been carried out.

B-Borough was another authority which similarly recorded a desire to maintain good professional–parent relationships, but there the onus was firmly placed upon parents to register any grievance with officers of the LEA. Such an attitude extended out into the schools and it was in B-Borough that one head teacher claimed that the accessibility of the CEO and the presence of his telephone number on the school name board provided sufficient safeguard for parents' rights. The guidelines for parents, a four-sided A4 duplicated sheet, made few concessions to a lay understanding of the procedures and adopted the line that, regrettably, parents would find them difficult because of their formality and the fact that they were 'cumbersome and time-consuming'. The general tenor of the document is captured in the section concerned with parents' rights to give their views, which was situated in the middle of a long paragraph headed 'Notification of assessment':

> The Authority will then write to the parents confirming that an assessment is being considered and inviting them to forward any comments they may wish to make or any independent specialist reports they have obtained, before the decision is made on whether to proceed with the assessment. For those parents who would prefer to speak to someone rather than convey their views in writing, the Authority will be happy to make the necessary arrangements.

At the time of the study, no written translations of these documents were available despite the presence of a large and fluctuating ethnic minority.

The three booklets produced for parents in A-Shire were targeted upon (a) all parents whose children attended their schools, (b) those whose children already attended special schools and (c) those whose children might require a statutory assessment. The first booklet included the statement on the abolition of categories already referred to and gave details of a 'Warnock five-stage assessment' process in which stages four and five constituted the statutory assessment. The document for parents of children possibly requiring such an assessment included details of the professionals likely to be involved and, in a strange contrast with observable policy, a pro-integrationist statement. The general tone of the document was rather formal and implied a close liaison with parents only where there was a dispute. The A-Shire document produced for schools did, however, emphasize the new position:

> . . . before the Act, it was good practice to involve parents . . . it is now the law of the land to do so
> (Notes for schools: A-Shire, May 1983)

Despite its less sophisticated appearance, the information provided for parents in C-Shire was much more accessible. The presentation was based upon a series of questions, such as:

Does my child have special needs?
When is formal assessment necessary?
Who else is involved?

The answers to these often included details absent from the documents available from other authorities. Typical of this was the inclusion of the social services department among those to contact during a statutory assessment, together with the reassurance:

If a social worker is already helping your family, there is nothing to worry about: your social worker will discuss the assessment with you, and will *not* give any information without your permission.

The information provided for parents by E-Borough was very condensed. For example, a description of the procedures was contained in a few paragraphs on a single page. Despite the introduction of a questionnaire to assist parents to make their views clear, there was no indication in this documentation that the LEA viewed parental contributions as valuable or desirable.

Other aspects of the local procedures often underlined the relatively marginal role that parents are allowed. Typical of this was the exclusion of parents from case conferences about their children in B-Borough, confirming some parents' beliefs that the Act had yet to give them access to the full information upon which decisions about their child were being taken. Two of the authorities had a pre-school counselling service for parents and this appeared to offer the best model of informing and involving parents. The extent to which the success of this service was based upon the formal roles performed by the staff and the degree to which it reflected their personal commitment and professional stance were difficult to determine.

As with so much that has been described earlier in this chapter, LEAs obviously found difficulty in adapting professional and administrative practice to the new role offered to parents by the Act. Although in some cases the new ideas had not yet been recognized, or had been rejected, it was clear that, in general, the Act's emphasis on partnership for parents was recognized. It was also clear that the transition from reconceptualization to changed practice had yet to begin in many areas of LEA practice. Previous patterns of working, sets of beliefs about parents and their willingness and capacity to play a larger part in decisions about their children with special educational needs, professional certainty and paternalism all had a part to play in the process. It seemed certain that even the small change in the balance of power between professionals and parents brought about by the Act had yet to be realized in a number of authorities.

## THE EFFECTIVENESS OF IDENTIFICATION, ASSESSMENT AND THE MEETING OF SPECIAL EDUCATIONAL NEEDS

Policies and practices concerned with special educational needs and provision and with the statutory assessment procedures will be described in more detail in Chapters 6 and 7. We are more concerned here with the understandings of those involved in carrying out those policies and practices.

In marked contrast to the ambiguities apparent in local responses to the definition of special educational needs and rights issues built into the Act, the implementation of the procedural elements of the legislation was much more easily observable. Chapter 6 will note the emphasis which LEAs placed upon the provision of documentary guidelines for their staffs and the lower frequency with which they provided material for other professional audiences in health authorities and social services departments.

Most authorities were able to implement the new procedures 'on time'. B-Borough, one of the detailed study LEAs, was one of the small group of authorities not meeting the DES deadline for implementation, 1 April 1983. The efficiency with which the Act's procedures were introduced was, of course, variable. C-Shire, another detailed study area, provided an example of a rather hesitant introduction of its new procedures.

Apart from such faltering, the elements of identification and assessment seemed to have been translated effectively into guidelines. More problematic, as Chapter 7 will make clear, was whether the principles of effective service delivery had received a similar response.

## SUMMARY AND CONCLUSION

This chapter has explored ways in which the principles promulgated by the 1981 Education Act have been incorporated into local thinking about special educational needs. The extent to which these ideas have been translated into practice will be explored in Chapters 6, 7 and 8. These chapters will indicate that, while the ideas which led to the new approaches to identification and statutory assessment appear to be on the way to becoming firmly embedded in the new local procedures, other aspects of the principles underlying the legislation appear to be less easily converted into practice.

Thus, while few would appear to reject the principle of a partnership with parents — indeed there were examples of LEAs incorporating this aspect of the legislation into their guidelines for schools — later chapters will describe how this has yet to affect practice in a number of important ways. The translation of the rights of children with special educational needs into a feature of everyday practice appears to be an even more distant prospect.

Lastly, the translation into practice of the new conceptualization of special educational needs appears to be problematic. The relative definition, achieving a balance between what the child can and cannot do, and distinguishing between within-child and environmental factors, appears to be proving difficult to operationalize at the local level.

# Chapter 6

## Policies and Practices

### INTRODUCTION

The beguiling simplicity of the policy–practice dichotomy is not easy to sustain. Even the boundary between the oral and the written does not discriminate adequately since, within some local authorities, even agreed policies may be left unwritten. Some policy is clearly a source of potential conflict between a permanent body of officers and a changing power group of elected members. In such circumstances policies are hidden and can often only be identified from practice. In the real world, there is often a blurring of the boundary between policies and practices and the reader's attention is drawn to the operational definition adopted by the team. This sought to avoid any ambiguity by the inclusion into 'policy' of written and oral statements and those actions capable of routine verification from practice.

This chapter describes the way LEAs established and sought to implement policies in the following topic areas:

- planning for implementation
- patterns of provision
- issues associated with integration
- in-service training to promote implementation
- aspects of accountability
- parental involvement
- collaboration between health, education and social services.

Policy and practice as it relates to statutory assessment under Sections 5 to 8 of the 1981 Education Act will be explored in detail in Chapter 7.

### PLANNING FOR IMPLEMENTATION
#### Local policy

To what extent and in what ways could the LEAs studied be said to have consistent policies? Even the definition of policy outlined above is problematic in the real world, as will quickly become apparent.

In E-Borough, most professionals recorded their support for a policy of mainstream special educational needs placement. There were several examples of integration schemes in the borough, including a long-standing scheme for the integration of hearing-impaired children into mainstream schools. However, differences in policy emerged in terms of 'competing' activities. Thus, there were a number of developments which clearly contributed to the policy: for example, the creation of head of department status for special needs co-ordinating teachers in mainstream secondary schools and the fostering of primary school special needs support services. Others, such as an extension of separate specialist nursery services and the introduction of new special-school-based 16+ courses in competition with those already existing in mainstream colleges of further education, appeared to undermine the policy. There was no evidence that such disparities were the result of differences in the consensus about integration as an aim of the special educational needs service (pre-school, primary, secondary, further), and at times the incongruities were recorded by participants with concern and frustration. Even within a relatively small, tightly administered authority like E-Borough, it appeared that competing initiatives sometimes survived. This appeared to happen despite the fact that they overtly ran counter to the current prevailing 'official' policies. These practices appeared to be a more accurate reflection of past policies which, in theory, had been superseded.

In each of the five detailed study LEAs, clear, authoritative statements were absent in some special needs policy areas. This was identified as damaging by some professionals, particularly in C-Shire, because the lack of a clear policy allowed an authority to delay meeting the needs of children and perhaps even to avoid meeting the responsibility to provide for them. Others recorded that the informality possible in the absence of a rigid policy framework allowed individual needs to be met more sensitively because of the lack of constraints. This latter view was also stated unequivocally by some C-Shire professionals who felt that the individual and institutional initiatives encouraged by the absence of an imposed overall LEA policy gave richness and variety to 'the system'. It was also clear that some officers considered that, in order to maintain services, it was essential to ensure that elected members did not have a totally clear impression of local policy or its real cost. 'Hidden' policies had, in this view, some political value since they allowed or encouraged the allocation of greater funding to special services. In such circumstances, 'no policy', *'laissez-faire'* and 'hidden policy' themselves became *de facto* policies. (On a broader front than special education, 'creative accounting' has been seen as an appropriate response to financial stringency and budgetary control.)

The distinction between C-Shire and the other four authorities, where clear written policies were more routinely available, deserves some emphasis. Different professionals offered different explanations, including the ideological, the economic and the creative (e.g. experimenting with new approaches). Whichever was the true explanation, the effect in C-Shire of directing resources away from the statutory procedures and towards provision did produce a markedly different model of practice. It is possible that the more localized planning of services, which appeared to be a product of these approaches, could lead to less control of policy from the centre, since clear policies can be monitored more easily than *ad hoc* local developments.

**Developing the LEA response**

Although there were some similarities between the policies of different LEAs, it is not surprising that there were differences in the way they had been developed. The five detailed study LEAs had adopted different approaches to planning for implementation, depending partly on the size and compactness of the authority and partly on the past history of relationships between the parties involved.

*Working party activity*

One common strategy was to bring together a working group with a specific policy development and implementation function. The working group in A-Shire, for example, reflected a careful balancing of the central and regional elements in a large authority. From the regions it was seen, perhaps inevitably, as being weighted in favour of the centre. It included administrators, advisers, a psychologist and, once the DHA had recovered from the trauma of reorganization, a representative doctor. No one from the social services department was routinely included, though the department worked closely with the LEA educational welfare service and it had been represented at meetings on an occasional basis. There was also no role allocated to elected members, and a senior member of the working group stated that policy creation was 'the role of professional officers . . . it distorts things if you listen too closely to . . . members'.

The membership of the group was planned well ahead of the Act and, though there were some changes in personnel, it allowed the authority to produce a quick initial response to the legislation, to monitor and modify detail as appropriate. Here, as in other authorities, the delay by the DES in providing Circular 1/83 was identified as a factor inhibiting full and careful forward planning. The consultative structures available in A-Shire also allowed the possibility of the wider involvement of head teachers and teachers. Despite such apparent invulnerability from attack, the working group was still seen, at least by some in the regions, as in the control of 'those at the centre who wish to change nothing'. However, it must be recorded that in no other authority studied was there an implementation group with access to such a broad spectrum of opinion.

Despite the establishment of a working group in B-Borough well ahead of the implementation date, and the involvement of members from all the contributing services, inter-professional collaboration could not be established. It was in B-Borough that implementation was delayed by means of an official statement of policy. The procedures introduced as a result of the 1981 Act were eventually implemented 16 months after the 1 April 1983 start date. This placed B-Borough among the 16 per cent of LEAs that, according to our questionnaire survey, did not implement the new statutory procedures on time and among the 3 per cent that did not implement them within six months of the starting date. The 'negotiations' in B-Borough were protracted, but much of the argument was heated and the involvement of the different disciplines appeared to do little to lessen the differences between them. However, the two-tier structure which resulted from their deliberations was a model of multi-disciplinary involvement in decision-making and in the evaluation of outcomes (see Chapter 9).

*The central co-ordinating group*

In D-Shire, the authority's response to the Act was produced by a central special educational needs administrative group. This group was inevitably much smaller than that in A-Shire and included a more limited range of professions and perspectives. Again, preparations preceded the placing of the Act on the statute book; indeed, much of the planning was completed well ahead of any need to implement. The dynamics of the process were uncontentiously described:

> The proposals . . . have tended to arise out of a very close working relationship between the (Senior Special Needs Administrator) the (advisers) and the psychologists. There has been a sensible balance between ambitious schemes and what is financially possible . . . (LEA administrator)

E-Borough's response to the Act was also planned by a small, centrally placed group. In this case, due to the smaller size of the authority, it consisted of a triumvirate of administrator, psychologist and adviser. The realities of working within an LEA where resources were clearly stretched to the ultimate meant that much of the documentary material about the Act was also prepared by the administrator. The adviser for special educational needs also carried responsibility for a number of curriculum areas, two of which would, elsewhere, be seen as constituting a major burden. Such was the range of advisory responsibility he had undertaken that special educational needs emerged as only one of a number of important current initiatives, even in the year the Act was implemented.

Although the scarcity of resources was clearly a factor in determining what was already available in terms of provision and in influencing the planning of response to the Act, other factors also played an important part. One of these was the close relationship in time between implementation of the 1981 Education Act and a major reorganization of the authority's primary and secondary schools. A second factor was the partnership between officers and members in E-Borough. Although the implementation of the Act was seen almost entirely as an administrative process, members were much more closely involved in contributing to the thinking about the nature of policies than in the other LEAs studied.

*Incremental implementation*

In C-Shire, there was some evidence of 'alternative' policies being generated as proposals by various individuals. One implementation document was circulated to schools, subjected to amendment and eventually withdrawn. By the time our study was carried out, a set of procedures, evolved by a newly appointed officer, formed the overt basis for action within the authority. By that stage, however, a set of *de facto* policies had arisen as a result of different ways of working at various levels within the authority. Consultative meetings at a regional level were still taking place, and some areas of the special needs services, such as the Special Needs Advisory Teaching Service, had evolved through such a consultative process on an authority-wide basis.

*Common themes*

With one notable exception in B-Borough, a factor common to all these very different approaches to policy formulation was the negligible role allowed to health and social services personnel. The joint DES/DHSS nature of Circular 1/83, the necessary involvement of health and social services professionals in multi-professional assessment, and their part in providing for those with special educational needs were apparently not seen as sufficient reason for including them in discussions. The one other example which came nearest to full multi-service involvement was in E-Borough, where health and education authorities were coterminous and there was a history of collaborative working between individuals from all three services. Even there, the interaction between the different services appeared to fall short of shared policy formulation. To do justice to the borough, it is important to acknowledge that attempts to bring about dialogue concerning the relationship between health and other local policy objectives had received no response from the regional health authority.

In each of the five authorities, there was some evidence of 'competition' between education and social services departments which appeared to sour the relationship. This was not necessarily the reflection of a real battle for resources within the local authority, nor was it an important issue between senior officers. What was perhaps more disturbing was that in B-Borough, where the policy-making body established specifically to respond to the Act had included representatives from all major professions, not only had implementation been significantly delayed compared with most other LEAs, but also there appeared, at that time, to be no withdrawal from the entrenched uni-professional position taken up by some.

A further feature, common to all the detailed study LEAs, was the way in which the voluntary sector was excluded from the planning process. While there are quite clearly extensive problems involved in any attempt to co-ordinate the activities of statutory and voluntary organizations (for example, those identified by Abrams (1984) ), the involvement of even a single voluntary representative at an early stage could be seen to bring mutual advantage. This was confirmed by participants in our meetings for administrators, some of whose authorities had provided a role for voluntary organizations at the stage of planning for implementation.

Still more obvious is the potential benefit to be gained from the early involvement of head teachers and teachers. Such an association would maximize the likelihood of procedures being understood and accepted and, in the most favourable circumstances, would gain commitment. Yet in three of the five LEAs there was not even a token involvement of head teachers and teachers. The, perhaps inevitable, consequence was that at least some of those working in schools attacked the local procedures and the way in which they had been implemented.

While time was inevitably a factor inhibiting extensive consultation (authorities commonly reported that the lateness of the Circular ensured that the fine detail of some of the procedures had to be created as they were being implemented), central, top-down, policy-making was the well-established routine in many LEAs.

## CHANGES IN THE PATTERN OF PROVISION FOR SPECIAL EDUCATIONAL NEEDS AFTER THE IMPLEMENTATION OF THE ACT

**Table 6.1.**   *Reasons given for changing patterns of provision*

| Reason for change* | % of LEAs (n = 76) | % reasons given (n = 126) |
|---|---|---|
| Integration/mainstreaming | 37 | 22 |
| Increasing awareness of special needs | 17 | 10 |
| Resulting from LEA policy change | 16 | 10 |
| Parental pressure | 12 | 7 |
| Falling rolls | 12 | 7 |
| Specific out-to-in policy | 10 | 6 |

* Response to open comment: LEAs could record four reasons. Most of the 23 different reasons were recorded by five or less authorities. Only those changes recorded by 10 per cent or more of LEAs are included.

The Act was just one of a number of possible factors leading LEAs to review and amend their patterns of provision for special educational needs. Five of the six most commonly recorded reasons for change could be directly attributed to the Act (Table 6.1). The most commonly mentioned cause for change was the movement towards introducing more integrated places for children with special educational needs (37 per cent of LEAs). Others included a growing awareness of special educational needs (17 per cent), post-Act changes in LEA policy (16 per cent), parental pressure for change (essentially change to mainstream) (12 per cent) and the switch from using 'out-county' places towards the provision of more places within the LEA (10 per cent). All of these were changes that could be related to, if not caused by, the Act. Falling rolls, recorded by 12 per cent of LEAs, were identified as the only major independent influence on changes in provision. It must be accepted, therefore, that in the view of local administrators the greatest influence on emerging patterns of special provision was the Act, either directly or indirectly. Such a view needs to be set into context. The most important influence within LEAs must be the nature of provision existing prior to the Act, since so large a fraction of the available resources will necessarily be 'tied up' in existing plant and personnel. No matter how far down the path towards the Warnock ideal of good practice an LEA had proceeded, or how enthusiastically it had determined to reorganize in response to the Act, in the first years such change must represent only a small fraction of provision unless the pace of change is to achieve an almost revolutionary quality. That at least one authority has aspired to a change of such proportions is a matter of public record. Elsewhere, change has inevitably been less dramatic, though whether this is identified as inertia or stability will, to some extent, depend upon the observer.

As we have seen in Chapter 5, the most recently available public information on the proportion of the school population provided with a Statement indicated that only 11 per cent of LEAs provided Statements for 2.1 per cent or more of their school population. Rather more (21 per cent) produced Statements for 1.3 per cent and below of their school population (see Table 5.1). Thus, while it was reported to the team, from a number of different areas of the research, that the Act would lead to a greater proportion of children being given a Statement than the 1.8 per cent previously ascertained under the special education procedures, there was little evidence that this had occurred.

While it was apparent that the largest group of LEAs reporting changes in the proportion of children with special educational needs allocated to different types of provision recorded movement to the 'mainstream', a number of other important changes were also apparent. Some changes appeared to be related to the age of the children, others were more universal and some appeared to be affected by the nature of the special educational needs displayed. Responses to our questionnaire survey indicated that, even in those areas where there appeared to be a near-consensus concerning the nature of a particular change, there were always some authorities changing the patterns of allocation to different types of provision in ways that ran counter to the consensus. For all types of provision, it was possible to find some LEAs electing to direct children to the sort of provision that most other LEAs were choosing to run down. For many types of provision there were clearly different types of policy being applied. For example, there appeared to be least consensus about provision for children identified as emotionally and behaviourally disturbed.

In order to identify reasons for the nature of the change (or the lack of it), provision is considered in respect of each age range.

## Provision for those under two years of age

Our detailed studies had indicated that great differences existed both between and within authorities in respect of provision for children aged under two years, with some authorities offering very little to this age group. There is a great deal of literature on early intervention and the value of an early understanding and treatment of certain medical conditions is unquestionable. However, it appeared from the practice, if not from the stated policy, that early educational intervention was not similarly unquestioned. Perhaps inevitably, much early intervention originated from medical or social services. Perhaps it was also inevitable that our research confirmed hypotheses that early intervention was essentially an urban phenomenon.

Responses to our national survey indicated that the developments in provision most

**Table 6.2.** *Types of provision where LEAs recorded major changes in the proportion of children aged 0–2 years with special educational needs since April 1983*

| Type of provision | Number of LEAs† | % LEAs with | | | |
|---|---|---|---|---|---|
| | | No provision | Increased proportion | Decreased proportion | No change |
| Portage schemes | (n = 61) | 30 | 51 | 0 | 20 |
| Opportunity playgroups | (n = 48*) | 35 | 21 | 0 | 44 |
| Parental play advice/ counselling | (n = 64) | 28 | 42 | 0 | 30 |
| DHA paediatric assessment centre | (n = 57) | 16 | 28 | 0 | 56 |
| LEA special nurseries | (n = 65) | 49 | 12 | 0 | 38 |
| LEA mainstream nurseries | (n = 64) | 67 | 16 | 0 | 17 |

† Missing cases and those who don't know are not included to simplify the table. Their numbers can be obtained by subtracting this total from 76
* Sixteen authorities recorded 'don't know'.

likely to receive an increased proportion of children were 'home-based' services. Fifty-one per cent of LEAs recorded an increased allocation of children receiving a Portage-style intervention, 30 per cent had no such schemes within their LEA and 20 per cent recorded no change (Table 6.2). The only type of provision other than Portage schemes, where an increased allocation of children was commonly recorded, was in the proportion of children being referred for parental play advice and counselling, where larger proportions of the population were given services in 42 per cent of LEAs.

The picture of 'under-two' provision following the Act was completed by the 67 per cent of LEAs that reported no use of mainstream nurseries for children of that age with special educational needs, and the 49 per cent that had no special nursery provision for the age group. Opportunity play groups were used by 65 per cent of LEAs, 21 per cent recording an increase in their use.

There were differences between shire and metropolitan authorities in respect of changes in provision for those under the age of two. Most of those recording an increase in the allocation of such very young children to particular types of provision were urban LEAs. The two most commonly recorded changes in the use of resources that showed this metropolitan–shire distinction were an increased use of Portage schemes (being recorded by 53 per cent of metropolitan authorities as opposed to 41 per cent of shires) and an increased use of parental play advice and counselling (identified by 51 per cent of metropolitan boroughs and 28 per cent of shire counties).

To summarize, the dominant feature of provision for the 'under-twos' was an increase in 'Portage'-style schemes and parental play advice and counselling, i.e. support for children in their own homes.

**Provision for those aged two to five years**

Portage schemes and parental play advice and counselling were also the two major types of provision where changes in the proportion of children with special educational needs were recorded for those aged two to five years. For this age group, the proportion of LEAs recording no provision of either type had dropped to 25 and 21 per cent respectively, while those reporting an increase in the proportion of children receiving the services formed 53 and 51 per cent respectively (see Table 6.3).

Apart from the increased use of mainstream nurseries, which will be referred to in the next section of this chapter, the major finding about changes in provision for this age group was the large proportion of LEAs making greater use of segregated provision in its many forms. This included increased use of opportunity play groups (32 per cent of LEAs), DHA paediatric assessment centres (31 per cent), day and residential schools for those with severe learning difficulties (23 per cent) and LEA special nurseries (18 per cent of LEAs). However, this is likely to reflect an increase in the numbers of children receiving some provision, as opposed to no provision at all, rather than a move towards increased segregation of this age group.

In order to obtain an accurate picture of change, it is important to recognize that, even for this immediately pre-school age range, there were types of segregated provision where quite large numbers of LEAs reported a decrease in the proportion of children with special educational needs being allocated places. Most commonly recorded among these was a reduction in the use of hospital school places, an area where

**Table 6.3.** *Types of provision where LEAs recorded major changes in the proportion of children aged 2–5 years with special educational needs since April 1983*

| Type of provision | Number of LEAs† | % LEAs recording | | | |
|---|---|---|---|---|---|
| | | No provision | Increased proportion | Decreased proportion | No change |
| Portage schemes | (n = 59) | 25 | 53 | 0 | 22 |
| Opportunity playgroups* | (n = 47) | 23 | 32 | 2 | 43 |
| Parental play advice/ counselling | (n = 63) | 21 | 51 | 0 | 29 |
| DHA paediatric assessment centres | (n = 57) | 7 | 31 | 2 | 60 |
| Hospital schools | (n = 63) | 43 | 0 | 21 | 37 |
| LEA special nurseries | (n = 62) | 39 | 18 | 0 | 44 |
| LEA mainstream nurseries | (n = 66) | 11 | 44 | 2 | 44 |
| Day/residential schools for SLD | (n = 65) | 5 | 23 | 11 | 62 |
| Day/residential schools for MLD | (n = 65) | 24 | 9 | 22 | 46 |
| Day/residential schools for PH | (n = 64) | 23 | 14 | 13 | 50 |

† Missing cases and those who 'don't know' are excluded to simplify the table. Their numbers can be obtained by subtracting this total from 76.
* Sixteen authorities recorded 'don't know'.

no LEA registered taking an increased number of places and 43 per cent did not use hospital schools at all. Day and residential schools for children with moderate learning difficulties were being allocated a decreased proportion of children in 22 per cent of authorities. Day and residential schools for those with physical handicaps and with severe learning difficulties were reported as receiving a decreasing proportion of young children by 13 and 11 per cent of LEAs respectively.

To complete the national pattern of pre-school provision for children with special educational needs, the high proportion of LEAs reporting 'no change' in the proportion of 2 to 5-year-old children placed in their day and residential schools for severe learning difficulties (62 per cent), for physical handicap (50 per cent), or for moderate learning difficulties (46 per cent) deserves attention. This may reflect the switch from hospital to LEA provision already noted, as well as the switch from residential to day placement.

The concentration, in metropolitan authorities, of the incidence of the increased use of provision noted for the under-two-years age group was not repeated for those between the age of two and five. For this age group, the only notable metropolitan/shire distinction was in respect of the far higher use of day nursery places in metropolitan authorities. The extent to which day nursery placement was of value, particularly for those children with severe special educational needs, was questioned by parents and some professionals in the project's detailed studies.

## Provision for children of primary age

Apart from a widespread increase in the placement of children with special needs in

**Table 6.4.**   *Types of provision where LEAs recorded major changes in the proportions of primary children with special educational needs since April 1983†*

| Type of provision | Number of LEAs* | % LEAs recording | | | |
|---|---|---|---|---|---|
| | | No provision | Increased proportion | Decreased proportion | No change |
| Mainstream schools | (n = 62) | 0 | 76 | 5 | 19 |
| Home tuition | (n = 64) | 8 | 30 | 2 | 61 |
| Day/residential schools for EBD | (n = 66) | 15 | 23 | 17 | 45 |
| Designated special units for EBD | (n = 64) | 38 | 23 | 3 | 25 |
| Day/residential schools for SLD | (n = 66) | 0 | 8 | 29 | 64 |
| Day/residential schools for MLD | (n = 65) | 2 | 2 | 49 | 48 |
| Day/residential schools for PH | (n = 65) | 14 | 8 | 26 | 52 |
| Independent schools for SLD | (n = 65) | 34 | 5 | 20 | 42 |
| Independent schools for MLD | (n = 64) | 33 | 0 | 30 | 38 |
| Independent schools for PH | (n = 64) | 28 | 0 | 19 | 53 |
| Independent schools for EBD | (n = 63) | 17 | 14 | 32 | 37 |
| Hospital schools | (n = 63) | 38 | 0 | 33 | 29 |

† Changes in provision for sensory impairment appear separately on Table 6.5.
* Missing cases and those who 'don't know' are excluded to simplify the table. Their numbers may be obtained by subtracting n from 76 for each type of provision.

**Table 6.5.**   *Major changes in the proportion of primary children with sensory impairment receiving the different types of provision*

| | Number of LEAs* | % LEAs recording | | | |
|---|---|---|---|---|---|
| | | No provision | Increased proportion | Decreased proportion | No change |
| (a) *Provision for visual impairment* | | | | | |
| Own day/residential school | (n = 65) | 59 | 2 | 17 | 23 |
| Own designated special unit | (n = 64) | 63 | 16 | 9 | 13 |
| SE provision in other LEA(s) | (n = 65) | 20 | 3 | 20 | 57 |
| Independent SE provision | (n = 64) | 17 | 5 | 28 | 50 |
| (b) *Provision for hearing impairment* | | | | | |
| Own day/residential school | (n = 66) | 59 | 0 | 20 | 21 |
| Own designated special unit | (n = 67) | 4 | 27 | 28 | 40 |
| SE provision in other LEA(s) | (n = 65) | 18 | 2 | 32 | 48 |
| Independent SE provision | (n = 64) | 20 | 3 | 42 | 34 |

* Missing cases and those who 'don't know' excluded to simplify the table. Their numbers can be obtained by subtracting n from 76 for each type of provision.

mainstream schools (recorded in 76 per cent of LEAs), other changes in the allocation of primary age children to the different types of provision were much more varied (see Table 6.4). With the exception of increasing placement of children in special units for the hearing-impaired (see Table 6.5), the pattern of provision reflected a lack of change. The most common provision for which 'no change' appears to have taken place was in day and residential schools for those children with severe learning difficulties (64 per cent of LEAs), physical handicaps (52 per cent), moderate learning difficulties (48 per cent) and emotional and behavioural disturbance (45 per cent). For all except the last type of provision, where change had occurred, it was most likely to consist of a decreasing proportion of primary children attending day and residential schools. For those with emotional and behavioural disturbance no clear trend emerged; 17 per cent of LEAs recorded a decrease in use and 23 per cent an increase. A similar proportion recorded an increase in unit provision for this group.

Some 32 per cent of LEAs recorded a decreased use of independent special schools for children with emotional and behavioural disturbance, and 30 per cent reported less use of independent schools for those with moderate learning difficulties. This also offered some confirmation of the importance of the 'out-to-in' policies identified in the detailed studies. However, for each type of independent provision, these changes contrast with the large proportion of LEAs recording no change in their use. For example, 53 per cent of LEAs recorded no change in respect of the use of independent schools for those with physical handicaps and 42 per cent identified no change for children placed in independent schools for those with severe learning difficulties.

Three other features of provision for primary children with special needs deserve attention. The first of these is the 30 per cent of LEAs recording an increase in the proportion of children with special educational needs being provided for via the home tuition service. The second is the 33 per cent of LEAs where a declining proportion of children were in hospital schools; the 38 per cent of LEAs without access to a hospital school should also be taken into account here. The third feature was the overall pattern of provision for those with sensory impairment (see Table 6.5).

The newly emerging patterns of provision for primary age children with hearing and visual impairment provided an example of types of special needs where there were no clear indicators of the direction of change. There was an increasing use of unit provision and a consequent 'running down' of other forms of provision in some LEAs. Children with a visual impairment were not usually being catered for in the LEA's own 'special' provision, since 63 per cent of LEAs reported having no special units and 59 per cent reported having no special schools. Some 80 per cent made use of special provision in other LEAs, and 83 per cent made use of independent schools. It is clear that some LEAs commonly used these last two types of provision to meet the needs of the visually impaired, the allocation of children to them being recorded as unchanged by 57 and 50 per cent of LEAs respectively. However, for those LEAs who recorded a decrease in use of these schools, discovering where those children were reallocated remained a problem. Although some were accounted for by the 16 per cent of LEAs noting an increasing proportion of children attending their own special units, it would appear that many of the children with a visual impairment were receiving their primary education in mainstream schools.

There appeared to be a greater range of provision available for the larger population of the primary aged hearing-impaired children, though even there 59 per cent of authorities recorded no provision of day or residential school places (and a further 20 per cent reported a major decrease in the use of the institutions they had). However, 40 per cent of LEAs reported no change in the proportion of children with a hearing impairment in the LEA's own special units and 48 per cent reported no change in the proportion receiving special provision in another local authority. The first of these, the LEA's own designated special units for the hearing-impaired, emerged as the only type of provision where some LEAs reported an increasing allocation of children (27 per cent). It may also be that children with a hearing impairment will be among the increased proportion of children of their age range receiving their education in mainstream reported by 76 per cent of LEAs.

With one exception, there were no major differences in the types of provision made for this age group by shire and metropolitan authorities, nor in the changes in the proportions of children being allocated places in them. The exception was provision for children with emotional and behavioural difficulties. Some 50 per cent of shire authorities recorded no change in the proportion of children allocated special unit provision, compared with the 25 per cent of metropolitan authorities reporting no change.

## Provision for children of secondary age

Despite the often repeated axiom that the mainstream placement of children with special needs so soon after the Act remains essentially a primary age phenomenon, and the evidence from our detailed study authorities, a move towards mainstream was the change most commonly recorded by LEAs in respect of their secondary populations (see Table 6.6).

No other change was noted by more than half the authorities. Indeed, only four other types of provision were noted by any significant fraction of LEAs as receiving an increased proportion of children. Further, only provision via the home tuition service (reported as increased in 47 per cent of LEAs) and the increased proportion of children placed in day and residential schools for the emotionally and behaviourally disturbed (noted by 27 per cent) could be seen as having any real impact on the national pattern at secondary level.

In contrast, the types of secondary provision which were noted as less used by LEAs were the LEAs' own day and residential schools for those with moderate learning difficulties (reported by 45 per cent of LEAs) and independent schools for those with moderate learning difficulties and for those with physical handicap (each used for a decreasing proportion of pupils in 37 per cent of LEAs). Some 33 per cent of LEAs reported less use of special schools in other LEAs for those with moderate and severe learning difficulties, and 28 per cent of LEAs noted a decline in the use of the LEAs' own special schools for those with physical handicap. The 35 per cent of LEAs reporting a decline in the proportion of children placed in hospital schools and the 16 per cent of LEAs reporting a decrease in use of the authorities' own day and residential schools for those with emotional and behavioural difficulties must also be added to this list.

Changes in the pattern of provision for those with sensory impairment seemed largely to replicate those already described for children of primary age (see Table 6.7). Thus, for those with a visual impairment, the majority of LEAs recorded no day or residential schools (60 per cent) or designated special units of their own (70 per cent). Some 64 per

**Table 6.6.** *Types of provision where LEAs recorded major changes in the proportion of secondary children with special educational needs since April 1983†*

| Type of provision | Number of LEAs* | % LEAs recording | | | |
|---|---|---|---|---|---|
| | | No provision | Increased proportion | Decreased proportion | No change |
| Mainstream schools | (n = 62) | 0 | 76 | 8 | 16 |
| Colleges of FE | (n = 61) | 3 | 75 | 2 | 20 |
| Sixth-form colleges | (n = 59) | 42 | 22 | 0 | 36 |
| Home tuition | (n = 64) | 5 | 47 | 3 | 45 |
| Own day/residential schools for EBD | (n = 64) | 9 | 27 | 16 | 48 |
| Own day/residential schools for MLD | (n = 64) | 0 | 3 | 45 | 52 |
| Schools for MLD in other LEAs | (n = 61) | 21 | 0 | 33 | 46 |
| Independent MLD schools | (n = 63) | 25 | 0 | 37 | 38 |
| Independent schools for PH | (n = 62) | 15 | 2 | 37 | 47 |
| Own day/residential schools for PH | (n = 64) | 17 | 8 | 28 | 47 |
| Hospital schools | (n = 62) | 32 | 2 | 35 | 31 |
| Schools for SLD in other LEAs | (n = 61) | 18 | 0 | 33 | 49 |
| Own day/residential schools for SLD | (n = 64) | 0 | 9 | 22 | 69 |

† Changes in the use of provision for sensory impairment are recorded in Table 6.7.
* Missing cases and those who 'don't know' excluded to simplify the table. The numbers may be obtained by substracting n from 76 for each type of provision.

cent reported unchanged use of special provision made by other LEAs and 58 per cent reported no change in the proportion of children in independent schools for the visually impaired. These types of provision were, in any case, the least used. Mainstream placement appeared to have increased for children with a visual impairment since, while only 10 per cent of LEAs recorded an increasing use of their own designated special units, decreasing proportions of children were noted in all other types of provision for visual impairment:

− own day and residential schools, 13 per cent of LEAs
− their own units, 7 per cent
− special provision in other LEAs, 21 per cent
− independent provision, 30 per cent.

Overall, 76 per cent of LEAs recorded an increase in the proportion of children with special educational needs in their mainstream schools and it is likely that a proportion of these will be children with visual impairment.

While the pattern was largely replicated for secondary children with a hearing impairment (for example, 59 per cent of authorities recorded having no day and residential schools), rather fewer had no designated special units (9 per cent). Although a decline in the proportion of children placed in all types of provision was recorded by

**Table 6.7.**   *Major changes in the proportion of secondary children with sensory impairment receiving the different types of provision*

| | Number of LEAs* | % LEAs recording | | | |
|---|---|---|---|---|---|
| | | No provision | Increased proportion | Decreased proportion | No change |
| (a) *Provision for visual impairment* | | | | | |
| Own day/residential schools | (n = 63) | 60 | 0 | 13 | 27 |
| Own designated special units | (n = 62) | 70 | 10 | 7 | 13 |
| SE provision in other LEAs | (n = 61) | 15 | 0 | 21 | 64 |
| Independent provision | (n = 60) | 12 | 0 | 30 | 58 |
| (b) *Provision for hearing impairment* | | | | | |
| Own day/residential schools | (n = 63) | 59 | 3 | 14 | 24 |
| Own designated special units | (n = 63) | 9 | 28 | 17 | 46 |
| SE provision in other LEAs | (n = 63) | 17 | 0 | 37 | 46 |
| Independent provision | (n = 63) | 8 | 2 | 43 | 48 |

\* Missing cases and those who 'don't know' are excluded for the sake of simplicity. To calculate their numbers
  subtract n from 76 for each type of provision.

some LEAs, 28 per cent reported an increase in the proportion receiving provision via the authorities own designated special units.

While there appeared to be only minor differences between shire and metropolitan authorities in the changes in the use made of the different types of provision for children with visual impairment, there were rather larger differences in respect of those with a hearing impairment (see Table 6.8). Children with a hearing impairment were increasingly likely to be placed in designated units in shire authorities. An increased proportion of children were allocated to units by 39 per cent of shires, compared to 17 per cent of metropolitan authorities. All shire authorities had such units, whereas 17 per cent of metropolitan authorities did not, possibly because the shorter travelling distances in metropolitan areas made it possible to use facilities in neighbouring boroughs. It may also be the case that these authorities place more children with hearing impairment in mainstream schools.

There were also differences between shire and metropolitan authorities for a few other types of special needs provision. Two types of provision in particular were used differently by quite large groups of authorities. The first of these were schools for those with a physical handicap. While 25 per cent of shires had no special day or residential school provision for those with a physical handicap, this was the case in only 11 per cent of metropolitan authorities. However, shire counties were slightly more likely to record an increase in the proportion of children being allocated to PH schools where they had them (11 per cent compared to 6 per cent in metropolitan authorities). Another aspect of secondary special needs provision where there appeared to be a shire and metropolitan difference was in the schools provided for children who, under the old category system, were designated as 'delicate'. Although shires were rather more likely not to have day or residential schools of this type (61 per cent compared to 47 per cent of

**Table 6.8.** *Major changes in the use of unit provision for sensory impairment by type of authority*

| | % LEAs | |
|---|---|---|
| | Metropolitan (n = 34) | Shire (n = 28) |
| (a) *Allocation to unit provision for visual impairment* | | |
| No provision | 70 | 70 |
| Increased proportion | 6 | 14 |
| Decreased proportion | 6 | 7 |
| No change | 18 | 8 |
| Totals | 100 | 99* |
| Missing cases | 9 | 5 |
| | (n = 35) | (n = 28) |
| (b) *Allocation to unit provision for hearing impairment* | | |
| No provision | 17 | 0 |
| Increased proportion | 17 | 39 |
| Decreased proportion | 17 | 18 |
| No change | 49 | 43 |
| Totals | 100 | 100 |
| Missing cases | 8 | 5 |

* Rounding error.

metropolitan authorities), they were more likely to record no change in the allocation of children to them where they existed (29 per cent compared to 19 per cent).

Although a rather confused pattern emerges from the analysis of our questionnaire data given above, the main findings appear to be that, on the whole, there has been little change in the patterns of provision available in LEAs and in the proportions of children being allocated to them. Where change has taken place, it appears to be in the direction of a decline in the proportions of children attending residential schools in other LEAs and an increase in the proportions of children with special educational needs receiving education in units or in mainstream placements. The issue of integration is considered in more detail in the next section.

## THE ISSUE OF INTEGRATION

### Local policy

To some extent, the placement of children with Statements in a mainstream setting relies upon those who make the decision distinguishing between needs, provision and placement. The principles which led to the need for this separation have been described in Chapter 1. Our detailed studies underlined the difficulties inherent in achieving such a formulation of special educational need. Problems seemed to arise from a number of factors such as:

  (i)   previous patterns of practice
 (ii)  the conceptual difficulty encountered in separating the three
(iii)  the need to consider realistic alternatives for the child

(iv)   the need to consider and offer to parents options which do not give rise to expectations which cannot be met.

Local policies which, to some extent, distinguished between children not in terms of their special educational needs, but on the basis of where they were to be placed, were another problem area. In such circumstances, 'integration' was often a *de facto* alternative to a Statement. It should not, however, be assumed that mainstream placement without a Statement indicated an unsupported placement. Nor was it true that a mainstream placement together with a Statement meant that a child was receiving additional resources. The team found examples to nullify both hypotheses.

Pressures to link the Statement to special school placement were, in some authorities at least, matched by contrary pressures;

> There is an inexorable move towards more ordinary school provision. Considerable moral pressure as well. We do what we can. A well established special school system makes this more difficult than in LEAs (without our) level of provision.
> (Shire authority)

> Increasingly, pupils with special educational needs are being placed in mainstream schools. In order that pupils' needs may be met . . . it is important that each school has a specialist member of staff to co-ordinate provision . . . that satisfactory levels of staffing are maintained . . . that all teachers [are] afforded the opportunity to receive in-service training . . . that special school staff provide support . . . when a youngster reintegrates. . . . Additional resources are required.
> (Metropolitan borough)

## Changes in the allocation of children

Despite such constraints, our national questionnaire survey showed that 68 per cent of LEAs reported an increase in the proportion of children being placed in mainstream

**Table 6.9.**   *Major changes in the proportion of pre-school and primary age children with special educational needs in mainstream settings since April 1983*

| | %LEAs | | |
|---|---|---|---|
| | Metropolitan (n = 39) | Shire (n = 27) | English LEAs (n = 66) |
| (a) *Mainstream nurseries* (children 2–5 years) | | | |
| No provision | 8 | 14 | 11 |
| Increased proportion | 46 | 42 | 44 |
| Decreased proportion | 3 | 0 | 2 |
| No change | 43 | 44 | 43 |
| Totals | 100 | 100 | 100 |
| | (n = 34) | (n = 28) | (n = 62) |
| (b) *Mainstream primary schools* | | | |
| Increased proportion | 71 | 82 | 76 |
| Decreased proportion | 6 | 4 | 5 |
| No change | 23 | 14 | 19 |
| Totals | 100 | 100 | 100 |

**Table 6.10.** *Major changes in the proportion of secondary children with special educational needs in mainstream schools and colleges by type of authority since April 1983*

| | % LEAs | | |
|---|---|---|---|
| (a) *Mainstream schools* | Metropolitan (n = 34) | Shire (n = 28) | English LEAs (n = 62) |
| Increased proportion | 68 | 85 | 76 |
| Decreased proportion | 11 | 5 | 8 |
| No change | 21 | 10 | 16 |
| Totals | 100 | 100 | 100 |
| (b) *Sixth form colleges* | (n = 33) | (n = 26) | (n = 59) |
| No provision | 42 | 42 | 42 |
| Increased proportion | 18 | 26 | 22 |
| No change | 39 | 32 | 36 |
| Totals | 100 | 100 | 100 |
| (c) *Colleges of FE* | (n = 34) | (n = 27) | (n = 61) |
| No provision | 6 | 0 | 3 |
| Increased proportion | 66 | 85 | 75 |
| Decreased proportion | 4 | 0 | 2 |
| No change | 23 | 15 | 19 |
| Totals | 99* | 100 | 99* |

* Rounding error.

settings. Not surprisingly, the only exception to this was for children under the age of two, for whom the necessary emphasis was on gaining access to provision of any type. The movement toward mainstream placement was readily apparent for children aged 2 to 5 years, where 44 per cent of LEAs recorded an increasing proportion of the children with special educational needs being given places in mainstream nurseries. As shown in Table 6.9, the trend continued for primary aged children where 76 per cent of LEAs reported an increased proportion of children being placed in mainstream schools.

The trend survived the transition to secondary school, as indicated in Table 6.10, despite contrary indications from the detailed studies and from other research conducted prior to the Act's implementation (for example Swann, 1985). For the secondary age group, 76 per cent of LEAs reported an increase in the proportion of children with special educational needs being placed in mainstream schools and 75 per cent an increase in those placed in colleges of further education. Table 6.10 also shows an increase in the allocation of children with special educational needs to mainstream sixth form colleges in 22 per cent of LEAs.

The degree to which the changes in proportions recorded by LEAs represent significantly different numbers of children now receiving their provision in mainstream schools rather than special schools remains somewhat problematic. These reported changes in the use of the available provision are based upon the record provided by the LEAs and reflect variable degrees of change from LEA to LEA. What is more certain, however, is that where clear indications of change are universally recorded, they will in time, given a sufficiently sensitive recording system, begin to show in official statistical returns. The United States mainstreaming experience indicated that fundamental changes in patterns of provision take years rather than months to accomplish.

**Other indications of integration**

Although, as was made clear earlier, the proportion of children acknowledged as having special educational needs within the meaning of the Act has, on the whole, changed little from practice prior to the Act, it appears that they are now more likely to be educated in a mainstream setting, especially if they live in a shire authority.

However, the boundary between special and mainstream remains and is reflected in the 38 per cent of the LEAs where it was usual practice to withdraw a Statement where a child was moved from special to mainstream school. The Statement of one mainstream-placed child, whose parent was interviewed by the team, specified no additional provision to support the child within the mainstream setting. The parent reported that the child, an infant with Down's Syndrome, received nothing more than the usual attention of the class teacher at school. More positively, the provision of a Statement meant that there was continued monitoring of a child at least in the initial phases of reintegration. Only 10 per cent of authorities had not produced a procedure to be followed where a Statement was to be withdrawn, emphasizing the general importance attached to formalizing movement between special and mainstream settings.

As will be discussed in Chapter 8, parents frequently believed that local authority practices were only changed as a result of continued pressure. Parents seeking integrated placement for their children were well represented in this group. The extent to which any apparent resistance to such pressure is brought about by a professional or even a paternalistic wish to provide the most appropriate resource for the child, by a need to use resources economically or by a resistance to integration in principle will, of course, vary both within and between LEAs. The research team were aware that in some detailed study authorities, parents were offered the stark choice of either a Statement with resources in a special school or no Statement and no extra resources for integration into the mainstream. In their interviews with parents, the team met only those who felt it necessary to accept the first option (apart from the exception noted above).

It is important to remember that for many authorities there was a very clear boundary between special and mainstream education prior to 1983, although some LEAs had made great progress in introducing a more flexible approach to meeting special educational needs. However, for those who had not, change will not be achieved at a stroke.

The slowness with which change can be introduced into an institutionally based special educational needs service was reflected by the large numbers of authorities recording no change in the proportion of children allocated to the different types of provision, though this will include those authorities who had already made changes before 1983. In the case of children with severe learning difficulties it was, for example, the unchanging nature of the pattern which predominated. Similarly, quite large minorities of LEAs recorded change in the direction opposite to the general trend, and the area about which there was least evidence of any consensus was that concerning the different types of provision made for children with emotional and behavioural difficulties.

Despite these reservations, many of the changes in the allocation patterns of children with special educational needs appeared to represent a trend towards a greater use of mainstream placement. This trend was continued by reported changes in the pattern of

Table 6.11. *Substantial changes in teaching/support staff since 1 April 1983*

| Nature of change | % of LEAs recording substantial staff changes | | | | | |
|---|---|---|---|---|---|---|
| | Peripatetic advisory support teachers | SEN teachers in mainstream schools | Special unit teachers | Special school teachers | Special school teachers in mainstream support | Welfare assistants (NTAs) |
| | (n = 66) | (n = 65) | (n = 69) | (n = 66) | (n = 67) | (n = 70) |
| Substantial increase | 52 | 37 | 39 | 14 | 31 | 77 |
| Substantial decrease | 1 | 0 | 0 | 18 | 0 | 0 |
| Redeployed into post | 7 | 6 | 6 | 2 | 9 | 0 |
| out of post | 0 | 0 | 0 | 2 | 0 | 0 |
| No substantial change | 37 | 40 | 52 | 59 | 43 | 17 |
| No staff of this type | 3 | 17 | 3 | 6 | 16 | 6 |
| Total | 100 | 100 | 100 | 101* | 99* | 100 |
| Missing cases | 10 | 11 | 7 | 10 | 9 | 6 |

* Rounding error.

**Table 6.12.**  *Substantial changes in support staff by type of LEA*

| | % LEAs | |
|---|---|---|
| | Metropolitan (n = 36) | Shire (n = 32) |
| (a) *Changes in peripatetic advisory/support teachers* | | |
| Substantial increase | 40 | 63 |
| Substantial decrease | 0 | 3 |
| Redeployed into post | 8 | 6 |
| No substantial change | 47 | 28 |
| No staff of this type | 5 | 0 |
| Totals | 100 | 100 |
| Missing cases | 7 | 1 |
| | (n = 39) | (n = 31) |
| (b) *Changes in welfare assistants/non-teaching auxiliaries* | | |
| Substantial increase | 64 | 90 |
| No substantial change | 28 | 6 |
| No staff of this type | 8 | 3 |
| Totals | 100 | 99* |
| Missing cases | 4 | 2 |

* Rounding error.

staffing involved in the delivery of special educational needs services. Details of these changes appear in Table 6.11.

Some 77 per cent of LEAs recorded a 'substantial increase' in the number of non-teaching auxiliaries (NTAs) and 52 per cent recorded a substantial increase in peripatetic advisory and support teachers. All NTAs were recorded as new employees, and increases in their numbers and in the number of peripatetic advisory and support teachers were much more common in shire counties than in metropolitan authorities (see Table 6.12). Some 31 per cent of LEAs also recorded substantial increases in the number of mainstream-based special needs teachers and 39 per cent in the number of teachers employed in special units.

While it may be assumed that much of the activity of these additional staff will be directed towards mainstream support of special needs, the increases should be set against the 17 per cent of authorities that recorded no special educational needs teachers in mainstream schools and the 16 per cent that recorded no mainstream support being provided by special school teachers. It must be recognized that such responses should not necessarily be taken to imply that such activities are not taking place within these LEAs, only that, if they are, they do not receive official recognition.

To summarize: some 18 per cent of authorities recorded a substantial decrease in numbers of special school teachers, with less than 2 per cent registering their redeployment. It is not possible to identify whether such changes represented large numbers of staff, though they were claimed as 'substantial' by the LEAs; nor is it possible to determine whether the changes were the result of retirement, redundancy in the face of falling rolls in the special schools, or 'natural wastage' from the profession. Combined

**Table 6.13.**   *Changes in funding for special educational needs since 1 April 1983*

| | % LEAs | | |
|---|---|---|---|
| | Metropolitan (n = 42) | Shire (n = 32) | English LEAs (n = 74) |
| (a) *Proportion of education budget directed to SEN* | | | |
| Remained the same | 31 | 19 | 25 |
| Decreased | 5 | 0 | 3 |
| Increased | 64 | 81 | 72 |
| Totals | 100 | 100 | 100 |
| Missing cases | 1 | 1 | 2 |
| | (n = 43) | (n = 32) | (n = 75) |
| (b) *Gross spending on SEN* | | | |
| Remained the same | 7 | 9 | 8 |
| Decreased | 2 | 0 | 1 |
| Increased | 91 | 91 | 91 |
| Totals | 100 | 100 | 100 |
| Missing cases | 0 | 1 | 1 |
| | (n = 38) | (n = 30) | (n = 68) |
| (c) *Relationship between increase and inflation* | | | |
| Kept pace with inflation | 32 | 26 | 29 |
| Failed to keep pace | 16 | 0 | 8 |
| Exceeded rate of inflation | 42 | 67 | 54 |
| Don't know | 11 | 7 | 9 |
| Totals | 101* | 100 | 100 |
| Missing cases | 5 | 3 | 8 |

* Rounding error.

**Table 6.14.**   *Educational spending by type of LEA (n = 76)*

| Spending group† | % respondent LEAs | |
|---|---|---|
| | Metropolitan (n = 43) | Shire (n = 33) |
| 1 | 23 | 0 |
| 2 | 23 | 3 |
| 3 | 0 | 12 |
| 4 | 2 | 3 |
| 5 | 12 | 15 |
| 6 | 14 | 21 |
| 7 | 5 | 9 |
| 8 | 16 | 27 |
| 9 | 5 | 9 |
| Totals | 100 | 99* |

† 'Spending group' is an independent variable derived from Public Education Statistics 82–83 Actuals (CIPFA), so that Group 1 includes authorities appearing in the top quartile for spending on both primary and secondary age children and Group 9 includes those appearing in the bottom quartile for both.
* Rounding error.

with the other changes, their effect may be to move the emphasis in special education staffing towards mainstream placement.

## THE FUNDING OF SERVICES

Considering the lack of direct central government resources to implement the Act and the limited use of redeployment by local authorities, it is perhaps surprising to find as much change as was apparent. Without a local reallocation of resources over the previous two and a half years, even the changes noted would have proved impossible, and the reallocation was made even more notable by the period of financial stringency in which it took place. Not only did nearly three-quarters of LEAs direct an increased proportion of their education budget to special educational needs (72 per cent), but also nine out of ten LEAs reported an increase in gross spending on special educational needs. In 29 per cent of LEAs this increase was reported to have kept pace with inflation and in a further 54 per cent it exceeded inflation (see Table 6.13).

An analysis of funding by the type of authority (Table 6.14) disclosed that the shire authorities, which were relatively more lowly funded, had gained ground relative to the metropolitan LEAs, particularly in respect of the proportion of the education budget directed to special educational needs and the relationship of the increased sums to the current rate of inflation.

## IN-SERVICE PREPARATION AND TRAINING FOR THE ACT

While mainstream placement clearly has its political, psychological and social importance, it will, in the end, be the quality of the education provided that will allow the proper judgement of integration. It is to be hoped that the fears about the quality of mainstream provision expressed by some respondents in our detailed study authorities, most particularly those made in respect of the rapidly developed 'special needs courses' in colleges of further education, will not be realized.

Training plays a crucial role in the implementation of any new policy and this was also the subject of one aspect of our study. Information in this area was collected in the questionnaire survey and in the detailed studies. Two facets of in-service work were explored: the holding of seminars and workshops and the production of written guidelines.

Despite their widespread exclusion from LEA planning groups, head teachers were the most common target for specific training about the Act (see Table 6.15). Thus, mainstream head teachers were given induction training in all but 4 per cent of the 84 per cent of authorities that provided some training, perhaps reflecting the importance accorded to their role in the statutory procedures. Although the proportion of LEAs giving training to special school head teachers and special unit heads was much lower than this, at 68 and 49 per cent respectively, it was clear that a 'top-down' model was being used in respect of the introduction of the Act to teachers. It was also confirmed that those working in mainstream settings were identified by more LEAs as higher priority targets for such Act-related in-service activity than teachers in special schools and units.

**Table 6.15.** *Specific training to help implement the Act*† (n = 76)

| Audience for training | % of LEAs* |
|---|---|
| Administrators | 41 |
| Clerical officers | 39 |
| Psychologists | 62 |
| Inspectors/advisers | 43 |
| Peripatetic/advisory/support teachers | 57 |
| EWO/ESWs | 49 |
| Mainstream: | |
| head teachers | 80 |
| SEN teachers | 71 |
| other teachers | 58 |
| governors | 32 |
| Special unit: | |
| head teachers | 49 |
| unit teachers | 43 |
| Special school: | |
| head teachers | 68 |
| teachers | 54 |
| governors | 54 |
| Welfare assistants/NTAs | 28 |
| DHA(s) personnel | 38 |
| SSD personnel | 33 |
| Parents | 11 |
| Voluntary organizations | 11 |

† Eighty-four per cent of LEAs recorded that they had offered some training and there was little difference between metropolitan and shire authorities.
* LEAs may respond for each audience, the percentage is of all LEAs not just the 84 per cent offering training.

The proportion of LEAs providing training declined from 71 per cent in respect of mainstream special educational needs teachers, to 58 per cent for other mainstream teachers, to 54 per cent for special school teachers and 43 per cent for teachers in special units. Peripatetic, advisory and special educational needs support teachers were provided with a specific induction to the Act by 57 per cent of LEAs.

Considering the vital role allocated to school governors by the Act, the proportion of LEAs providing induction training for special school governors (54 per cent) and for those of mainstream schools (32 per cent) was disturbingly small. Such exclusion appeared unaffected by the statutory nature of new duties. Such a low level of provision cannot be taken as an indication that LEAs were content that school governors could carry out their new role without such training. Indeed, the focused studies suggested that their capacity and willingness to carry out such duties was questioned, at least in some authorities.

Similar reservations must be expressed about the training opportunities offered to health and social services personnel closely associated with the 1981 Act procedures. Only 38 per cent of LEAs provided an introduction to the Act for staff from DHAs and still fewer provided training for staff from social services departments (33 per cent).

The extent to which parents or workers in the voluntary sector were considered to be real partners was indicated by the very small proportion of LEAs (11 per cent) which produced any training experience for them.

There were quite marked differences between the proportion of LEAs giving training to other LEA professionals concerned with special educational needs. Psychologists were the only professionals for whom a majority of LEAs provide Act-related training (62 per cent). For all other groups only a minority of LEAs considered that there was a clear need for an induction. Thus, 49 per cent of authorities provided such training for educational welfare officers, 43 per cent for inspectors or advisers, 41 per cent for administrators and 39 per cent for clerical officers.

Such patterns were reflected in the audiences offered information by the detailed study authorities. Although staff from district health authorities serving E-Borough and D-Shire recorded the usefulness of the meetings to provide information, elsewhere meetings were more usually restricted to the staff of the education authority. Such meetings in other detailed study authorities were targeted in a number of different ways. The head teachers of special schools were often collected together from across an authority, whereas head teachers of the much larger number of primary schools were usually seen on a more localized basis. Training for secondary head teachers and teachers was often provided for on an institutional basis.

The early phase of in-service activity concerned with the implementation of the Act had been pursued with varying degrees of enthusiasm within the five authorities and participants' judgements of it varied from 'early, thorough and professional' (primary head teacher, A-Shire), through 'providing in-service meetings on the Act when requested' (administrator, D-Shire), to 'a quick tour round the schools in the Autumn Term' (adviser, C-Shire). Dissemination was, without exception, a top-down activity, confirmed in the focused studies as didactic and allowing little discussion, and was condemned in a number of authorities by those subjected to the experience. In one case at least, the condemnation was almost explosive in force, the activity being identified as:

> Going through the motions . . . As an effective form of communication it is rubbish!
> (mainstream head teacher, A-Shire)

Despite such accusations, it was apparent that considerable importance was attached to the in-service exercises in all authorities. The Act was seen in A-Shire and E-Borough as providing an increased momentum to the LEA's efforts and in D-Shire it was specifically identified as producing an outstanding opportunity to follow through the effects of in-service work into the schools and ensure that it had achieved the appropriate response.

The extent to which the Act qualitatively or quantitatively affected in-service training was quite difficult to determine. C-Shire had been conducting 'Awareness Courses' for a considerable time before the introduction of the Act, but at the time of study these were being subjected to criticism from contributors and attenders alike. Some of those contributing to the courses feared that they were unable to change people's attitudes through this approach. Criticism also suggested that it had not proved possible to provide a skill-based follow-up to the courses, to develop, through increased awareness, the capacity to meet the needs of children with special educational needs newly recognized within the classroom.

The 'awareness' aspects of some training provided in A-Shire were subjected to a similar attack, even where some of these had culminated in skill-based elements such as pupil assessment and curriculum development. By the judicious use of supply teachers, one region of A-Shire had provided such training for one teacher from each of the region's mainstream infant and primary schools and the scheme was, at the time of the study, being extended to secondary teachers. However, despite the successful completion of such a course of training based in a nearby special school and the consequent accolade of expertise within the school, a teacher interviewed by one of the research team remained adamant that within-child factors were the only cause of special educational needs within the school. This provides an example of the difficulties of bringing about attitudinal change.

The different elements in the special educational needs in-service course were quite clearly identified at the outset in E-Borough and the programme was described as being intended:

(i) to increase understanding of the nature of handicaps and special needs
(ii) to train teachers to identify and assess special needs and to determine where specialist advice and assistance is necessary
(iii) to give guidance in the management of children with special needs in the ordinary classroom.

This programme would be 'provided through [teachers' centres] over three terms . . . taken by external lecturers and local staff with experience.'

The programme was proposed for 'the majority of serving teachers' and stated to be the equivalent of a week's duration. Elsewhere, most effort was put into a top-down (as opposed to a cascade) approach to special educational needs in-service work, focusing on, for example, head teachers. While such an approach was certainly pragmatic, in view of current financial stringency and the large numbers involved, it was based upon certain assumptions, for example, that:

(a) the head teachers had accurately received the information
(b) that they could accurately transmit it
(c) that they would transmit it
(d) that the audience was in turn able to receive and apply the information accurately.

None of these assumptions was routinely confirmed by those giving evidence to the project, and it is not clear whether this model of in-service training would lead to changes in practice.

Among the professionals, it was possible in a number of authorities to find examples of psychologists using the Act as a focus for their own in-service activity. For example, in A-Shire the schools psychological service held a two-day conference devoted to various aspects of their own work with the Act. Psychologists elsewhere appeared to have identified less in the Act which could form an appropriate focus for professional development. Nor was it possible to find any other professional group involved in similar self-help activities.

In at least three of the detailed study areas, national or local voluntary organizations had held some form of public meeting concerned with the Act and its implementation attended by LEA representatives.

A final aspect of implementation strategy, which has already been touched on in respect of parents, was the production by the local authority of documentary material. Details of this were collected on a national basis, initially six months after the Act was placed upon the Statute Book and then again after a further two years had elapsed.

**Table 6.16.**   *LEAs providing documentary information about the Act for specific audiences at implementation: 'internal' memoranda/information sheets*

| Audience | % of LEAs giving information | | |
| --- | --- | --- | --- |
| | Metropolitan (n = 42) | Shire (n = 29) | Total (n = 71) |
| Advisers/inspectors | 62 | 59 | 61 |
| Educational psychologists | 71 | 79 | 75 |
| Education welfare officers | 64 | 62 | 63 |
| Head teachers (special schools) | 90 | 86 | 89 |
| Head teachers (mainstream) | 95 | 90 | 93 |
| Teachers (special schools) | 45 | 41 | 44 |
| Teachers (mainstream) | 50 | 45 | 48 |
| School governors | 64 | 66 | 65 |
| Elected members | 64 | 55 | 61 |
| DHA personnel | 57 | 66 | 61 |
| Missing cases | 15 | 10 | 25 |
| Response rate | | | 74% |

It was possible to distinguish three major types of documents. These were those with the function of:

(a)   giving basic, but sometimes, restricted information to those working within the LEA and other special needs professionals — 'internal documents'
(b)   giving 'public' information to the professionals and to others such as parents
(c)   documents concerned with some aspect of the 1981 Act procedures, such as the recording of assessment information.

Shire counties were, in general, rather less likely initially to have produced 'internal' documents than were metropolitan authorities, although the proportion of each type of authority producing such information for each of the audiences was remarkably similar (see Table 6.16). The production and circulation of internal letters, memoranda and restricted circulation booklets reflected LEA priorities already identified in the provision of in-service courses. Thus, head teachers were the most commonly identified audience, with mainstream school head teachers being given information in this way by 93 per cent of LEAs and those from special schools by 89 per cent of LEAs. The 'top-down' approach was confirmed in this aspect of preparation for the Act by the reduction in the proportion of LEAs providing documents specifically for teachers (48 per cent for those in mainstream schools and 44 per cent of LEAs for teachers in special schools).

To some extent, the absence of a training experience for governors was compensated for by the production of, albeit limited, written information, with some 65 per cent of LEAs offering guidelines in this way.

Among the non-school-based LEA staff, psychologists were targets of internal briefing documents in 75 per cent of LEAs. Educational welfare officers were also provided with such documents by 63 per cent of LEAs and advisers and inspectors by 61 per cent of LEAs. This last proportion was replicated for personnel employed by district health authorities, who were the only major recipients of 'restricted information' who were not members or employees of an LEA. Elected members, who had not emerged as a major target for training associated with the Act, were provided with this

**Table 6.17.** *Changes in the documentary information provided by LEAs about the Act for specific audiences two and a half years after implementation: 'internal' memoranda/information sheets*

|  | % of LEAs providing | | | | | |
|---|---|---|---|---|---|---|
|  | (a) Updated information | | | (b) Information where none before | | |
| Audience | Metropolitan (n = 36) | Shire (n = 29) | Total (n = 65) | Metropolitan (n = 36) | Shire (n = 29) | Total (n = 65) |
| Advisers/inspectors | 11 | 24 | 17 | 3 | 3 | 3 |
| Educational psychologists | 19 | 31 | 25 | — | — | — |
| Education welfare officers | 17 | 20 | 18 | — | 10 | 5 |
| Head teachers (special) | 31 | 41 | 35 | — | — | — |
| Head teachers (mainstream) | 33 | 41 | 37 | — | — | — |
| Teachers (special) | 8 | 10 | 9 | 3 | 10 | 6 |
| Teachers (mainstream) | 11 | 14 | 12 | 3 | 14 | 8 |
| School governors | 14 | 14 | 14 | — | — | — |
| Elected members | 17 | 24 | 20 | — | — | — |
| DHA personnel | 17 | 21 | 18 | — | 3 | 5 |
| Missing cases | 21 | 10 | 31 | 21 | 10 | 31 |

sort of document by 61 per cent of authorities overall and by 55 per cent of shire counties. A few authorities considered that the implementation of the new legislation required both governors and elected members to be offered some training, and the team were able to observe the positive achievements of a few of these exercises. However, training was not offered in the majority of LEAs and in many there was no written information specifically formulated to help them take on their proper role.

Two years after the Act had come into force, few of those authorities that had not originally produced 'internal' information documents for the range of different audiences had changed their practice. Thus, none of these authorities had subsequently produced information for head teachers in mainstream or special schools, or for school governors or elected members. The proportion of authorities newly producing such documents peaked, in respect of circulars provided for mainstream teachers, at only 8 per cent.

Such a picture of very limited change, summarized in Table 6.17, was not repeated for authorities which had produced internal guidelines from the start. The major targets for such revised internal documents were head teachers, both mainstream in 37 per cent of LEAs and special school in 35 per cent of LEAs. Psychologists (25 per cent) and elected members (20 per cent of LEAs) were also given updated information. It was more common for such revisions to be carried out in shire authorities than in metropolitan boroughs. For example, the revision of internal memoranda for mainstream head teachers had been undertaken by 41 per cent of shire counties compared to 33 per cent of metropolitan authorities.

As indicated above, LEAs also provided 'public' information which was made available to some of the audiences provided with confidential information elsewhere. Therefore, it should not be assumed that, because an LEA had not provided, for example, mainstream teachers with a specially targeted internal memorandum concerning the Act, they had not given them any information. Clearly, it was also possible for any person working in the special needs area to obtain copies of such public documents. However, what was clear from LEA responses was that copies of such public documents were not routinely issued to elected members or to school governors.

During the period immediately after implementation, a majority of LEAs produced public documents for parents. Of those responding to our request for information, 76 per cent had produced documents for parents of children with special educational needs

**Table 6.18.** *LEAs providing 'public' information sheets/circular letters about the Act for specific audiences at implementation*

| Audience | % of LEAs giving information | | |
|---|---|---|---|
| | Metropolitan (n = 42) | Shire (n = 29) | Total (n = 71) |
| All parents | 57 | 45 | 52 |
| Parents of children having SEN | 74 | 79 | 76 |
| Special schools/teachers | 40 | 45 | 42 |
| Mainstream schools/teachers | 50 | 34 | 44 |
| Other services | 38 | 41 | 39 |
| Voluntary organizations | 10 | 28 | 17 |
| Missing cases | 15 | 10 | 25 |
| Response rate | | | 74% |

**Table 6.19.** *Changes in the 'public' information sheets/circular letters provided by LEAs about the Act two and a half years after implementation*

| Audience | % of LEAs providing | | | | | |
| --- | --- | --- | --- | --- | --- | --- |
| | (a) Updated documents | | | (b) Documents where there were none before | | |
| | Metropolitan (n = 36) | Shire (n = 29) | Total (n = 65) | Metropolitan (n = 36) | Shire (n = 29) | Total (n = 65) |
| All parents | 19 | 14 | 17 | 3 | 3 | 3 |
| Parents of children having SEN | 47 | 45 | 46 | 3 | 7 | 5 |
| Special schools/teachers | 14 | 10 | 12 | — | 10 | 5 |
| Mainstream schools/teachers | 8 | 7 | 8 | — | 17 | 8 |
| Other services | 3 | 10 | 6 | — | 3 | 2 |
| Voluntary organizations | 6 | 10 | 8 | — | 3 | 2 |
| Missing cases | 21 | 10 | 31 | 21 | 10 | 31 |

and 52 per cent for all parents. Only a minority released such documents specifically to mainstream teachers (44 per cent), special school teachers (42 per cent), other services (39 per cent) and to voluntary organizations (17 per cent) (see Table 6.18).

As has been the case with documents having a restricted circulation, two years later few LEAs provided documents where none had been produced before (Table 6.19). This was true even in the case of information for parents of children with special educational needs (5 per cent) and parents in general (3 per cent), despite the legal obligation to provide such information. Interestingly, the audience most commonly identified by shire authorities as now receiving information where it had not done so before was mainstream teachers (17 per cent) and special school teachers (10 per cent of LEAs).

A revision of the publicly available information was much more common, most importantly updating the information provided by LEAs for parents of children with special educational needs in 46 per cent of LEAs, and for all parents in 17 per cent of LEAs. They had undertaken far less revision in the documents produced for teachers, and revised information was produced for mainstream teachers by only 8 per cent, and for special school teachers by only 12 per cent of LEAs.

The third area of document production related to the Act was the provision of forms for the recording of information. While these were much more commonly available than information documents, they did show similar patterns of revision.

By the date of implementation of the Act, the majority of LEAs had forms for the recording of a child's special educational needs (72 per cent) and for the recording of the assessment of those needs (82 per cent). Some 79 per cent had Statement forms and 59 per cent had review forms available by that date (Table 6.20).

Only in respect of review documents was there any marked increase in the proportion of LEAs producing documents after two years. Revised forms for identification had been produced by 15 per cent of LEAs, for assessment by 18 per cent, and for the Statement by 20 per cent.


## THE ISSUE OF ACCOUNTABILITY

As has already been suggested, the Act increases the accountability of local education authorities for the special needs services they provide, in a number of crucial ways. The extent to which this measure of accountability extends to health authorities appears to be much more open to question.

LEA awareness of this aspect of the legislation emerged in the project's early discussions with administrators and professionals in all three services, and was confirmed in the detailed studies. The vast majority of authorities were clearly cautious in their initial responses to the Act and many administrators attending meetings set up as part of our research strategy reported the intervention of their legal advisers. A major factor, at the stage where the procedures evolved and the documentary information about the Act was being prepared, appeared to be a wish to avoid using any words or form of words which did not match exactly those used in the Act and Regulations. The extent to which legal advisers consulted the content of Circular 1/83 was not clear.

What might be described as an overly legalistic approach at this stage of implementation appeared to be based on a number of fears. The combined power of the 1980 and

**Table 6.20.** *LEAs providing forms for the recording of specific information*

| Purpose of record | % of LEAs producing forms | | | | | | | | |
| --- | --- | --- | --- | --- | --- | --- | --- | --- | --- |
| | (a) At time of implementation | | | (b) Two and a half years after implementation | | | | | |
| | | | | (i) Updated | | | (ii) Issued where none before | | |
| | Metropolitan (n = 42) | Shire (n = 29) | Total (n = 71) | Metropolitan (n = 36) | Shire (n = 29) | Total (n = 65) | Metropolitan (n = 36) | Shire (n = 29) | Total (n = 65) |
| Identification | 74 | 69 | 72 | 8 | 24 | 15 | 0 | 0 | 0 |
| Assessment | 81 | 83 | 82 | 17 | 28 | 18 | 0 | 0 | 0 |
| Statement | 76 | 83 | 79 | 17 | 24 | 20 | 0 | 3 | 2 |
| Review | 48 | 76 | 59 | 9 | 21 | 14 | 6 | 7 | 6 |
| Missing cases | 15 | 10 | 25 | 21 | 10 | 31 | 21 | 10 | 31 |
| Response rate | | | 74% | | | 65% | | | 65% |

the 1981 Acts which ensured the publication of information by local education authorities meant that, perhaps for the first time, an LEA's written pronouncements about special needs provision were available to provide a bench-mark for service delivery. The second contributory factor was the introduction of an appeals procedure which was already proving to be contentious in the relatively 'simple' area of parental choice of school. Concern was expressed in many quarters about the capacity of such an unpredictable process to deal with all the complexity of special needs decision-making. The introduction of appeals direct to the Secretary of State added further caution. A third dimension was the way the Act gave parents access to the information used by LEAs to make special needs decisions. For the first time, the whole assessment process could be followed and the nature of the process subjected to analysis and criticism. A further factor, confirmed by much that administrators said, was a concern for the 'unrealistic' expectations of parents — a fear that they would unrelentingly and unreasonably seek to exploit the new framework. While such fears proved to be largely groundless, some authorities felt that they were under pressure from their local newspapers. For example, two of the detailed study authorities were the subject of local press campaigns at the time they were visited.

Many LEA administrators recorded their frustration at the way in which the concern for strict legality affected the language used in standard letters to parents. They thought that the resulting formality alienated parents, and the need to ensure that they were informed of their rights actually prompted conflict. However, it was not possible to find direct evidence to support such views.

Despite this early emphasis upon the legality of the wording used, there were examples of practices and, by implication, policies which ran counter to the drive towards more accountability.

For example, those local authorities failing to provide school governors with documentary material about the Act might be said to have impaired their capacity to fulfil their additional responsibilities. While authorities might argue that they have evolved alternative mechanisms for ensuring that children with special needs are identified and, once identified, have provision made for them, the Act clearly intended that school governors should have direct responsibilities in these areas.

The focused studies carried out by the project had indicated that, for some authorities at least, monitoring the delivery of special educational needs services was a task beyond their staffing resources, particularly where it involved provision in other LEAs, health or social services settings, independent schools or voluntary organizations. The problems appeared particularly acute for large rural shires, where the distances involved presented major problems, and for small metropolitan authorities where the restricted number of officers ensured that each had to undertake a multiplicity of tasks.

Chapter 7 will discuss the production of the Statements of special educational needs. In the context of accountability, it is important to recognize that at least two distinctive views were current concerning the way in which that document acted as a means of rendering the LEA accountable. One allocated that function to the Statement because of the insight it provided into the LEA response to the needs of the child, most particularly to the resourcing implications of the LEA response. The second saw the content of the document in a more instrumental way, viewing the Statement as providing an agenda for a fairly precise intervention which, because of regular review, could be effectively monitored in terms of its application and outcome. Both views accepted the direct legal accountability conferred by the document. However, the extent of this can also be questioned, since it offers a restriction to 'rights' of parents, as well as a safeguard of the rights of children.

Those Statements seen by the team (drawn largely from the detailed study authorities) suggested that, as they were currently being formulated, the documents did little to further either model of LEA accountability. As they were currently being prepared, some Statements appeared masterly in their non-specificity and in the lack of help which they offered to anyone seeking to evaluate local practice.

There were a number of factors which contributed to that state of affairs:

- the efforts of the LEA administrators to avoid 'the traps', for example, of committing the LEA to expenditure it could not afford
- the sheer volume of work and the consequent need to obtain relief by routinization
- the carry-over from previous professional practices, particularly in respect of confidentiality.

There can be little doubt that confidentiality and accountability (at least in the forms currently adopted) were seen as mutually incompatible.

The delivery of special educational needs services within the schools and colleges provided some excellent examples of good practice. In some schools, great efforts were being made to achieve clarity as well as comprehensiveness in the recording of progress and its communication to parents. There were also authority-wide attempts to achieve a greater accountability. Two examples illustrate some of the different methods used. In E-Borough, 'special educational needs' appeared as a routine item on all meetings of school governors. In A-Shire, each step along the road towards the preparation of a Statement was logged by means of a series of related pupil record forms.

The remit for this project precluded detailed studies of practice within schools and it was difficult to identify anything other than the most superficial attempts at accountability for practices within individual schools. In one particular school visited by the team, while children from the 'special needs unit' had been placed in mainstream classrooms for part of their school day over a number of years, we were unable to identify any coherent attempt to monitor the overall balance of curriculum offered to them.

At the LEA level, the openness of the new way of working was still proving difficult for some, and it was possible for parents to provide examples of some rather strange practices. Often, it must be admitted, such actions were carried out with good, if misguided, intentions. Among examples of this type were:

(a)  the refusal of any school place for a 5-year-old until parents agreed to an assessment
(b)  the completion of a psychological assessment before parents had been informed of the LEA wish to begin procedures
(c)  medical advice written without a recent examination and without parental discussion
(d)  the use of a lengthy 'assessment placement' without parental involvement
(e)  the holding back of completed Statements until immediately before the start of a new term
(f)  the production of a Statement which conferred no additional resources to the child.

From many of our interviews with parents, it appeared that the legal formalities, such as the wording and sending of letters, the provision of advice by medical, psychological and education advisers and the provision of a Statement, were on the whole observed. However, in order to accommodate the work load and the pressures inherent in the task, it was possible to identify many occasions on which shortcuts and a circumvention of the ideals of good practice outlined in the Circulars often brought the whole local approach to accountability into question, as well as conflicting with the principles underlying the Act.

## PARENTAL INVOLVEMENT

The availability of information about the Act, the local procedures and the LEA approach to special needs provision has already been detailed and can be seen as providing the minimum starting point for any parental involvement as suggested by the Act. It will be recalled that, despite the legal obligation to achieve this first step, a number of authorities had yet to provide information for parents. (Only 55 per cent of LEAs provided information for all parents and only 81 per cent provided such information for parents of children with special educational needs, two and a half years after the introduction of the Act.) The quality of the information produced has been the subject of criticism elsewhere (Rogers, 1986).

A second phase of involvement requires an LEA to listen to parents as well as informing them, and this was more difficult to achieve for some LEA staff. While most parents whom we interviewed did, at the end of the procedures, accept the outcome of the assessment, there were many who felt that they had not been involved in the decision-making process in any substantial way. Most were silent, and this was sometimes taken as agreement. In their interviews with the team, parents often made it clear that silence did not mean assent and many recorded their unhappiness about both the lack of information and the lack of voice they were 'allowed'.

Clearly the quality of the relationship between parents and professionals is crucial and, because of the imbalance of power, professionals must necessarily accept major responsibility for it. The professionals are many in number, they have access to knowledge and expertise, and they are routinely involved in procedures that parents of children with special educational needs often meet only at the time their child is assessed. In the final analysis, the professionals will, in all except the tiny minority of cases, also control access to resources. Even where they do not, control will not pass to the parents.

Despite this, the detailed study LEAs did, in general, adopt the proper legal line. They also attempted to avoid appeals wherever they could. Although the emphasis on avoiding appeals had clear implications for the relationship between parents and the LEA, it had led to some professionals over-riding their professional judgement about the most suitable placement for a child. In some cases, pressure by the LEA to persuade parents to accept a particular placement was seen as 'coercion'.

Although these reservations represent important constraints on accountability to parents, some had grasped the opportunities offered by the Act and, though they had yet to achieve parity with the professionals, some parents identified movement towards a more equal partnership as a realistic target.

## CO-OPERATION BETWEEN EDUCATION, HEALTH
## AND SOCIAL SERVICES DEPARTMENTS

This chapter has already identified the extent to which professionals from health and social services were, in effect, excluded from LEA planning for the Act. The differences in administrative structure between the three services, outlined in Chapter 4, did little to facilitate involvement in planning or to help reach the mutual understanding so essential to effective multi-disciplinary collaboration. Two factors appeared to be most damaging to the achievement of multi-disciplinary planning for the Act. One was the contiguity of the implementation of the Act and the reorganization of the health authorities which, in many areas, brought about the severance of the personal and professional links which would have facilitated the introduction of the new procedures. The second was the distancing of social workers from the other contributing professionals. The fact that both the social services department and the education authority were part of the same authority appeared to do little to reduce the gap between them. The resulting competition for resources was claimed by some to have actually increased in the prevailing economic climate.

There were obvious differences in policy and practice in the three disciplines, for example, over the simple question of whether the child was the focus, as was usually the case for educational and health professionals, or whether it was the family, as was more often the case for social workers. In some cases, such differences led to conflict, and there were also disputes over which authority should take financial responsibility for provision.

While some administrators rejected the importance of interdepartmental battles, there were clearly major questions requiring resolution; for example, whether education authorities should seek to supply 'health' services to those children whose needs indicated that they were necessary. The context for many such conflicts was the requirement for speech therapy. Similar difficulties arose in some authorities over whether education or social services departments should accept the costs of residential placement.

Competing definitions of special educational needs and differences in the interpretation of the requirements of the Act and regulations were not helped by unclear boundaries between the professional roles of such staff as clinical and educational psychologists, and educational welfare officers and social workers.


## SUMMARY AND CONCLUSION

This chapter has explored the difficult area of local policy and practice related to the 1981 Education Act. It has recorded a number of aspects which offer clues to central and local administrations seeking to provide an effective special needs service within the framework of the legislation.

The research has indicated the problems faced by local authorities seeking to respond to a delayed Circular of Guidance. It has also identified the narrowness of the constituency which LEAs consulted during the preparation of the local response.

The system of services described by LEAs was influenced, to some extent, by pre-existing patterns of provision. These were so difficult to change that patterns laid down prior to the Maud reorganization of local government in 1974 were still observable in some authorities. Despite this, changes in the allocation of children to different types of provision and changes in the recruitment of teaching and support staff reported by LEAs suggested an accelerating move towards mainstream placement.

In-service training and written guidance material produced by LEAs had their shortcomings and these were, in the detailed study areas at least, often recognized by providers and users alike.

The project was able to identify only limited movement along the road towards greater parental involvement in the decision-making about their children's needs and provision. Even well-informed, articulate and determined parents found the local procedures difficult. This theme is discussed further in Chapter 7.

Multi-professional involvement in many LEAs also appeared to be token in nature and the extent to which this was reflected in the part played by the various professionals in the local procedures is considered in the following chapter.

# Chapter 7

## The Identification and Assessment of Children with Special Educational Needs

### INTRODUCTION

This chapter explores the issues surrounding the identification and assessment of children with special educational needs and the decision-making processes concerned with the statutory procedures for making Statements following the 1981 Education Act. It includes an analysis of the relationship between continuing professional assessment and the statutory assessment required to make a Statement, the processes involved in decision-making about special educational needs and the allocation of provision. Inter-authority and inter-professional co-operation and collaboration are also considered. A more detailed analysis of the effects of the Act on the roles of professionals, administrators and parents will be discussed in Chapter 8.

### THE FUNCTIONS OF ASSESSMENT

Assessment is a decision-making process whereby a child's strengths and weaknesses are evaluated in order to come to a clearer understanding of the nature of his special educational needs, in relation to environmental resources, and the provision which could best meet those needs. The 1981 Act makes a clear distinction between (a) assessment as a continuous feature of a school's attempts to help children with difficulties and (b) assessment which takes place in order for an LEA to determine the provision which should be made in a particular case, where the resources available to a school have not met a child's needs (Circular 1/83).

The Warnock Committee envisaged a five-stage assessment procedure which involved an increasing level of expertise from the class teacher, through the specialist teacher and the psychologist, to a multi-professional assessment which was linked to the drawing up of a record of needs. However, as Welton *et al.* (1982) have pointed out, a distinction must be made between 'professional' decision-making about the nature of a child's needs and how they should be met and 'administrative' decision-making about the allocation of resources.

Circular 1/83 makes a distinction between the continuous process of assessment that takes place as professionals attempt to understand the nature of a child's needs, and to meet them, and the statutory procedures which must be followed if a Statement is to be made. The function of the statutory assessment is to collect advice on a multi-professional basis, and from that advice come to a decision about whether a Statement of Needs is necessary and, if so, what provision is to be made. Continuous assessment can be, and often is, multi-professional, but it is not concerned with the writing of Statements, though obviously it can lead to statutory assessment and provision of a Statement.

Circular 1/83 (para. 4) advises LEAs that, in drawing up a Statement, a clear distinction must be made between:

   (i)   the analysis of the child's learning difficulties
   (ii)  the specification of his special needs for different kinds of interventions, facilities or resources
   (iii) the determination of the special education provision to meet these needs.

The separation of (iii) from (i) and (ii) indicates the separation between the decisions about the nature of a child's needs and decisions about the allocation of provision.

The Circular also emphasizes that assessment is a continuous process and that, in most cases, it shall be for the school rather than the LEA to assess and meet the special educational needs of children. It is only in cases where a school's interventions do not seem to meet the child's needs that formal statutory procedures should be considered.

Thus, there appear to be two distinct functions of assessment. First, there is the process whereby education and health authority professionals involved with the child attempt to come to some understanding of the child's difficulties and needs, and evaluate the child's response to intervention in his normal setting, whether at home, at school or elsewhere. Such evaluations may take place in pre-school play groups or opportunity groups, or in speech or physiotherapy sessions provided by the health authority, or as part of a Portage programme or assessment by a district handicap team.

The second function of assessment is as a process in which the findings from individual professionals' assessments are considered by the LEA, in order for it to come to a decision about the allocation of 'extra' resources to an individual child.

As discussed in Chapter 4, the definition of 'extra' resources will vary from LEA to LEA and so, therefore, will the threshold at which professionals assessing a child will come to the decision that the statutory assessment procedures should be initiated. This is acknowledged in the Circular 1/83 which says:

> The deciding factors in determining what constitutes additional or otherwise different provision are likely to vary from area to area depending on the range of provision normally available in an authority's schools. As a general rule, the Secretary of State expects LEAs to afford the protection of a Statement to all children who have severe or complex learning difficulties which require the provision of extra resources in ordinary schools, and in all cases where the child is placed in a special unit attached to an ordinary school, a special school, a non-maintained special school or an independent school approved for the purpose.
> (Para. 14)

This makes it clear that one of the functions of the statutory assessment procedures is to provide the 'protection of a Statement' to any child who is provided with 'extra' resources or is relocated out of mainstream into special education. The Act acknowledges that decision-making of this kind must be accompanied by safeguards for children and parents; parents must be given an opportunity to make their views known to the LEA and must be given copies of the Statement and advice from professionals upon which decisions recorded in the Statement are made. Therefore, the functions of the statutory assessment procedures are not related just to the allocation of resources to children, but also to the allocation of children to resources. That is to say, special schools and units are resources which are already there, regardless of whether they are allocated to a particular child, so they are extra resources allocated in advance of the needs of any individual child. In fact, the qualifications mentioned in the 1981 Act indicate that children should be allocated to these resources, rather than be supported in mainstream if this is more cost effective. The statutory procedures make it possible for such decisions to be open and challengeable, and do not just represent an attempt to produce a more efficient form of decision-making for professionals and administrators.

The involvement of parents, which is mandatory under the statutory assessment procedures, should be sought at an early stage of any assessment, according to Circular 1/83:

> In looking at the child as a whole person, the involvement of the child's parent is essential. Assessment should be seen as a partnership between teachers, other professionals and parents in a joint endeavour to discover and understand the nature of the difficulties and needs of individual children. Close relationships should be established and maintained with parents and can only be helped by frankness and openness on all sides.
> (Para. 6)

So, another function of assessment is for all concerned, including parents, to come to a negotiated understanding of a child's needs. In order to do this, the Circular recommends that a sharing of information should take place, during the continuous as well as the statutory process of assessment.

However, given the relative status of parents and professionals, there are problems in achieving such a partnership, even if information is shared. These have been acknowledged by Wolfendale (1985), who has developed a checklist to enable parents to structure their observations and comments about their children.

Weatherley (1979) identified several difficulties for parents as participants in the 'core evaluation process' which took place under the special education legislation in Massachusetts. These were multi-professional meetings, the culmination of an assessment process which had taken place in the last weeks leading up to the meeting. The difficulties were:

(i) the parents were outnumbered by professionals
(ii) they were outsiders in an on-going group
(iii) there were status differences in terms of education and social class.

Similarly, our research showed that parents were unequal partners in the assessment procedures, and a majority of the parents we interviewed did not feel that they had been able to make a significant contribution to the decision-making process. In cases where the parents had definitely disagreed with the LEA's decision, none had appealed. They had accepted what the LEA was prepared to offer. In these cases, the assessment process had appeared to the parents as coercive and had served to legitimize a decision in which they had played no part.

Thus, in addition to the overt functions of assessment (the analysis of a child's learning difficulties, the monitoring of the effectiveness of interventions, and decision-making about the allocation of resources), there are other covert functions which relate more to the processes of negotiation and socialization that occur as parents and professionals interact in order to achieve certain ends. These ends involve, not only meeting the needs of individual children, but also the efficient management of resources and the reconciling of a variety of different interests, including those of parents, teachers, psychologists, health and social services professionals, administrators and politicians.

## THE IDENTIFICATION OF SPECIAL NEEDS

The first stage in any process of assessment is the identification of children with learning difficulties. The 1981 Act is precise about where the duty to identify lies:

> It shall be the duty of every local education authority to exercise their powers under this Act with a view of securing that, of the children for whom they are responsible, those with special educational needs which call for the local education authority to determine the special educational provision that should be made for them are identified by the authority. Section 4 (1)

Circular 1/83 advises that:

> LEAs should provide guidance to all maintained schools in their area on the arrangements for identifying, assessing and meeting special educational needs. This guidance should relate to the identification of special needs, assessment procedures, channels of communication for referrals and advice on the specialist services available for referrals. (Para. 8)

Our survey of the documents produced by LEAs in response to the legislation, carried out in 1983 and again in 1985, indicates that the majority of LEAs had issued guidance on identification and referral to their schools. New procedures were initiated in each of the five LEAs which we studied in detail. These new procedural guidelines emphasized the role that schools had to play, not only in identifying, but also in providing for children with special educational needs.

For example, in A-Shire, a set of pupil record forms had been introduced. These forms were used to monitor the progress of all pupils at certain stages in their school career. Two forms were designed for use for children who appeared to have learning difficulties. The first was a record of those interventions that had been tried to help a child with learning difficulties. The second was a referral form, but could only be used once the first form had been filled in and showed that all strategies available within a school's resources had been tried and had failed.

A similar clear statement of the stages of assessment and the role which the school had to play in meeting children's needs was found in D-shire.

In E-Borough, the Special Needs Action Programme (SNAP) had been introduced into primary schools with the object of improving school-based identification, assessment and provision.

B-Borough produced a 'Booklet of Guidance for Professionals' which summarized the Act and gave details of B-Borough's response. As previously described, B-Borough has a 'Board' which decides special education policy and a 'Panel' which makes decisions about initiating formal procedures and making Statements. The functions of these two were explained in the booklet. It also summarized the main themes of the Warnock report, gave details of the range of special educational provision available in the Borough and gave 'sources of information'.

The difficulties in C-Shire, of providing a co-ordinated response, have been described in Chapter 4, and initially these led to conflicting advice being given to schools. This resulted in a certain amount of confusion for head teachers, which did not appear to have been completely resolved, even though a new revised system had been devised and circulated.

It is likely, then, that schools in most local authorities were given a clear picture of what was expected of them in terms of their duties to identify children with special needs. However, it appeared from our research that, in many schools, staff were less clear about their responsibility to meet those needs within the resources of their school. Some heads thought that the new procedures for referral introduced by the LEA were an attempt to block referrals and to force schools to cope without giving them extra resources. In some areas there appeared to be long delays between schools asking for 'outside professional advice' and this being made available. This, coupled with the trend, documented by Gipps *et al.* (1987), for 'remedial' and 'support' teachers to try to provide for pupils with special educational needs through support for their class teachers, put extra pressures on schools at a time when resources were not available. The present project found there to be a high level of frustration expressed by teachers, who felt that nothing was being done to meet the needs of the children they had identified.

Some LEAs employ authority-wide screening procedures. Gipps *et al.* (op. cit.) found that 71 per cent of authorities use some form of screening. They found (and this was confirmed by our study) that there were marked differences between authorities in the way in which the information gained by screening was used. It was not always used for the purpose of identifying children with special educational needs, but rather to monitor 'standards' throughout an authority.

For example, in A-Shire, children were given NFER tests in the first and third years of junior schooling and in the third year of secondary schooling, to monitor standards, rather than to identify individual children with learning difficulties or as a basis for directing extra resources to particular schools. In B-Borough, screening had been used to allocate extra resources to schools where a large proportion of children had low scores on standardized reading tests, although this system was thought to be unsatisfactory and was in the process of being altered. In C-Shire, the support service used the results of screening tests to allocate extra help to individual children.

Although the primary duty to identify children with special needs lies with the education authorities, the health authorities also play a major role in identifying children under five, particularly those with severe handicapping conditions. In the areas in which we conducted detailed studies, we found that health authorities had well-established screening procedures for children. However, in some sparsely populated areas, procedures were less well developed, and in one health authority we visited there was no school health service; the functions of the clinical medical officers were performed by GPs.

Once a health authority has identified a child who has or might have special educational needs, it has a duty, after discussion with the child's parents, to inform the education authority. Most authorities had well-established procedures for doing this, and these appeared to work effectively, to the extent that in some areas the education departments were informed about children a few days after birth. However, some medical officers expressed reservations about the desirability of informing the education authority about very young children. Some parents expressed a reluctance about having this information passed on, and this placed doctors in a difficult position. Some doctors also worried about the consequences of 'labelling' a child at a very young age. Overall, there appeared to be a fair degree of mutual confidence and respect between education and health as far as the identification of children was concerned. What was more problematic, however, was whether identification of children with special needs ultimately led to appropriate provision being made. This was more a question of the allocation of resources than the efficiency of systems of identification.

## ASSESSMENT AND INTERVENTION WITHIN GENERALLY AVAILABLE RESOURCES

Even though authorities may have had adequate procedures for identification and referral, such referrals did not always lead to children's needs being met, particularly in areas with insufficient resources. In authorities where there was a limited range of provision available within mainstream schools, assessment and intervention within the mainstream setting was not always an option, even if children were identified. In some authorities, there appeared to be a tendency to provide very little until a Statement had been made. We were given several examples of children whose parents had had to fight very hard to gain any help for them, and where help was only made available after statutory assessment had taken place.

This was particularly true of pre-school children. In those LEAs with very few nursery schools, any provision for children under the age of five provided by the LEA would be in a segregated setting. In areas with very little pre-school provision, authorities had to rely very much on provision offered by social services day nurseries or by opportunity groups and playgroups. In some areas of A-Shire, for example, there were very few nursery schools, and the only educational provision available was in schools for pupils with severe learning difficulties, which were not suitable for some children. Provision was made in 'opportunity groups' and social services day nurseries, but this was not always strictly educational, and some parents we interviewed had serious reservations about the appropriateness of what was being offered. One solution to this problem in A-Shire had been the provision of a 'special class' in an infant school. This took children with special needs from the age of three years, thus avoiding a long journey to the nearest special school for this age group, that might otherwise have been necessary.

In LEAs with a wide range of provision, there were more options available to the LEA and the parents. For example, in B-Borough many schools had units for children with special needs attached to them. Some of these were 'designated' units, which meant that children had to be given Statements to go to them; others were 'non-designated', which meant that children could transfer to them without a Statement. This resulted in a more flexible approach to children with special needs. The same was true of D-Shire, which had a wide range of options available for pre-school children, including help from a teacher-counsellor, Portage schemes or nursery placement.

D-Shire also provided a support service for children with specific learning difficulties in mainstream schools.

However, D-Shire differed in its approach from B-Borough, in that it tended to make most of this provision available only to children who had Statements. This was in order to protect the service from 'cuts', but had the effect of introducing severe delays into the system. At one stage, the pre-school teacher–counsellor service almost disappeared because no children were being referred to it. Eventually, the LEA had to change its policy and make this service available without a Statement.

In contrast, C-Shire had adopted a policy of 'minimal statementing'. This meant that very few children with special needs came forward for statutory assessment. Almost every assessment and allocation of resources was deemed to be 'within generally available resources'. The authority had produced an assessment procedure, which was identical to the statutory assessment procedures in every way, except that no Statement was produced for the majority of children who went through it. 'Assessments for all and Statements for none' was the slogan adopted for this tactic. Only children who were in separate special schools (mainly schools for children with severe learning difficulties) or who were placed 'out-county' were given Statements. Many children with moderate learning difficulties or behaviour problems were being educated in mainstream schools, with support. However, since this support was not protected by a Statement, it could be, and sometimes was, removed without full consultation with the school or the child's parents.

**Provisional placements**

Circular 1/83 states that children may be placed in special schools and units on a provisional basis in order for an assessment to be carried out. The Circular states that such placements are permissible if a child has severe emotional or behavioural problems, or if the assessment is likely to be protracted. Of authorities answering our questionnaire, 63 per cent said that they sometimes used provisional placement, and 28 per cent said that they often used it. There were three authorities who said that they *always* used provisional placement.

We found a wide use of such placements in some of the detailed study authorities and it seemed that the criteria set out in the Circular were not always being followed.

For example, in E-Borough, of the nine children with Statements whose parents we interviewed, five had been admitted to schools for assessment. Some of these assessments had been going on for over a year. Some of the parents had been given the impression that these placements were 'temporary' and were disconcerted to find that subsequently, when the Statement was drawn up, temporary placement had become permanent.

In C-Shire, two of the three young children who had been admitted to a school for children with severe learning difficulties, whose parents we interviewed, were already in the assessment unit attached to that school.

In one area of A-Shire, two out of five children whose parents were interviewed had been admitted to schools for children with moderate learning difficulties for assessment. One was admitted at the age of 12 years, having just been identified by his new comprehensive school as unable to read or write. The other was a child with Down's

Syndrome whose parents had wanted integrated education for her, but could not persuade the educational psychologist to agree. As she was over the age of five and was not in school, the placement in the special school was presented to the parents as the only option available. In these cases, it seems that provisional placement was being used to place children in special schools quickly, because it was felt that assessment and intervention in mainstream were inappropriate.

The Act makes provision for such assessments to take place, but in some cases it may be that children's rights to education in an integrated setting could be undermined if they are moved from the mainstream for assessment, or in the case of younger children, if they are never given the opportunity to experience education in the mainstream. It seems that often such placements reflect the lack of suitable provision for children with special needs in mainstream and that the choice is between no provision or segregated provision, particularly for under-fives.

It may also be the case that such placements are used to 'get the parents used to the idea' of special education for their child. This was one of the reasons put forward by the head of a school for children with moderate learning difficulties in E-Borough, who accepted children from the mainstream for trial periods of up to two terms.

From comments made at some of the feedback meetings held to verify our research findings, it appears that provisional placement is also used when the authorities' formal procedures are subject to delays. The Circular envisages that some assessments are 'likely to be protracted', but presumably because some children's cases are complex, rather than because local authority procedures are inefficient.

It seems, then, that provisional placement is being used in several ways: as a tactic to persuade parents that placement in a special school is acceptable; to make speedy provision where none exists in mainstream; as a method of pre-empting the results of assessment; and as a way of speeding up the process of placement, when there are delays in the system.

## THE THRESHOLD OF REFERRAL FOR THE STATUTORY ASSESSMENT

What marks the point at which the decision to initiate the statutory assessment procedures is taken? The starting point for such a decision must be that local education authorities have a duty to ensure that children have their special educational needs met and a duty to assess if there are 'prima-facie' grounds to suspect these needs cannot be met through generally available provision. If the statutory assessment shows that this is the case, the LEA must make a Statement. The relative definition of special educational needs and provision, discussed in previous chapters, indicates that such a decision-making point will vary from authority to authority, and even from area to area within an authority, depending on the type of need and the range of provision available. It will also depend on authorities' policies about which types of provision require Statements to gain access. As described earlier, there seem to be wide variations in LEA policies on this, ranging from one extreme where anything provided in mainstream was not the subject of a Statement, to the opposite extreme where provision specifically excluded by the Circular, such as that provided in tutorial units, was protected by a Statement. Thus, not only is there a difference between LEAs in their levels and types of provision, but there is also a difference in their interpretation of what 'made generally' means.

The establishment of a 'prima-facie' case as advised in Circular 1/83 is closely connected to this relativity, and consequently the criteria used vary widely between LEAs. Such inconsistency is not, of itself, a bad thing, since the requirement to produce a Statement was intended to iron out differences in levels of provision by forcing LEAs with little 'generally available' provision to meet individual children's special needs by providing extra resources through a Statement. However, the local policy decisions about which resources should be made available through the Statement disallow the possibility of such flexibility, and the result is that there are widely differing standards throughout the country.

One fairly straightforward way of making the decision to initiate the statutory procedures is to respond to parental requests for an assessment under Section 5 of the Act. Of authorities responding to our questionnaire, 53 per cent reported that they always carried out a Section 5 assessment following parental requests, and 34 per cent said that they often did so. One problem with this was that it led to the parents expecting a Statement and, since this was not always the outcome, led to conflict at a later stage.

Another method of coming to such decisions was through a panel meeting which considered the evidence for a 'prima-facie' case. This method was used in 33 per cent of the metropolitan boroughs and 15 per cent of the shire counties. A panel was used in one of the LEAs that we studied in detail. One of the problems was that the evidence was filtered before it got to the panel: through the schools psychological service, who summarized it, and by the Statementing Officer, who summarized the summary. It was described as 'like a game of Chinese Whispers'. However, it did provide a forum for multi-disciplinary discussion at an early stage, which could explore likely options. The panel also met later to discuss the draft Statement.

In 75 per cent of LEAs, the decision to initiate the formal procedures was delegated to one person, usually either an administrator (56 per cent of authorities) or an educational psychologist (16 per cent of authorities). However, many administrators added that they would consult their educational psychologist before making the decision.

One fairly consistent signal for the initiation of the statutory assessment procedures seemed to be the impending movement of a child from one stage of education to another. Among the children whose parents we interviewed, it seemed that, in many instances, the decision to assess was prompted by the fact that the child was about to move from infant to junior school, or from junior to secondary school, and it was thought that he or she 'just would not cope' in the new school. This sometimes led to problems, as there was often not enough time for the procedures to be completed before the end of term, and parents and children were left wondering which school they would be attending after the holidays. Since it is now common practice for children to visit their 'new' school, many of these children became very anxious when they could not do so. Timing is an important consideration when procedures are started at a point of transition for a child.

The establishment of a 'prima-facie' case appears to rely on a complex interaction of factors, and the ability to meet the child's needs in the context of the 'generally available' provision is only one of these. Other factors include the LEA's policy on what provision is restricted to those children who have Statements, parental wishes, and the age of the child related to the stage of schooling.

The decision to initiate the procedures is most commonly taken by an administrator.

This was the case in 53 per cent of authorities responding to our questionnaire. Thus, it can be seen that it is regarded as primarily a bureaucratic, rather than a professional, decision, though most children being considered for statutory assessment will have been referred by a professional: either a head teacher, a psychologist or a medical officer.

## THE STATUTORY ASSESSMENT PROCEDURES

The 'formality' or 'bureaucracy' of the procedures for assessing children for a Statement and for arriving at decisions about provision to meet needs has been one of the chief criticisms levelled against the 1981 Education Act. It is said that these procedures 'cut across good practice', 'cause delay' and 'cause confrontations with parents'. However, as noted earlier, the form of the procedures was designed to give parents certain rights and to make LEAs open and accountable for the decisions they make about the education of children with special needs.

Our findings indicate that it is not necessarily the nature of the procedures themselves, but the way in which they have been implemented in some LEAs, which has caused the problems. The time taken for producing Statements varies widely between LEAs, some reporting an 'average' time of 12 weeks or under and others an 'average' of over 36 weeks. So, on average, some LEAs are taking three times as long as others to complete Statements. The main reasons given by administrators for delays in producing Statements were:

> the complexity of the procedures (14 per cent)
> delays in receiving medical advice (22 per cent)
> delays in receiving other professional advice (17 per cent)
> work load (20 per cent).

The form of the procedures themselves is cited as a reason for delay by only 14 per cent of administrators, the other main reasons reflecting practice in implementing them.

As far as confrontations between parents and the LEA are concerned, figures published by the DES indicate that the majority of LEAs have not had appeals to the Secretary of State. Of the 53 appeals up to March 1985, 15 were from a total of three LEAs (five each) and another nine were from three LEAs (three each). Again, this appears to indicate that local factors, rather than something inherent in the procedures, cause confrontation.

Indications from our interviews with parents are that they were not particularly bothered about the formality or the bureaucracy of the procedures. They saw these as only to be expected in any dealings with 'officialdom'. This aspect of the 1981 Education Act seems to have been seen as a problem mainly by professionals and administrators, perhaps because they wish to achieve a more positive relationship with parents and feel inhibited in doing this by the procedures.

**The initiation of the procedures**

Circular 1/83 advises that the serving of formal notice under Section 5 of the Act should not be the first indication to parents that their child has learning difficulties. Many authorities try to soften the impact of the first formal letter by stipulating that it should be delivered by hand. This was the case in just under half of the authorities we surveyed. Inevitably, such visits are time consuming, and one of our detailed study authorities decided to revise the practice when it discovered that, although the letters were being given to the educational psychologists involved with the children so that they could deliver them, the psychologists were then putting the letters in the post! Some authorities use educational welfare officers to perform the task of visiting and counselling parents whose children are being assessed, but in other areas, psychologists are reluctant to give this responsibility to the welfare service. In our five detailed study authorities, we came across a range of ways of delivering the letter. In those areas where the letter was posted, psychologists went to great lengths to inform the parents to expect a letter, and to advise them of its contents. In the sample of parents we interviewed, we did not come across any cases where parents had been unaware that the statutory procedures were to be initiated before receiving the first formal letter from the LEA.

The LEA is also under a duty to give parents details of the formal assessment procedures, the name of an LEA officer from whom they can obtain further information and their rights to make representations and submit written evidence.

A study by the Centre for Studies in Integration in Education (Rogers, 1986) has indicated that many authorities failed to give parents sufficient information to enable them to participate fully in the assessment process. Authorities tended to give parents information in stages, rather than giving them an overview, so that they would not know what was due to happen next. The language in which the parents' booklets were written was difficult to understand, and often there were no translations for non-English-speaking families. We have collected some excellent parents' information booklets in the course of our research, but there are also some very poor ones. In our five detailed study authorities, the standard of presentation and information given varied tremendously, and this appeared to have some effect on parents' sense of participation. When interviewed by the project, parents in the authorities which stressed parents' rights and the value given to their contribution were much more able to express their feelings, both positive and negative, about what had happened. In the authorities where there had been little emphasis on parental participation, parents were, on the whole, more distanced from what had occurred during the procedures and could remember less about what had happened.

Only 28 per cent of authorities responding to the questionnaire said that all or most parents contributed advice for the Statement. In our detailed studies, we found that the majority of parents had done so. In one of the authorities, a questionnaire designed by the medical officer was given to parents to fill in. It was intended to help them to participate in giving advice about their child. Although the professionals felt that the information given by parents in this way was very useful, it did not seem to increase the parents' sense of participation since very few of those interviewed could remember filling it in. In the other detailed study LEAs, many parents had written quite detailed letters; some gave their views about their child; others challenged advice from the professional advisers.

Circular 1/83 suggests that the LEA might wish to suggest the name of a voluntary organization or employee of a statutory body to help parents who might have difficulty in making representations. We found no evidence that voluntary organizations were being used for this purpose. The person most commonly used to help in this way was an educational psychologist or an education welfare officer. There was usually no *independent* adviser for the parents.

### Multi-professional assessment for the statutory procedures

As noted earlier, multi-professional assessment does not take place only during the statutory assessment procedures, but the form of multi-professional assessment required by the 1981 Education Act in this regard is quite specific. The Regulations require that the LEA should obtain, at the minimum, educational, medical and psychological *advice*. The functions and qualifications of the persons designated to give this advice are specified in some detail. 'Advice' must be *written* advice on features of the case which affect a child's special educational needs and on the ways of meeting those needs, and it must be made available to parents.

Circular 1/83 suggests what the content of the advice should cover:

   (i)   the relevant aspects of the child's functioning, including his strengths and weaknesses, his relation with his environment at home and at school and any relevant aspects of the child's past history
  (ii)   the aims to which provision for the child should be directed to enable him to develop educationally and increase his independence
 (iii)   the facilities and resources recommended to promote the achievement of these aims. (Para. 23)

The kind of information which might be included under these headings is detailed in an appendix to the Circular.

The quality of advice for Statements varies enormously. Parents found some of the remarks and phrases used by the advisers quite distressing, particularly if the advice had not been fully discussed with the parents before being forwarded to the LEA. For instance, much of the educational advice appeared to be wholly negative. Perhaps this is not surprising, since in referring a child, schools are describing the ways in which the child is failing within the school. Parents particularly resented remarks about their personal circumstances (e.g. the state of their marriage), or their attitudes (e.g. their lack of concern with their child's problems). Terms used to describe their children, such as 'mentally handicapped' and 'retarded', were also upsetting to parents. The tactic of saying something positive at the beginning of the advice had a noticeable effect on parents' attitude to the particular professional. For example, one educational psychologist always started her advice by saying something individual and positive about the child, such as: 'James is a lively and friendly little boy with big brown eyes'. This psychologist was particularly remembered by parents as having produced a 'fair' assessment of their child.

There were great variations in the amount of detail given in the advice. Medical advice tended to be fairly brief. There had been worries among medical professionals about confidentiality, and this may have had an inhibiting effect. On the other hand, it is likely that the majority of children who receive Statements (i.e. those with moderate learning difficulties and behaviour problems) do not have medical problems which affect their educational needs. Some doctors pointed out the absurdity of performing a medical examination on a strapping 14-year-old who had no history of illness.

The most detailed advice tended to be the psychological advice. Psychologists usually wrote their advice last, and had the benefit of reading the educational, medical and any other advice given. So, in addition to their own observations, they could take the views of others into account. Responses to the questionnaire indicate that the person most likely to summarize the advice and prepare a formulation of the child's needs for the draft Statement was either the administrator (45 per cent of authorities) or the psychologist (24 per cent of authorities). Indications from our detailed studies are that psychologists play a crucial role in formulating a view of the child's needs which is forwarded to the administrator who then drafts the Statement.

The multi-professional aspects of the formal assessment are not merely confined to sending advice to the LEA about particular children. There is a distinction to be made between professional assessment, the formulating of advice, and the decisions made upon the advice submitted. The formulation of advice is left in the hands of three designated officers, as outlined above. They may consult with others before writing their advice. In the case of the medical advice, the designated medical officer may summarize advice given by other health professionals, such as speech therapists or physiotherapists. This is the cause of much concern among health professionals, who feel that it is inappropriate for their advice to be summarized and subsumed under the general medical advice. Circular 1/83 suggests that speech and physiotherapy advice should be sought through the designated medical officer, and that any psychiatric advice should be included in the medical advice. Nursing advice, however, is sought separately, though a survey by the Society of Nurse Advisers (Child Health) suggests that 26 per cent of nursing advice is summarized by designated medical officers and not sent verbatim to the LEA. Our questionnaire indicates that 63 per cent of LEAs receive their advice direct from advising professionals in the health authority and 28 per cent receive advice collated by an administrator before being sent on, so it would appear that the advice in Circular 1/83 has not been followed in the majority of authorities, and that it does not reflect the practice that health professionals feel is most appropriate.

Circular 1/83 also stipulates that social services departments should be notified of the intention to assess a child. Our research found a great deal of uncertainty among social services personnel about how they should respond to such notification. There appeared to be problems about what type of information was relevant for the LEA, and conflicts of loyalty, where the social worker's client was the parent rather than the child. In areas where social services were part of a panel, or had close links with special schools, co-operation between them and the education department appeared to be less problematic. However, in many areas the role of social workers was unspecified, and since they were so stretched by other aspects of their work, they tended not to place a high priority on their involvement with the statutory assessment procedures.

## Decision-making for the Statement

Circular 1/83 places great emphasis on the desirability of inter-professional and inter-service co-operation in decision-making about the special educational needs of children. It suggests that there are two strategies for ensuring co-operation during the statutory assessment process. One is that professional advisers should submit their advice separately to the LEA. These reports should then be copied to all the professionals advising on the child's needs. We have termed this *collected* multi-professional assessment. The other method is through consultation among the professional advisers at a case conference. District Handicap Teams may provide a forum for such discussion, mainly in the instance of pre-school children with physical and multiple handicaps. We have termed this *collective* multi-professional assessment.

Responses to our questionnaire indicate that collective MPA, as defined by the Circular, is not used routinely in any LEA. Two authorities co-ordinated advice at a meeting with representatives from different services, but the majority of LEAs acted as receivers of advice from separate sources. At a later stage, when the advice had been collected, it was more usual for a panel of professionals to consider it. In 24 per cent of authorities this happened when the decision to make a Statement was under consideration, in 17 per cent of authorities when the formulation of the child's needs for the Statement was being discussed, and in 29 per cent of authorities when provision was being decided upon. In 18 per cent of authorities, the draft Statement was submitted to a panel for approval.

In the authorities in which we undertook detailed studies, we found a range of approaches to the co-ordination of advice for Statements.

In A-Shire, the initial letter was sent out by the administrator, and it was then left to the psychologist to collect the advice and write the draft Statement. This method was causing problems of workload for psychologists in A-Shire. This finding was confirmed by responses to a questionnaire survey of principal educational psychologists conducted by Pearson for the National Association of Principal Educational Psychologists. This survey was concerned with the impact of the 1981 Education Act on local authority psychological services (NAPEP, 1985).

In B-Borough, the Panel, a group of representatives from health, education and social services, met to consider whether procedures should be initiated for particular children, and then again after a draft Statement had been prepared. The case for initiating procedures was made by the educational psychologist and, at the time of our research, no case had been rejected. The draft Statement was prepared by a Statementing Officer (a teacher on secondment) (1), in consultation with a senior educational psychologist, and submitted to the panel for approval. In most cases, the members of the panel would have no direct knowledge of the child, and decisions were made on the basis of the advice submitted. This was multi-service decision-making, rather than multi-professional assessment.

In C-Shire, the procedures were co-ordinated by a special education administrator, appointed after a breakdown in the previous system. This officer collated the advice. The formulation of the child's needs and decision-making about provision was undertaken by area education officers in consultation with advisers. Psychologists were viewed as advising professionals, in the same way as medical and educational advisers, and did not have a part to play in the decision-making or in the formulation of needs. Decisions about 'out-county' placements were made by the Chief Education Officer.

In D-Shire, a core team of administrator, principal educational psychologist and three specialist advisers was involved in the decision-making. The advice from health and social services was sent direct to the administrator, though the main liaison and negotiation with parents was undertaken by the educational psychologist.

In E-Borough, the decision-making for the Statement was again undertaken by a triumvirate of adviser, administrator and psychologist.

Thus, it appears that the decisions regarding Statements and provision are mainly taken by officers of the LEA. Only in one of our detailed study areas was multi-service decision-making the norm. Multi-professional assessment for the formal procedures, in the form of case conferences, was not a routine occurrence in any of the authorities. However, that is not to say that the professionals did not meet in other circumstances to discuss children with special needs. In both D-Shire and A-Shire there were regular District Handicap Team meetings to discuss pre-school children with special needs, both with and without Statements. In E-Borough there were regular meetings of multi-disciplinary special schools admission panels, which discussed the placement of children with Statements. So, there appears to be a lot of inter-service contact, for a whole range of purposes, not all connected to the Statement procedures.

One omission, which may be crucial, was that not all LEAs appeared to inform the district health authority or the social services department of the outcome of the procedures. While all parents were given a copy of the child's Statement, only 69 per cent of health authority professionals and 50 per cent of social services departments were given copies. There have been complaints from the Society of Nurse Advisers, and from representatives of support services in the health authorities, that they are not informed of the outcome of the statutory assessment procedures, even if they have contributed. This may be due to lack of information from the LEA, or it may be that, though the information is given to the DHA or SSD, it is not passed on to those professionals who have been involved with the child.

Despite the frequent contact between services, the gulf in understanding between them still appears to be wide. Some of the reasons for this were outlined in Chapter 2. One advantage of the panel system adopted by B-Borough was that representatives from the three services had to sit down together and work out a co-ordinated approach for particular children, including an agreed formulation of their special needs and an agreed statement of the provision to meet the needs. In situations where these decisions are made by the LEA alone, conflicts over interpretations are less easy to resolve, and difficulties over the availability of non-educational provision can be more readily interpreted as incompetence or irresponsibility.

Circular 1/83 contains a section (Section VIII) which deals with co-operation between education, social services and health authorities. It expresses the hope of the Secretaries of State that:

> effective and constructive co-operation will help to make the best use of available skills and resources in providing for children with special educational needs under the Act.

Chapter 4 outlined the obstacles to such collaboration. Our detailed studies and the focused study of administrative roles indicate that the question of the allocation of resources by health authorities for children with special educational needs under Part V of the Statement of Needs is a major source of concern for LEAs and DHAs. It appears to be the case that many health authorities find themselves unable to match the demand for their services, particularly speech therapy and physiotherapy, for children with Statements. This puts education authorities in a difficult situation, since parents may question why speech and physiotherapy needs which have been noted in the advice of professionals are not being provided for in the Statement. More difficult still is that children may not be receiving speech therapy or physiotherapy which has been specified in Part V of the Statement. The ultimate responsibility for this provision lies with LEAs, yet they do not have the power to allocate the resources even though, under Section 3 of the Local Government Act 1972, health authorities have a duty to provide services to the local authorities.

**Parental involvement**

This topic will be dealt with in more detail in Chapter 8, but it is useful to make some comments here, as the involvement of parents in the formal procedures is one of the central themes of the legislation.

We have already noted the inadequacy of some of the information given to parents about the procedures. As a result, parents did not always have a full grasp of the process of assessment. LEAs differed in who acted as the 'named officer', required in Section 5(3) of the Act. Just over half gave the name of an administrator, almost a third gave the name of a clerical officer, and one-fifth gave the name of a psychologist. This person appears to perform a symbolic function only and was rarely contacted by parents, even when they had queries. They preferred to use someone they already knew, such as the psychologist or the pre-school adviser. As mentioned earlier, voluntary organizations were not presented to parents as agencies who could help them through the procedures.

In some LEAs, there seemed to be little awareness of the needs of parents who could not read or speak English. Those authorities responding to the questionnaire reported that they would call upon the services of a translator or an interpreter, if this appeared to be necessary. Only six authorities stated that they would offer translation of the documents. More than one in five authorities said that they had no arrangements and that they had not yet had a situation where the home language of the parents of a child being assessed was not English. In one of the authorities in which we conducted a detailed study, 17.1 per cent of the population were from ethnic minority groups, mostly Asian. This borough offered the services of an interpreter 'if asked to'. The Statementing Officer reported that, up to the time of our visits, no one had asked for help of this kind. Another research project working in the Borough at the same time, conducting a survey of parental response, had to rely heavily on the services of the interpreters to interview the parents of children with Statements. The fact that ethnic minority parents do not ask for help does not necessarily mean that they understand the information they are being sent by the LEA.

Circular 1/83 envisages that parental involvement in assessment 'provides an opportunity to reach an agreed understanding of the nature of a child's learning difficulties', though such agreement is not always easy to achieve. In our detailed study authorities, we did, indeed, come across parents who had achieved a very good relationship with a key professional, usually a teacher or a psychologist, and for these parents the assessment procedures had been a satisfactory experience. However, the majority of parents we interviewed were either dissatisfied or extremely upset about certain aspects of the way in which they had been treated during this time.

These feelings seemed to centre round a perception that they were being coerced into accepting provision for their child that they did not want, or that they were being rushed into a decision without being given sufficient information. In many cases, the 'frankness and openness' exhorted by Circular 1/83 appeared to be lacking. This seemed to be a problem particularly where professionals were unsure of the best way of meeting a child's needs, or where the LEA did not have the exact provision which the parents felt was necessary, and so felt that they had to recommend the parents to accept something else. Thus, the lack of frankness seemed to be related to the lack of opportunity to provide a choice, which ultimately was a question of resources.

## Statements and advice

The distinction between professional assessment, formulating advice and writing Statements has already been explored. Circular 1/83 attempts to explain the reasons for these distinctions:

> A similar understanding is required of the respective roles and functions of professional advisers and LEA administrators. Professional advice should not be influenced by considerations of eventual school placement to be made for the child, since that is a matter to be determined by the LEA at a later stage. Because of this, any discussions individual advisers have with parents about the child's needs should not be such as to commit the LEA, or pre-empt their decisions about the provision and placement to be made for the child. (Para. 35)

There are two interpretations of this passage. One is that it leaves professionals free to exercise their judgement about a child's needs and the type of facilities and resources which would meet those needs without regard to the question of the availability of resources. The other is that it is an attempt to prevent professionals from exercising their judgement about the particular provision to be made available by the LEA. The tensions between these two approaches highlight the difficulties inherent in attempting to meet individual needs within a system which has to provide a service for a population of children within a limited budget.

These tensions and differences in interpretations were manifested at the inter-service meetings which were held at the University of London Institute of Education as part of our research strategy. There was one school of thought that maintained that it was naive, even hypocritical, to expect professionals to write about needs with no regard to the likelihood of provision being made. Administrators who expressed this view were quite candid about the fact that professionals had been told not to put into advice the need for facilities which could not be made available. This practice was followed in health, as well as education, authorities.

The counter view was that professionals should be quite free to express their views about children's needs in the way they saw fit, and that it was up to the LEA to resolve any conflicts which might arise with parents because of lack of provision.

The Statement and its appendices are supposed to provide a measure of accountability in LEA decision-making, in that discrepancies between the advice contained in the appendices and the formulation of needs in the Statement are open and challengeable. The extent to which this becomes possible depends on the way Statements are formulated.

We had access to the Statements and advice on those children whose parents we interviewed, around 50 in all, so we were able to make a comparison of the way in which our five detailed study authorities approached the writing of Statements.

In A-Shire, the Statements we saw tended to be worded in general terms. For example:

**II   Special educational needs**
As set out in appendices A, C, D & E.

**III   Special educational provision**
J. requires a great deal of remedial teaching in order to develop basic literacy and numeracy skills. He is fairly well motivated and with consistent help should make progress.

**IV   Appropriate school or other arrangements**
Day placement in a school for children with moderate learning difficulties.

**V   Additional non-educational provision**
Transport.

It is interesting to note that none of the Statements we had access to in A-Shire named a particular school, despite the fact that Circular 1/83 stipulates that the LEA must name the school they are proposing for the child, if it is known. Also, in two cases where speech therapy was recommended in the advice, it did not appear in the Statement. One might argue that such vagueness in the wording of the Statement reproduced above left the parents in a difficult position if they wished to appeal against the provision their child was receiving, since it did not commit the LEA to provide any specific resource. It should be noted here that A-Shire is a relatively low-spending authority with a limited range of provision for special educational needs.

In contrast, B-Borough's Statements were much more detailed:

**II   Special educational needs**
G. needs access to a full curriculum in an environment where there is an awareness of her limited distance vision, appropriate equipment for enlarging material she is studying and the support of a teacher of the visually impaired.

**III   Special educational provision**
The provision for G. is a mainstream comprehensive school. She is to be treated at all times as an integral member of the class. Work will often need to be specifically prepared or enlarged so that G. can work alongside her peers. She will need to sit near a blackboard in a good light and the detailed recommendations of the peripatetic teacher of the visually impaired in the attached advice need to be followed closely. G.'s progress, and the appropriateness of the various aids she uses, will be kept under constant review by the peripatetic teacher.

**IV   Appropriate school and other arrangements**
B _ _ _ _ _ School for Girls

**V   Additional non-educational provision**
Medical surveillance, spectacles.

Despite the fact that Statements of educational needs should be specific for each child, it seems that, if the particular needs of a child can be met by providing additional resources in a mainstream setting, Statements are detailed, whereas if the needs can be generally met within a certain type of provision, for example, a school for moderate learning difficulties, the needs and provision are formulated in a more general way. There is a tendency for Statements of the latter kind to use certain stock phrases to describe needs and provision. For example, in E-Borough, two children, one with mild epilepsy who had been having difficulties in mainstream and one who had been receiving remedial help in mainstream, had their needs and provision to meet those needs formulated in exactly the same words:

**II   Special educational needs**

A.'s [M.'s] special educational needs are marked by learning difficulties particularly in reading skills and number.

**III   Special educational provision**

A. [M.] needs a curriculum which can be geared to the pace of her development. She requires teachers who are trained and experienced in the education of slow-learning children and a teacher/child ratio more advantageous than that available in mainstream school.

**IV   Appropriate school or other arrangements**

The most appropriate school for A. [M.] is W _ _ Senior School

If Statements can be written in such general terms, it is evident that they cannot be effective as instruments of accountability. It would be difficult to challenge such a Statement, unless there was some obvious discrepancy between the advice given and the formulation of needs, or the parent wished to challenge the content of the advice itself. As we have previously pointed out, it is difficult for most parents to do this effectively, because of their lack of knowledge or confidence.

The impression given by many of the Statements we saw in the course of our research is that they were solely concerned with the relocation of children, and that they were written from part IV backwards. That is, the provision is decided, then the requisite formula is slotted into part III and part II to justify the placement. A previous research project (Wedell *et al.*, 1981) found that the SE procedures were being used in a similar way, and that decisions about placement were usually taken before the SE procedures were initiated.

Thus, it seems that the linking of the advice, the Statement of needs and the provision is often tenuous. The range of provision available in many authorities is such that there is little choice or flexibility, and Statements tend to be worded in vague and generalized terms in order that LEAs are not made liable to provide resources that they cannot readily make available.

This is particularly true when the provision required is not under the control of the LEA, such as speech therapy or physiotherapy. Circular 1/83 appears to indicate that the LEA is ultimately liable to provide anything which appears on the Statement. That being so, LEAs are understandably reluctant to commit themselves to provide such services, even if the advice for the Statement clearly indicates that they are needed. Health authorities are in the seemingly fortunate position of not having a legal responsibility to provide services that they control if those services are in short supply. It has been suggested that LEAs could 'buy in' sessions from the health authority, but LEAs are understandably reluctant to do this since it would set a precedent, and in the long term would do nothing to overcome the problems of lack of resources for children with special educational needs in the community health services. Furthermore, a recent High Court judgement (2) appears to indicate that LEAs are not entitled to use their funds in this way.

The differences in approach between LEAs are highlighted when a child with a Statement moves from one LEA to another. Circular 1/83 suggests that the receiving authority can request the transfer of the Statement from the old authority. The new authority can use the advice supplied by the old authority in order to make a formal assessment. However, the new authority is under no obligation to meet the child's needs in the same way as they were met in the old authority. Parents were most likely to notice the differences in approach between authorities. In A-Shire, a parent who had moved from the North of England found noticeably less willingness on the part of the LEA to make provision for his severely handicapped pre-school child. A parent moving into D-Shire from another LEA found help more readily available in D-Shire.

## Amendments to statements

The Act makes it possible to amend or to cease to maintain a Statement without further assessment, after consultation with the child's parents, if the child's needs change. The advice in Circular 1/83 seems to indicate that this refers, in particular, to children in special schools who might be moved into mainstream schools. Of authorities responding to our questionnaire, 38 per cent said that it was usual practice to withdraw a Statement if a child transferred into mainstream. It seemed more customary that moves into mainstream were for a trial period first, and that withdrawal of a Statement would not take place unless a child had settled back into mainstream satisfactorily. Some 87 per cent of authorities said that they had evolved a procedure to be followed when amending or ceasing to maintain a Statement. Surprisingly, in view of the legal obligation to consult parents, only 81 per cent always did so. Less than 60 per cent consulted the district health authority, and 80 per cent consulted the psychologist. However, some LEAs commented that such decisions would only be made following an annual review or a full re-assessment and, of course, parents who are unhappy with any proposed changes can request a full re-assessment.

## Annual reviews

The obligation to review provision 'at least annually' is the only reference to reviews in the Act. Circular 1/83 is not much more prescriptive, advising merely that:

> Reviews should normally be based on reports prepared by the school the child attends including, where appropriate, the views of other teachers and professionals who work with the child. They should be seen as part of a process of continuous assessment, and should include the views of the child's parent wherever possible.
> (Para. 55)

Most LEAs appear to have offered advice or guidance to schools on the way in which annual reviews should be conducted. Of LEAs responding to our survey, 90 per cent required a copy of the annual review to be sent to the LEA, and 82 per cent required a copy to be sent to parents. The involvement of parents was not as widespread as one might have expected, given the circular's advice. Some 85 per cent of authorities invited comments from parents. The range of levels of commitment to the involvement of parents went from:

> They are always invited. If they do not attend, schools staffs try to make a home visit to discuss the review. As a last resort the review is posted to them.

to:

> Arrangements to involve parents? None that I know of.

However, it seemed that most LEAs tried hard to make sure that parents were at least informed of the outcome, even if they did not participate in the review.

In the LEAs we studied in detail, there had been several different approaches to setting up the annual review procedure. In all cases it involved an element of in-service training for special schools. In A-Shire, schools had been invited to design their own forms and procedures. These had then been used as a basis for a training day for the heads of all special schools in the authority.

In D-Shire, the advisers visited the schools for which they were responsible and helped them to formulate their aims and objectives as a first step towards deciding what was relevant to include in the annual review. It was described as a very good opportunity to get schools to evaluate what they were offering.

In B-Borough, a close watch was kept on the way schools were conducting annual reviews. These were done on a cyclical basis so that, for example, a special school with 160 pupils would have to do about six reviews a week. The reviews involved parents and all professionals who were involved with children, such as speech therapists and physiotherapists.

There seemed to be more of a problem about conducting annual reviews of children who were in mainstream placements or non-LEA provision. As far as mainstream schools were concerned, it was felt that teachers often did not realize what was required and, since they were so thinly spread, there was little opportunity for in-service training of these staff. This was a particular problem in authorities, such as C-Shire, where there were a number of children with special educational needs in mainstream schools with extra resources who did not have Statements. Under these circumstances, there was no statutory obligation for the authority to monitor the progress of these children.

Provision in non-LEA schools or schools in other LEAs also posed problems, not least of parental involvement. A-Shire, which used a lot of non-LEA provision, held an in-service course for the head teachers of the schools in which they placed children, to inform them of the LEA's requirements. Nevertheless, it was difficult to get a standardized approach from schools which the LEA could not control. This was part of the difficulty in monitoring the quality of education being offered by these schools. Although HMI had inspected and approved (or not) all schools wishing to continue as independent special schools after the 1981 Act, it was still felt that LEAs had a responsibility to ensure that children whom they placed in such schools were receiving the education they required, and it was not always possible for officers of the LEA to have first-hand knowledge of the schools in which they were placing children.

On the whole, it appeared that annual reviews had been a focus for making schools more accountable to parents, children and the LEA for the education they were offering. The annual review was being used as a means to evaluate the schools' curriculum and to monitor children's progress. Some teachers found it difficult to accept a more rigorous approach, but most found that it had brought genuine improvements in the quality of education they were providing.

## Mandatory re-assessment

Regulation 9 of the Special Educational Needs Regulations 1983 states that:

> Where an education authority maintain a statement in respect of a child whose educational needs have not been assessed since before he attained the age of 12 years and 6 months then, during the period of 12 months beginning with the day on which he attains the age of 13 years and 6 months, the authority shall reassess those needs.

These re-assessments have become known as the 13+ re-assessments. The purpose of this re-assessment is to:

> enable attention to the arrangements to be made for the child during the remainder of his time at school, to his preparation for the transition to adult life, and to the nature of the further education, vocational training, employment or other arrangements to be made for the child when he leaves school.
> (Circular 1/83, Para. 56)

There is much debate among local authority and health authority personnel about whether 13+ is the right time to have such a re-assessment. Some feel that it is too late for planning educational goals. Others feel that it is too early for thinking about prospects at 16+. However, there is no consensus among those who feel that around the age of 13 is the wrong time as to what age would be more appropriate. Since it coincides with the time at which most children in mainstream schools are making option choices and being introduced to the idea of thinking about career choices, it does not seem inappropriate for some children, at least, who are in special schools to be given a similar opportunity. This applies especially to children who may be considered for transfer to mainstream school at this stage.

In one of our detailed study authorities, we came across a partially sighted child who expressed the wish to transfer into mainstream school at 13+. The re-assessment allowed her to be placed in mainstream for a trial period, and to make her option choices with the other children. When it was demonstrated that she could cope in mainstream, a new Statement was written for her giving details of the facilities she needed. If the transfer had been any later, she would have run into difficulties in being slotted into option groups.

Authorities differed in the way in which they approached the 13+ re-assessment. Most authorities (94 per cent of those responding to our questionnaire) had specified a procedure to be followed. Some 79 per cent said that it was identical to the Section 5 assessment. However, the range of personnel involved differed widely. Although most involved the head teacher, the psychologist and the health authority, only 55 per cent asked for a contribution from the careers officer for the handicapped, and only 20 per cent asked the child for his or her views. Some 89 per cent asked parents for their views.

We did not interview many parents of children who had been re-assessed at 13+. Where we did, there seemed to have been a genuine attempt to take a prospective view and to suggest options for post-school opportunities. This applies to two children with severe learning difficulties in D-Shire and two children in B-Borough (including one already mentioned, who moved into mainstream).

There did seem to be a problem with children who were first assessed under the procedures after the age of 13, who would not qualify for 13+ re-assessment. Parents of these children (mainly children with emotional/behavioural problems) were often concerned about 'what was to happen next' after the child left school. It would, perhaps, be appropriate for first assessments of older children to take account of some of the concerns of the 13+ re-assessment, and make suggestions for future post-school goals.

## APPEALS

The last resort for parents who cannot resolve their differences with the LEA is to appeal. There is a two-stage procedure for this: appeals to a local appeal committee constituted under the 1980 Education Act and appeals to the Secretary of State. If an LEA refuses to make a Statement on a child, parents who wish to appeal do this directly to the Secretary of State without going through a local appeal. If the parents wish to appeal against the provision specified on a Statement, they must first appeal to a local appeal committee.

### Local appeals

Circular 1/83 expresses the hope that appeals will 'seldom prove necessary and that they will be seen only as a last resort'. This view seems to be shared by many LEAs, whose officers reported that they avoided appeals wherever possible, since they were incredibly time consuming and stressful for both officials and parents. In our detailed study authorities, several professionals reported that they had, on occasion, even gone against their professional judgement about the best placement for a child because the parents would not accept that placement.

Nevertheless, responses to our questionnaire indicate that half the authorities who answered had had at least one appeal against a Statement since the implementation of the 1981 Act. The total number of (local) appeals recorded by LEAs was 129, but only three authorities recorded more than three local appeals.

The recommendations of appeal committees are not binding on LEAs, and there has been some criticism that they are merely symbolic and do not represent a genuine attempt to make LEAs' decisions challengeable. This view is reinforced by the composition of the committees, which tend to be made up of a majority of LEA members. The Law Society Group for the Welfare of People with Mental Handicap (1985) has suggested that the balance in appeal committees should be changed so that LEA members are in a minority.

Responses to our questionnaire indicate that, in 73 per cent of cases, the appeal committee upheld the decision of the LEA. In the 27 per cent of cases where it asked the LEA to reconsider, 66 per cent had amended the Statement. Following an unsuccessful appeal, 66 per cent of parents did not take the matter further. Only 33 per cent made an appeal to the Secretary of State.

### Appeals to the Secretary of State

Thus, it seems that the local appeal is quite an effective mechanism for filtering out parental requests for changes to provision. In the year April 1985 to March 1986 there were 23 appeals to the Secretary of State under Section 8(6). In 57 per cent of these cases the Secretary of State confirmed the Statement made by the LEA, and in 27 per cent the LEA was asked to amend the Statement. The outcome of the remainder had not been decided at the time the figures were published (April 1986).

Appeals under Section 5(6) of the 1981 Education Act (i.e. against an LEA decision not to issue a Statement) were dealt with more slowly. In 52 per cent of these appeals, there had been no decision by April 1986. Of those that had been decided, half were in the favour of the LEA, and only 10 per cent in favour of the parents. For the rest, the LEA was reconsidering its decision following 'informal discussions'.

It would appear, then, that it is very unlikely that parents who are in dispute with an LEA about the placement made for their child under the 1981 Act procedures will be able to have that provision altered by means of an appeal. Of the original 129 local appeals recorded by LEAs in our questionnaire survey, 44 had appealed to the Secretary of State. Of these appeals, 11 (25 per cent) had resulted in the LEA being directed to amend the Statement, and 23 (52 per cent) had resulted in the Statement being confirmed. The remainder are yet to be decided.

As mentioned earlier in this chapter, many of the parents we interviewed were unhappy with the placement made for their child, even though they did not appeal against it. It appears that most of those parents would have preferred provision to have been made in a mainstream setting. So LEAs should not take the absence of an appeal as an indication that parents are entirely satisfied with all aspects of the educational arrangements made for their children. Despite the legislation, which was intended to enhance parental participation in decision-making, it is still the case that the LEA and its officers are in an extremely powerful position when it comes to the allocation of resources to children with special educational needs.

## SUMMARY AND CONCLUSIONS

It seems that children with severe and obvious handicaps are identified efficiently, as they were before the passage of the Act. However, there have been changes in the expectations of the educational requirements of some children. For example, many parents, and some professionals, consider that children with Down's Syndrome should be offered education in mainstream schools, particularly at the infant stage. Therefore, a 'diagnosis' of Down's Syndrome no longer means that a child will automatically be placed in a special school. This also applies to other forms of serious handicap, where parents can express their opinion about the best placement and will sometimes make unilateral decisions to place children in, for example, a Steiner school, and then ask the authority to assess the child. We came across several instances of such action by parents in our detailed studies.

For the majority of parents, though, such assertive action was not possible. They were given the opportunity to express their views and many of them did so, but in a time of shortages of resources for education, which have been well documented by many organizations, including HMI, the options available to parents in terms of choices of provision have been severely limited.

The nature of the procedures, and the delays built into them, has been a source of irritation to some LEAs. However, delays are often due to local factors and the ways in which LEAs conduct their formal assessments, rather than to inherent difficulties in the Act. Major delays of over a year or more were uncommon, and were usually the result of appeals.

Different policies about establishing a 'prima-facie' case led to inconsistencies within LEAs about levels of provision for children. The Act had done very little to even out the differences in educational opportunities for children in different authorities.

Co-operation between professionals in different services has been little affected in practice, though the balance of power in decision-making appears to have shifted. Administrators are, at least on the face of it, most likely to make decisions about Statements.

There is still a wide gulf in understanding between personnel in the different services, particularly with regard to the allocation of resources.

Annual reviews have provided an opportunity for schools to evaluate their curriculum and monitor more closely the objectives and outcomes of the education they are offering. Parental involvement is sought in most cases.

Statutory re-assessments can be a powerful mechanism for deciding future educational goals for children, though the annual review procedure should ensure an annual consideration of such goals. Many LEAs are still working out the best way of making use of the opportunities the 13+ re-assessment can offer. Some are still unconvinced that 13 is the right age for such a re-assessment.

LEAs do not see appeals as a good mechanism for resolving conflicts with parents. Very few parents who appeal have the provision on their child's Statement changed. As a result of this, some parents have opted to use the route of the judicial review to challenge LEA decisions.

Although, as far as we can tell, LEAs are meticulous about sticking to the letter of the law when conducting a formal assessment under the Act, many parents still find that it is difficult for them to be involved as active participants, and many LEAs do not take positive steps to ensure parental involvement.

NOTES

(1)  This is now a permanent post.
(2)  *R. v. Oxfordshire LEA ex parte W.*

# Chapter 8

## Participants' Experience of the 1981 Education Act

### INTRODUCTION

This chapter is concerned with the feelings about and evaluations of the working of the 1981 Education Act of those who have been involved in its operation at the local level. These include parents and children as well as professionals, administrators and other local and health authority officials. Also included are those standing outside the local authority structure, such as voluntary organizations and pressure groups. These observations are based on personal accounts given in interviews and group discussions with a wide range of respondents, both from our detailed study areas and from other areas represented at meetings held in London and sparsely populated rural shires. A more detailed account of our research methodology is given in Chapter 3.

These data are not quantifiable, but they give an invaluable insight into the perceptions of the effects of the 1981 Act of those whose relationships and working practices have been determined by its provisions.

One major change which the Act was designed to bring about was a much closer involvement of parents in the decision-making processes concerning their children's educational needs. The procedures for the statutory assessment and issue of Statements for children were designed to ensure that no decisions are taken without parental knowledge and involvement.

In addition, the Act requires that a range of professional expertise be brought to bear upon the assessment of children's learning difficulties. Circular 1/83 describes the roles and responsibilities of the various parties to the multi-professional assessment. It also provides a clear statement of the government's view of the importance of co-operation between education, social services and health authorities.

The 1981 Education Act provided the framework for changes in the roles of parents, professionals and administrators. The extent to which these changes have resulted in behaviour which is in line with the intentions of the legislators and the spirit of Warnock will depend upon the personal and professional relationships established at a local level. Baroness Young, the Minister of State at the time the Act was passed, observed:

The law is not the place . . . where feeling can be enshrined. Legislation can insist, for example, that the parents must be consulted over the provision made for their child, but it cannot ensure that this is always done with as much understanding as we would all like. As the Warnock Report so rightly recognized, nothing . . . would be fully effective without changes in attitudes. (1)

It is the behaviour of the 'street level bureaucrats' (as Weatherley (1979) termed them) that will determine the experiences of all those involved with the operation of the 1981 Act. However, as Weatherley (op. cit.) indicated, it was not just attitudes, but also administrative structures and access to resources which determined professional behaviour. It would be misleading to attribute all shortcomings in the implementation of the legislation to individual failures. As was pointed out in previous chapters, the way in which the Act was implemented was the result of a complex interaction of factors, including historical, structural, social, economic, professional and individual elements.

So individuals' actions will be constrained by a number of factors. These will include:

– their place within (or outside of) the organizational structure
– their perception of their role (or roles)
– their power, influence or autonomy
– their professional (or other) socialization
– the resources (personal as well as organizational) which they can command
– their negotiating or bargaining skills
– their interpretation of and personal commitment to the courses of action suggested by the 1981 Act and its accompanying regulations and circulars.


## PARENTS AND CHILDREN

The implications of the legislation were examined in Chapter 1. However, it may be useful here to focus on some of the issues concerning the rights given to parents and children.

The legislation is quite specific about the role of parents of children with special educational needs, and about the steps that should be taken to involve them in the decisions that are made about the education of their children. These include the right to see the advice upon which the LEA bases its decisions about provision and the right to make their own representations about the educational needs of their child. As well as giving parents these new rights, the 1981 Act also recognizes that the right of children to have their special educational needs met is an important consideration. This being so, the Act takes away the rights of parents under the 1980 Act to a choice of educational placement. The ultimate decision about placement is given to the LEA.

The rights given to children under the 1981 Education Act are:

1.  to have their special needs identified (Section 4(1))
2.  to special educational provision to meet their needs (Section 2 (1))
3.  to education in an ordinary school wherever feasible (Section 2 (2))
4.  to interact with other children in school who do not have special educational needs (Section 2 (7))
5.  to a full assessment under the Act if the LEA rather than the school is proposing to decide upon the educational provision to be made (Section 5 (1))
6.  to an annual review of the provision being made (Schedule 1 Part 11, 4)

7.   to a re-assessment between the ages of 12 years 6 months and 14 years 6 months. (Education (SEP) Regulation 9)

The rights given to parents are mainly concerned with parental involvement in the statutory assessment procedures under Sections 5 to 10 of the Act.

The parents have the right to:

1.   be notified that the LEA are proposing to assess their child
2.   be given details of the procedures to be followed
3.   be given the name of an LEA officer from whom they can obtain further information
4.   be informed of their rights to make representations and submit evidence to the LEA before the assessment starts
5.   be given 29 days to make their representations.

If the LEA decides not to assess or, having assessed, decides not to make a Statement, the parents have the right to be informed in writing and given reasons. Parents must also be informed of their rights to appeal against the decision not to maintain a Statement. Parents have the right to refuse an assessment if their child is under two years old.

If the LEA decides to make a Statement of a child's special educational needs, it must give a copy of the proposed Statement to the parents, and give them 15 days to respond to it. If the parents wish it, the LEA must arrange meetings for them with an officer of the LEA and with those professionals who contributed to the Statement advice.

Once a Statement is finalized, parents must be given a copy together with a notice in writing of their right to appeal and the name of a person to whom they may apply for information and advice about their child's special educational needs.

Parents also have the right to request an assessment of their child's needs and, if the request is not unreasonable and it is more than six months since the previous assessment, the LEA is bound to comply. Health authorities have the duty to inform parents if they are of the opinion that a child has special educational needs, and the parents have the right to discussions with an officer of the health authority before the LEA is informed.

These duties placed on the education and health authorities and the rights they confer on parents are an attempt to ensure that parents are fully involved in the decision-making about their child's needs. The Circulars are more explicit about the spirit in which these duties should be carried out. The Circulars do not confer legal rights in the way that the Act does, but they attempt to describe 'good practice'. They provide a standard to evaluate the experiences of the parents whom we interviewed. Circular 8/81 takes a pragmatic approach:

> Although the Act lays down formal procedures for notifying parents, it should be possible for LEAs to satisfy these requirements while maintaining a sympathetic approach and developing a co-operative relationship with parents which will ultimately be in the best interests of the child concerned.
> (Circular 8/81, Para. 13)

Circular 1/83 seems to see the cultivation of a good relationship with parents as an end in itself:

> Assessment should be seen as a partnership between teachers, other professionals and parents in a joint endeavour to discover and understand the nature of the difficulties and needs of individual children. Close relations should be established and maintained with

parents and can only be helped by frankness and openness on all sides.
(Circular 1/83, Para. 6)

This circular goes further and recommends the involvement of children in this relationship:

The feelings and perceptions of the child concerned should be taken into account, and the concept of partnership should, wherever possible, be extended to older children and young persons.
(ibid.)

Circular 1/83 recommends contact with and involvement of parent well before any formal notice under Section 5 of the Act is issued:

The serving of the formal notice under Section 5 of the Act should not be the first indication to a parent that his child has learning difficulties.
(Circular 1/83, Para. 17)

The Circular also indicates an awareness on the part of the government that the concept of 'partnership' may involve the local authority in providing help for parents to exercise their rights:

Some parents may need help in making representations. It will be open to the LEA to suggest the name of a voluntary organisation or an employee of the statutory body who could help in this way, or to offer the parent the services of a named LEA officer to whom he could make his representations orally. Where representations are made orally, a written summary by the LEA should be agreed with the parent concerned.
(Circular 1/83, Para. 20)

Any evidence given by the parents must be given to the LEA's professional advisers.

Besides involvement in the assessment process described above, the Circular prescribes that parents should be fully informed about placement decisions and should have an opportunity to visit the school being considered *before* the Statement is finally made. Parents also have the right to see and comment on the draft Statement.

Parental involvement does not stop when the Statement is finally agreed and finalized by the LEA. Parents have the right to consult a 'named person', and also to express their views as part of the annual review. The review:

should be part of a process of continuous assessment and should include the views of the child's parents wherever possible.
(Circular 1/83, Para. 55)

As part of this review process, the LEA should be:

ready to allow for the possibility of transfers from a special to an ordinary school when some of the child's problems have been met.
(Circular 1/83, Para. 57)

So children have the right to a continuous monitoring of their educational provision, and the right to transfer out of special school, if this is appropriate.

To summarize, the general guidance in the circulars and the legal formulation in the Act were designed to give parents, and to some extent children, the right to participate in the decision-making about the nature of the child's difficulties and special educational needs, and the provision to be made to meet those needs.

The extent to which these goals were achieved may be illuminated by the accounts given to us in interviews by a sample of 50 parents of children with Statements. Their children represented a cross-section, in age and learning difficulties, of those with

Statements in the five detailed study local authorities. We contacted the parents of the 20 children in each authority most recently given Statements, and about half of these parents consented to see us. We interviewed the parents in their homes, using a focused interview which centred on their awareness of their child's learning difficulties and their perceptions of the process of identification, assessment and production of a Statement for their child.

The issues which arose during the interviews are grouped under the following headings:

(a)   Meeting the child's needs
(b)   The effectiveness of communication
(c)   The efficiency of service delivery
(d)   Legality in respect of the statutory procedures and rights
(e)   The respective roles of parents, administrators and professionals in decision-making about children's special educational needs.

## Meeting the child's needs

What were parents' views about the effectiveness of the procedures for meeting their children's needs? As was pointed out in an earlier chapter, meeting children's needs under the 1981 Act involves a series of decisions, starting with the identification of children with learning difficulties and culminating in making provision to meet their needs. The Circular indicates that parents should be fully involved throughout this process.

In almost all cases, parents had been aware of their child's difficulties and had been involved with professionals from the LEA or health authority for some time before the statutory procedures were initiated. Circular 1/83 suggests this should have provided ample opportunity for an exchange of views between parents and professionals in order to come to an agreed understanding of the child's needs. However, in many cases, there were unresolved differences between parents and the LEA staff concerned. These tended to centre upon lack of what the parents considered to be appropriate provision for their child.

In some cases, parents felt that the statutory assessment had been forced upon them because the LEA was unable to meet their children's needs adequately in mainstream. This applied particularly to children with moderate learning difficulties, some of whose parents felt that if there had been smaller classes, or extra remedial help in their schools, the children's needs could have been met in mainstream. A typical comment was: 'I don't think we were left with any choice. It was something we had to do for him.'

In other cases, parents acknowledged that their children had serious problems, but would have preferred education in an integrated setting with support, if the LEA had been willing to provide it. For example, the parents of a five-year-old child with Down's Syndrome had expressed a wish to have their child educated in her local infant school. This had been supported by the psychologist in the county from which she had just moved, but both the psychologist and the head of the infant school in her new LEA opposed the idea. The psychologist wanted to offer a place in a school for children with severe learning difficulties (apparently before he had even seen the child). The parents realized that, without support, placement in mainstream would not have met their child's needs, so they agreed to an assessment placement in a school for children with moderate learning difficulties. These parents, and others who had insisted on a placement against the advice of the LEA, felt very insecure. They felt that their children were 'on trial' and would be moved if they did not perform adequately. It was also the perception of some parents that their children's performance was looked at too precisely, and that non-handicapped children were not judged so rigorously.

Some parents of children with severe learning difficulties differed from the LEA in their perception of what type of special provision would best meet their children's needs. In many cases, these parents did not want placement for their children in the LEA school for children with severe learning difficulties. It was not possible for us to judge whether this was for reasons of stigma, or because of worries about the quality of what was on offer. However, the reasons they gave were that they wanted more specialized provision than that on offer at the local school; provision that they felt would meet their children's specific needs more adequately. In some cases, these parents had acted unilaterally and placed their children in their chosen school, and had then asked the LEA to assess and confirm the provision. In other cases, the parents had accepted what the LEA was prepared to offer, but were still unhappy about the decision.

Parents were unhappy about assessments which took place outside the children's normal home or school environments. They felt that in such circumstances their children tended to 'act up' and not perform tasks which they could usually do quite adequately. For this reason, parents did not like assessments by a child development or district handicap team, particularly if they were made to wait outside when the assessments were taking place. The following comments are typical:

> If I knew what I know now, I would have refused to take part in all those assessments and case conferences. . . . It was all so negative.

> I wish I could be in on more of it. We have to wait outside and then go in for a few minutes and just get told what they said. I would rather sit through it, even if I didn't understand all the words they said.

However, not all parents had negative feelings about the identification and assessment process. Some, who had been helped over a long period of time, were very positive in their comments. Parents who had achieved good rapport with head teachers or teachers in mainstream schools described how they and the school had evolved strategies to help their children over many years, and did not necessarily feel that the school had failed them because their children eventually had to move out of mainstream education. It was in cases where parents felt that their children had not received adequate help, or had not even been given an opportunity to try the placement that the parents had wanted, that feelings of frustration and injustice arose.

In most cases, the parents had welcomed the initiation of the procedures as a way of gaining extra resources for their children, particularly in areas where provision in mainstream was limited. However, there were criticisms about lack of resources, even after a Statement had been made. The lack of speech therapy was frequently mentioned as a source of concern to parents. This applied to all areas studied. Often speech therapy needs were noted on the advice, but not put on the Statement or, even if speech therapy was on the Statement, it was not being made available on a regular basis because of staff shortages. In some cases, particularly where children were in placements which were being closely monitored (if there had been a doubt on the part of the LEA that this was the best provision), parents were worried that lack of sufficient non-LEA provision would jeopardize their child's chances of success in that particular setting.

To summarize: parents recognized that statutory assessment was a route to gaining extra resources for their child and welcomed it on that basis. However, some parents were of the opinion that a Statement would not have been necessary had sufficient resources been available in mainstream for their children.

Most parents in our sample were satisfied that their children's needs were being met following a statutory assessment, though some of the parents were unhappy about the placements for their children. They felt that their children could have been educated in mainstream settings, with adequate support, or in placements more suited to their particular learning difficulties. Many of the parents felt that their views on this question had not been given sufficient weight by the LEA.

Some parents had grasped the significance of the legal status of the Statement as a way of bringing local authority decision-making out into the open and had requested Statements for that purpose. These were parents who had firm ideas about the provision which would best meet their children's needs.

**The effectiveness of communication**

Circular 1/83 makes it very clear that 'frankness and openness on all sides' are necessary in order to achieve a close relationship between parents and professionals. The assessment is viewed as a process during which information is exchanged in order that the nature of a child's needs and difficulties can be discovered and understood. Effective communication between professionals and parents plays a vital part in establishing this relationship.

The first communication between parents and professionals about children's special needs is likely to be at the initial stage of assessment within the school, since Circular 1/83 makes it clear that every effort should be made to contact parents before a Section 5 assessment is initiated. As reported in Chapter 7, in our sample, there were no examples of a formal letter stating the authority's intention to carry out a statutory assessment being sent to parents without initial discussions, though in some cases statutory assessment followed very quickly after the first contact.

It is well known that helping parents to understand the nature of their children's difficulties is a difficult task. Professionals often find it hard to negotiate a path between being evasive and being brutally frank about children's problems.

Although parents are often aware that their children have problems, they are very sensitive to the language used by professionals to describe them. For instance, one mother was very upset that the doctor had written on the medical advice that her child was 'mentally handicapped', particularly since the doctor had never used this description when talking to her:

> On one of the assessments it had got boldly written that S. is mentally handicapped, but no-one ever said that S. was mentally handicapped. They had all said, 'We don't know what's the matter, he's a bit slow.' I complained a bit about that, saying I'd rather people say to me first before writing letters having it printed all over, because the way it was printed, it wasn't very nice.

It seems that, if professionals are vague with parents about their children's problems, it causes difficulties at a later stage when parents have the opportunity to see the professionals' advice. This was the experience of several of the parents whom we interviewed; they had not fully realized what the professionals' views were until they had read them on the Statement.

Often, the problems which parents experienced appeared to them to result from the fact that professionals themselves were not sure of the nature of their child's difficulties, or the best way to help, but would not openly admit this:

> They tell you nothing, give you the idea there are no alternatives . . . they don't like to admit that they can't cater for every child's needs . . . they don't give anything freely, not even information.

Parents seem to be able to sense when professionals are on the defensive or being deliberately evasive. Professionals would probably get better co-operation from parents if they took them more into their confidence. The mother of a deaf child, in our sample, became extremely anxious at the delays which had occurred in her son's assessment. She did not find out until later that the educational psychologist had been delaying it deliberately in order to give her son a chance to establish himself in the mainstream nursery. If the psychologist had been able to communicate this to the parents at an early stage, then much of their anxiety might have been avoided.

It would seem that, frequently, difficulties in communication arise when professionals and administrators are faced with dilemmas, about either diagnosis or provision, which they do not feel confident to share with parents.

Some parents reported attempts by professionals to manipulate them into accepting provision which they did not really feel was right for their child, by withholding information about alternatives. For example, the parents of a child with muscular dystrophy wanted him to continue in mainstream education on transfer to secondary school, but were not given sufficient information about schools in the area which might have been suitable. They commented:

> We seemed to be looking at the wrong schools at the wrong time. Schools that were physically wrong.

In this case the child was eventually placed in a school for the physically handicapped.

Those working for LEAs are in a very powerful position regarding the access of parents to information. Although the Act and Circulars lay down that parents should have access to information and support to enable them to be fully involved, LEA staff are able to control the flow of information in order to achieve the outcome which they desire. The paucity of much of the information provided to parents about the 1981 Act and their role within it was noted in Chapter 7. Some parents had the resources or support from elsewhere to find out what the range of alternatives was, but these were the minority. Most were left with no choice but to accept what the LEA offered. As one parent commented:

> We were not really informed enough. Each time we were given no option really, and it is difficult to decide if it is the right school if you are only given one.

The keys to establishing effective communication between parents and professionals seem to be:

(i)    the recognition by professionals that parents can provide and understand detailed information about their child's needs

(ii)    the availability of adequate resources to avoid the necessity of professionals and administrators having to be defensive with parents

(iii)    adequate support for those parents who have difficulty with reading or writing, or with obtaining information from elsewhere

(iv)    a sensitivity on the part of professionals to the concerns of parents about their children

(v)    avoidance of negative comments about parents or children.

## The efficiency of service delivery

The perception of LEA officers that the new procedures are more bureaucratic and time-consuming than the previous forms of assessment was mentioned in Chapter 7. It was also noted that LEAs vary quite considerably in the average time they take to complete assessments.

Many parents mentioned the length of time taken by the statutory assessment as one feature of the process which they found upsetting, particularly if they were not informed of the reasons for delay. For example, one parent, who thought she had come to an understanding with the psychologist about her child's needs and the provision to be made for her, was highly critical of the length of time taken to issue a Statement:

> There was no doubt she [the child] needed to go there [to an MLD school]; that wasn't the point at issue. I was all for it . . . we'd all come to terms with it . . . but it was just all this red-tape business that had to be gone through. We had all the problems then of getting sorted out before the term ended, so I knew where she was going and I could explain to her where she was going. It was six months of absolute worry, and I was desperate.

Some parents felt that the LEA was deliberately stalling in order to limit their range of choice to make them so desperate that they would take what the LEA was offering:

> You were left in a corner. You were in a corner and couldn't do anything else.

In some LEAs, the length of time between Statement and allocation of provision was protracted because the placement was in an independent school which was not a special school. In these cases, approval for the placement had to be sought from the DES.

Whatever the reasons for delay, parents became very worried if they were not kept informed, and if they felt that, in the mean time, their children were not receiving any help for their special needs.

## Legality and rights

From the parental interviews, it appears that the legal formalities attached to the wording and sending of letters, the provision of advice by medical, psychological and educational advisers and the issuing of Statements were, on the whole, observed. However, within this framework, many short cuts and circumventions of the ideals of good practice suggested in the Circulars seem to have occurred.

In a few cases, assessments were made before parents were informed that the formal statutory procedures were being considered. Where this had happened, parents felt that their rights had been undermined, and in two cases they insisted that the assessment be done again. The confusion here may have arisen because parents were not aware of the distinction between continuous and formal statutory assessment. Nevertheless, the Circulars stipulate that parents should be informed about all assessments. Some parents were concerned that assessments carried out before the initiation of formal procedures were being used as the basis for the advice for the statutory assessment. In the case of one pre-school child, the psychological assessment had been carried out 18 months previously. The parent of this child would not accept the advice based on this assessment, and insisted that it be done again.

We have already noted the widespread use of provisional placements in some LEAs. The Act allows such placements, but in some cases it may be that children's rights to education in an integrated setting may be undermined if they are removed from mainstream education for assessment.

Some five-year-old children were denied placements in mainstream schools if they were in the process of being assessed for a Statement. Several children were kept out of school, or offered placements in special schools only, until their Statements were completed.

Problems with the timing of assessments for children who were due to transfer from one stage of education to another meant that sometimes parents were unable to visit the schools named on the Statements before they made their decision. One parent recalled:

> We didn't see anything of the Statement until she left nursery in the July. We had not seen the school. They seemed to think we would just take what was offered. We dug our heels in and R. had to go back to nursery for two weeks.

It seems that some parents were aware of their rights and were prepared to insist on them if necessary. However, many of our sample felt that the officers of the LEAs concerned had attempted to manipulate by withholding information and not being completely open with them about alternatives. Parents felt that the LEAs' actions were more concerned with not being made liable for extra expense, rather than with fulfilling their obligations to ensure that theirs and their children's rights were safeguarded.

**Parental roles in decision-making about children's special educational needs**

Despite being given rights of access to information about the procedures and to play a more active part in decision-making under the 1981 Act, many parents clearly felt that they were still a long way from achieving a positive role within the procedures. One mother commented:

> I would prefer that more was done when I was there. I think too much is done and written down and I don't know about it. I feel I'm too much left on the outside. I don't feel I know what's happening.

However, it was clear that some parents had been able to play a more active role in the decision-making. These were parents who had definite ideas about their children's needs, and the provision required to meet those needs. These parents had been able to negotiate with the LEAs to achieve what they wanted.

In other cases, though the parents had wanted to play a positive role in the decision-making and had expressed a preference about the provision they felt would best meet their children's needs, the LEA officers had not been able to satisfy them. However, the fact that they had access to the advice and could appeal if they wanted meant that their role within the decision-making was not a completely passive one. Several parents challenged the advice, on the grounds that it contained inaccuracies or distortions. One parent wrote a detailed letter to the LEA complaining that the advice on his son's condition was not impartial:

> . . . the overwhelming impression given by the medical and psychological advice is that they have already determined which school N. shall attend. The comments imply no insight into N.'s needs, but that he should fit into one of the education centres available regardless of whether it meets his needs.

These parents had had a meeting with the professionals who had written the advice to discuss the conflict, but felt that they had got little out of it:

> Nothing new came of the meeting. . . . Everyone just restated what they had already written.

In the sample we interviewed, no parent had gone to appeal or had even considered it, though some of them were dissatisfied with the provision made by the LEA. Having negotiated with the LEA and listened to the LEA's point of view, they were prepared to accept what was offered as a compromise.

It may appear that the majority of parents whom we interviewed felt that they were not able to influence the outcome of the procedures in any substantial way and had raised many negative issues. Certainly, the structures within the LEA and the DHA, and the long-standing relationships between professionals and administrators in both services, put parents at a disadvantage. However, there is no doubt that parents were able to raise these issues because they had been involved to an extent and had been given access to the professionals' views and to the decision-making process.

## THE ROLE OF VOLUNTARY ORGANIZATIONS

Representatives of the major voluntary organizations concerned with supporting children with special needs and their parents were interviewed by the research team, both during the pilot work for the project and as a focused study during the main data collection phase. Representatives of these groups were also invited to the meetings held to provide feedback and verification of some of our preliminary findings (see Chapter 3).

Voluntary organizations have played a strategic role in shaping the thinking which emerged in the Warnock Report and was incorporated in the 1981 Education Act. The importance of voluntary organizations as sources of information and support for parents was recognized in the legislation. Health authorities have a duty to inform the parents of any child they identify as having special educational needs of any voluntary organization which they consider may be able to give the parents advice or assistance. The importance which the government attaches to the role of the voluntary organizations in this respect is made clear in Circular 8/81:

> The Secretary of State for Social Services hopes that health authorities and voluntary organisations will increasingly develop links in support of both the handicapped child and his parents.
> (Para. 25)

Circular 1/83 makes several references to the way in which voluntary organizations could be of help to parents:

– to help parents make representations during the initial stages of the statutory procedures
– to make provision for children with special educational needs under the age of five
– to play a role in counselling parents of children under five with special educational needs.

The Circular states that voluntary organizations are being encouraged to provide full information about their services to DHAs and LEAs.

It was surprising, therefore, to find that the services of voluntary organizations in support of parents were not seen as particularly important by LEAs and DHAs. When asked about the role that voluntary organizations had played in discussions about the implementation of the 1981 Education Act in local areas, most officers replied that they had not been consulted. Some of the larger organizations, such as MENCAP and the Spastics Society, had formalized links with some local authorities, but on the whole LEAs seemed to be rather wary of too much involvement with voluntary organizations. Perhaps this reflects the dual role of these organizations: as providers of help to parents and as pressure groups for more resources within local areas.

It appears that many parents are not put in contact with an appropriate voluntary organization at an early stage in the procedures, since one of the most common observations made by their representatives was that parents contacted them too late, when they were already in dispute with the LEA. These representatives also remarked that they felt it was their duty to support the parents, even if they thought they were wrong, because the LEA appeared to be in such a powerful position and parents, even articulate, middle-class parents, were often at a loss to know how to handle the situation. Voluntary organizations regretted the fact that they were often in dispute with LEAs on behalf of parents, but recorded that even their initial contact with LEAs on behalf of parents frequently met with a hostile response.

Some voluntary organizations recorded that they had been able to achieve a good working relationship with particular officers within LEAs. These organizations were the cross-handicap groups, which were formed specifically to support parents of children being assessed; such groups were becoming more common. Other, more handicap-specific organizations were also finding themselves helping the parents of a wider range of children than was their original brief, simply because the need was there and no one was fulfilling it.

The voluntary organization representatives whom we interviewed remarked that they heard mainly of cases where things had gone wrong and, therefore, had an unbalanced view. Nevertheless, it was their experience that parents were not given sufficient information and support to be fully involved in the assessment procedures, and that LEAs who found themselves in conflict with parents often became hostile and unpleasant to deal with.

In a recent report (Wilson, 1986), the Society of Nurse Advisers commented that:

> . . . it is a matter for concern that this is an 'untapped resource'. These voluntary organizations could be unbiased and understanding agencies who could be advocates for the children and the parents of the handicapped child.

It seems that many voluntary organizations feel they are being put in the unfortunate position of coming into conflict with LEAs because of their role in supporting parents and, if they were offered a more positive role at an early stage, such difficulties would be avoided. However, one respondent observed that, if his organization were called upon to help all its potential clientele in this way, it would just not have sufficient resources to do so.

## THE EVALUATIONS OF LOCAL AUTHORITY PERSONNEL

There appeared to be a range of reactions within each professional group across LEAs, which indicates that, when evaluating the 1981 Education Act, most professionals tend to relate more to their own LEA than to their professional group. This is not surprising since, as we have already described, LEAs differ widely in their approach to the implementation of the legislation. We have already made cross-LEA comparisons of these different adaptations. The following observations attempt to describe the re-actions of different professional groups to the 1981 Act and their experiences of the ways in which it was implemented in their authorities.

### Educational psychologists

The central role in decision-making given to educational psychologists by Circular 2/75 has been made more precise, and in some ways curtailed, by the 1981 Education Act and its accompanying circulars. Psychologists have been given a specific role in giving professional advice to the LEA on the nature of a child's educational needs as part of the statutory assessment process, but they have been given no specific role in the decision-making about whether the child should be given a Statement, or what extra provision should be given to the child when a Statement is issued. The extent to which psychologists have been involved in these decisions and the nature of their involvement have been a matter for local authorities to decide.

The psychologist still plays a pivotal role in *defining* needs, since Circular 1/83 suggests that the psychologist should write his or her advice for the Statement after having received the advice of the other professionals involved with the child. However, the decisions about *meeting* needs have to be negotiated with those who control resources. In practice, this distinction is probably less clear cut than it appears to be, since the range of resources available in an authority will have been set up as the result of consultations between administrators and professional advisers, including psycho-logists.

The role of psychologists in determining an authority's special education policy varies throughout the country. In some areas, the psychological service has been at the forefront of sweeping changes, such as the integration of large numbers of children with special educational needs in mainstream schools. In other areas, it has played a large part in setting up the identification and assessment procedures required for the 1981 Education Act. In some authorities, psychologists have been extensively involved in in-service training programmes for teachers in mainstream and special schools, while there are other authorities where the schools psychological service has not been involved in any of these activities, but has confined itself to giving professional advice for the statementing procedures, the major part of their work being continuous assessment and intervention in schools.

These variations in response have also been noted by Pearson (1986) in surveys carried out for the National Association of Principal Educational Psychologists in 1983 and 1984. Pearson also found that many psychologists perceived themselves as having several potentially conflicting roles within the local authority: officer of the authority; independent professional; child advocate; and teacher trainer and evaluator. She concluded that there was increased stress and danger of burnout for psychologists.

Psychologists' evaluations of the usefulness of the Act for meeting children's needs varied, depending on the way in which their authorities had implemented the Act, but on the whole the psychologists we interviewed expressed concern that the bureaucracy attached to the formal statementing procedures cut across good practice and inhibited their relationships with parents. A major concern was that the statutory procedures introduced delays in meeting children's needs. If a psychologist had been involved with a child over a period of time, and had formed the opinion that the child had special educational needs, the initiation of the procedures would then entail a delay of perhaps six months or more while a Statement was being produced. This sort of delay was particularly unhelpful for very young children whose needs could change rapidly at this age, and whose progress could be greatly diminished if no provision were being made in the mean time. Psychologists working in LEAs that had policies about not providing extra resources without a Statement were especially critical of this practice.

Psychologists also reported feeling inhibited in their communications with parents because of the prohibition on discussing placement with them. They felt that it was not possible to discuss children's needs with parents without mentioning possible schools, and even taking the parents to visit the schools. It was in these circumstances where the potential conflict of roles between being an LEA officer, an independent professional and a child advocate arose. Psychologists were often the main source of information and contact between the parents and the LEA and, as such, were called upon to act as support for the parents. However, if delays or disputes caused problems, they found it difficult to reconcile their roles.

Psychologists appeared to feel very confident of their ability to communicate effectively with parents and wished to retain the roles of counsellor and supporter. This contrasts with our finding that other professional groups and parents did not find psychologists particularly effective communicators, a finding that was confirmed by a research project carried out by Sandow *et al.* (1986), which looked at parent–professional communication and the 1981 Act in one of the London boroughs. Sandow *et al.* reported that parents found it easier to relate to teachers, speech therapists and social workers than to educational psychologists. There appears to be a difference between psychologists' and parents' perceptions of the relationship between them.

The legality of their authorities' approaches or attitudes to parental rights did not appear to be a major issue with psychologists, who were mainly concerned with the professional aspects of their role and with the service they were able to give to their clients. The impression given was that, if the statutory procedures stood in the way of meeting children's needs quickly and effectively, they should be dispensed with. This may account for the high number of provisional placements in some authorities, which may be made on the recommendation of psychologists, in order that children would not be left without help for extended periods.

Psychologists in some authorities had been expected to take on the extra administrative burden which the statutory procedures were said to have generated. Many felt that this channelled their time and energies away from preventative work with children, and led to them having to spend more time processing children through the procedures.

Other changes in the role of the psychologist included the opportunity to become more involved in in-service training in mainstream schools. This was welcomed as a way of structuring the demands made upon the schools' psychological services by schools. However, it seems that, generally, educational psychologists did not feel that the 1981 Education Act had contributed to improved professional practice in their area of responsibility, since most felt they had been working 'within the spirit of the Act' anyway, and that the formalities introduced by the statutory assessment procedures inhibited rather than encouraged good practice on their part.

### Advisers

Not all authorities have an adviser for special educational needs. Responses to our questionnaire indicate that one in ten LEAs does not have such an appointment. A survey conducted in 1983 by the National Association of Advisory Officers in Special Education (Nichols, 1983) indicated that, among those LEAs which did have advisers in this area, 40 per cent would be involved routinely in the statementing procedures and have a major role in decision-making. The survey also found that 76 per cent of advisers had been involved in formulating policy for annual review.

Among the authorities we studied in detail, we found a variety of arrangements. In one authority, the adviser for special needs had a total of 11 curriculum areas as his responsibility, including English, drama and commerce. In another authority, there was a team of three advisers for special needs, including one with responsibility for special needs in the ordinary school. One authority had a senior adviser and three advisers for specific handicaps. Another had a senior adviser with overall responsibility, plus advisers for each area of the county, and the fifth had one adviser for special needs.

On the whole, advisers were positive about the effects of the 1981 Act, particularly upon the quality of education being offered in special schools. They felt that the Annual Review had given them the opportunity to undertake in-service work with special schools in order to encourage schools to be more specific about their curricular aims and objectives, and that this had led to children's needs being better met within the special school system. Perhaps because of this, many were ambivalent about integration. They felt that the expertise built up in special schools was too valuable to lose, and they also felt a loyalty to those special school teachers for whose professional development they were responsible. In one LEA, this ambivalence had led to conflicts between them and the schools' psychological service about the emphasis which should be put on the relative importance of integrated and segregated provision. They had also noted an increased awareness and interest in special needs on the part of teachers in mainstream schools, and increased demand for in-service training and awareness courses.

The advisory services in the LEAs in which we conducted detailed studies had been significantly restructured since the implementation of the 1981 Education Act. They had moved away from sending in 'peripatetic remedial' teachers to help pupils. Such teachers were now styled 'advisory' teachers and their role was directed towards supporting teachers and giving them the skills to help pupils in the classroom. This change, which has been documented by Gipps *et al.* (1987), has involved special needs advisers in a major restructuring of their service, a change which has not always been welcomed by teachers in schools.

On the whole, the reactions of advisers to the implementation of the 1981 Act appeared to be positive. It had provided an opportunity for a re-evaluation of the education being offered to children with special educational needs and, in some cases, to considerable changes in the way the service was structured.


**LEA administrators**

The reactions of administrators in the education, health and social services to the implementation of the 1981 Education Act have been the subject of a special enquiry during the course of our research project. This took the form of multi-disciplinary meetings of administrators from the three services to discuss issues arising from the implementation of the legislation. The observations of health and social services personnel will be dealt with in a later section. This section concentrates on the views of education authority administrators.

Administrators see themselves as standing at the epicentre of the tensions between the demands of parents, pressure groups, professionals and politicians. They have to resolve the conflicts inherent in managing a service when resources are restricted and when demand is accelerating because of an increasing awareness of the needs of children with learning difficulties. Despite these conflicts, the administrators who attended our meetings displayed a high level of commitment to the effective implementation of the Act and were positive about the benefits which this had brought for their services. These included:

- a higher status for special education
- an increased share of resources
- more pressure within the system for changes
- more opportunities for them, as administrators, to be involved in shaping the special education service.

There were also many problems brought about by the implementation of the Act. To the administrators, these appeared to derive mainly from the lack of resources available to fulfil their obligations to meet children's needs effectively. Administrators felt they lacked not only money, but also staff and, above all, time. This prevented them from providing the sort of service they would have liked. The Act had raised expectations among both parents and professionals and had led to greater pressure on resources to meet children's needs. This led to some children being given inappropriate provision. In some cases the authorities could not cater for children who had unusual special needs. In other cases, children with less severe learning difficulties, whose needs should have been met within ordinary schools, were being given Statements because the provision to meet their needs was not available in mainstream schools. There was some resentment about resources being misdirected to support schools which were not making adequate provision out of their own resources.

Administrators also pointed to the futility of going through the procedures if resources were not available. As far as statutory assessment and the writing of Statements were concerned, the lack of resources meant that there was pressure to formulate needs without being 'unrealistic' about provision. It was admitted that, in some cases, professional advisers were under pressure not to write down what a child really needed because the resources were not available.

There was concern about the lack of paramedical services, and about the consequences for education authorities of social services closing down some of their residential provision. The different resourcing policies within the three services made co-operation and rational planning difficult.

The administrators felt that all these pressures were distorting the allocation of resources and preventing a rational approach to meeting children's needs. The time demands of the procedures were inhibiting professionals from doing preventative work with children in mainstream schools; this in turn, was generating increased demand for assessment, so creating a vicious circle. Concentrating limited resources on the statutory assessment procedures also had the effect of making it difficult for professionals to justify preventative work. The system had become geared to crisis management and there was little time or money for new initiatives.

There were some problems which were specific to the procedures. These were mainly concerned with their bureaucratic nature, the time they took and the volume of paperwork they generated. The main cause of delay was identified as obtaining reports from professionals in the field. The administrators' workload was also increased by the amount of contact they had with parents. Their greater involvement in the procedures, and the fact that they now had access to the professionals' advice about their children, meant that parents were more demanding and put greater pressure on administrators.

Administrators perceived that their role had changed following the 1981 Education Act. They had become more involved in 'professional' decisions about the allocation of resources. They had to evaluate advice from the different professionals and to come to a decision based on that advice. There were worries expressed about whether they were having to make decisions which were outside their areas of competence. They welcomed and enjoyed the greater contact with parents that the Act had brought about, even though they found it stressful at times. They felt that it was part of their responsibility to provide opportunities for parents to participate in the procedures, but were often unclear about the best way to do this. As with professionals, there was a conflict between their roles as officers of the LEAs and as guides or advocates for parents.

The three years since the implementation of the 1981 Education Act had been a time of stress for administrators. They had been obliged to implement new legislation and introduce new procedures where the legal responsibilities of the parties concerned were unclear. It had been necessary to have delicate negotiations about the respective roles of professionals and administrators, and about the responsibilities and involvement of the three services, each of which had its own priorities. These problems were compounded by the lack of resources available for implementation.

Nevertheless, the administrators saw plenty of positive outcomes of the legislation:

(i)   It had given special needs a heightened profile within the education service.
(ii)  It had increased awareness of the needs of children with learning difficulties in mainstream schools.
(iii) It had increased the involvement of parents in decision-making.
(iv)  It had been a lever to obtain more resources for the special needs service, particularly for the under-five and post-16 age groups.

**The differences between administrative, psychological and advisory service responses to the 1981 Education Act**

It is interesting to compare the reactions of the three groups within the education service who were mainly concerned with the implementation of the legislation: psychologists, advisers and administrators. The preoccupations of the three groups and their attitudes to the legislation reveal the differences in approach which they adopt.

The main concern of psychologists appears to be the individual child and his or her difficulties. They do not appear to be overly concerned with the legal niceties of the Act or its role in safeguarding parental rights. They emphasize processes and relationships more than procedures and rights. Their view might be illustrated by the words of the principal psychologist in one of our detailed study areas:

> I'm sure we had multi-professional assessment right before. We used to concentrate on meeting the child's needs. In a small Borough we know our local service very well. The EP follows the child like a thread. You've got your hand on the pulse. The EP should be the named person. The child is always our responsibility. We should have kept to the SE procedures. If the Act turned up any children we had been missing, I would eat my words. . . . It's just about ruined my service. I'm sure we were keeping the spirit of the Act before. We had all the right ingredients: co-operation with parents; good relations with other services; plenty of resources.

Advisers, on the other hand, were more concerned with the quality of education being offered to children with special educational needs, and welcomed the opportunity the Act had given to bring about changes. The annual review had given them the opportunity to require schools to evaluate what they had been doing and to attempt to make the education they were offering more structured and accountable. Two advisers from one authority sum this up in very similar ways:

> The Act has given me more means and reasons to influence what goes on in schools. It has given us a new enthusiasm and influence. It has certainly structured what we do so much more. It certainly hasn't cut anything out. In-service training has changed. It has given a new emphasis to courses.

> I don't think that it introduced anything completely new or unexpected. It's given a nudge in the right direction to all sorts of things that were already happening, which have a beneficial effect on the curriculum. The 1981 Act must also be seen as part of an opening up of what is happening in schools. There is now greater accountability.

Administrators have an overview of the service and of the relationships between professionals, parents and the LEA. As already described, their evaluations of the Act were mainly positive, apart from the caveat that it was impossible to do justice to the legislation when resources available for implementation were so limited. They observed that, in many ways, the good intentions behind the Act were being thwarted, as professionals and administrators were forced to compromise good practice in an effort to comply with resource limitations.

## Teachers

Teachers are at the sharp end of the resources problem. In most cases, they *are* the resources. Children whose needs cannot be met in mainstream schools have difficulties mainly because the education offered in those schools is inappropriate. These difficulties can be tackled either by offering specialist help within mainstream or by removing a child from mainstream into a school where specialist teachers offer a more suitable curriculum.

The relative definition of special educational needs adopted by the 1981 Education Act indicates that difficulties in school should be viewed as an interaction between the child and his or her educational environment. Teachers, therefore, play a part in *creating* as well as in *meeting* needs. Mainstream and specialist teachers have different perceptions of the way in which the 1981 Education Act is operating, which probably reflect the ways teachers are used as resources by the LEAs.

### Teachers in mainstream schools

In Chapter 7, we noted that many authorities have introduced new systems for the identification of children with special educational needs within mainstream schools. These involve classroom teachers demonstrating that they had attempted to meet the children's needs within their classroom before they referred them for outside help. It was also noted that some teachers saw this as an attempt to stem the tide of referrals, and to force them to hold on to children who would be better placed outside mainstream schools.

However, there were also many teachers whose awareness of children's special needs had been heightened by in-service training, or by the new methods for identifying children with special needs which had been introduced to help children within their classrooms. Unfortunately, large class sizes or lack of resources within schools made this difficult for some teachers, and many expressed frustration that they had identified children, but were unable to give them the help they felt they needed:

> We have tried to go along with the idea behind the Act, but must feel guarded about it because we're not getting the full support which it is intended that LEAs should give. They're always trying to get away with spending as little money as possible and still getting their pound of flesh. It's extra work with no extra reward.
> (Head teacher, primary school)

The mainstream school teachers whom we interviewed in the course of our research were either head teachers, or teachers with responsibility for special needs. It is likely they would have more knowledge of, and interest in, children with learning difficulties. However, most schools had provided some form of training about the 1981 Education Act for their staff, and specialist teachers reported a greater awareness on the part of their colleagues and a greater willingness to refer to them for advice or help for children who were experiencing problems:

To date, it has been beneficial. There has been a change in teachers' attitudes. The staff are more aware of children with special needs, and have a sense of responsibility for them. It has created an awareness that we can and must help children.
(Head teacher, comprehensive school)

Some teachers said they had had initial fears that the 1981 Act would mean they would be asked to take on children with severe handicaps, and that they would not be able to cope. In the event, this had not happened. Although there were some schools which had accepted children with quite severe difficulties, staff had, on the whole, taken this in their stride. They were more concerned about children with less severe special needs who were in schools with no extra resources or back-up. It was felt that these children were the ones who were 'missing out'.

*Teachers in special schools*

Some teachers in special schools were worried that the emphasis of the Act on, as far as possible, meeting children's needs within mainstream schools would mean that their role within education would be diminished. There have been many discussions about a new role for special school teachers as advisers and support for their colleagues in mainstream schools (see, for example, Jones, 1983).

Policies on integration which have been adopted by LEAs have differed widely in their scope and effects, but on the whole special schools have emerged intact, and the role of teachers within them has not changed markedly. Most moves towards integration by local authorities have been gradual and limited. In some areas we visited in the course of our research, integration schemes had been running for several years before the 1981 Act was passed. In other areas, links between special and ordinary schools were still very much in their infancy. As with mainstream school teachers, the perceptions of special school teachers about the effects of the 1981 Act were very much influenced by local factors and policies.

The main impact of the Act upon special schools has been in the requirement to do an annual review and a 13+ re-assessment. The annual review was welcomed by the head teachers of special schools whom we interviewed. Many of them had already been giving parents an annual report, but they felt that the requirements of the annual review had sharpened their procedures for doing this and had increased their commitment to the involvement of parents.

Some special school heads had noted a falling off in admissions of children in the younger age groups, which they attributed to the tendency of schools to try to meet children's needs in the mainstream for longer than had previously been the case. For teachers in schools which dealt with children with severe learning difficulties, the Act did not appear to have made any difference to their clientele.

Most heads reported increased links with mainstream schools, but apart from one school for the deaf, which had a long-standing exchange scheme with mainstream schools, we did not encounter any schools where teachers were playing an advisory role for children with learning difficulties in mainstream schools. However, such schemes are becoming more common in many LEAs, and a research project, based at the NFER and directed by Seamus Hegarty, has been studying them.

**Governors**

We did not interview any lay governors in the course of our research. The observations made here are based on comments made during interviews with teachers and education officers on the role which governors were playing within the new framework of the 1981 Act.

Governors have a duty under the Act to ensure that, if any children in the school have special educational needs, the special educational provision they require is made for them. They also have the duty to ensure that all those who teach children with special educational needs are aware of those needs. They must also ensure that teachers are aware of the importance of identifying and providing for pupils with special educational needs in their school. The governing body is required to nominate a 'responsible person' to carry out these duties. This can be the head of the school, or a governor.

In practice, most authorities have advised their school governing bodies that the head teacher is the appropriate person to nominate for this task. Some governing bodies have also nominated a governor to take an interest in special educational needs, but these are a minority. Most head teachers whom we interviewed did not expect their governors to take a very active role, and did not feel that they had the competence to do so.

In one of our detailed study areas, members of the education and social services committees were on all special school governing bodies and this was felt to be very helpful in planning for future needs.

However, the main impression gained from interviews with LEA officers and with heads of schools was that they did not expect governors to take an active role in monitoring special educational provision for individual pupils in schools. Theirs was to be a passive role: to receive the report of the head teacher and to press for extra resources when needed, but not to 'act like a set of lay inspectors', as one LEA official put it.

**Elected members**

We interviewed elected members in only one of our detailed study areas, so most of the observations made here are based on reports of elected members' views from local authority officers.

Members were seen to be sympathetic to special education and to wish to be regarded as humane in their allocation of resources. As far as was possible, special education spending had been protected from 'the cuts'. This view was confirmed by the question-naire finding that spending on special education had tended to increase as a proportion of total education spending in the majority of authorities.

This positive attitude towards special education was shown by councillors of all political persuasions in shire counties and in metropolitan boroughs.

> Special education has not been a political football; the political will has come from the Labour Group, but there has been no real opposition.
> (Elected member, metropolitan borough)

However, it was felt by some local authority officers that elected members who acted for parents in putting pressure on the LEA on behalf of a particular child sometimes led to a distortion of the distribution of resources. It was felt that 'those who shout loudest get the resources', and that they were not always the most needy.

Elected members appear to have viewed the 1981 Education Act in a positive light. As it was an initiative coming from central government, based on the recommendations of the Warnock Report, it was generally felt that it must be a 'good thing' and that politicians should be seen to be supporting it.

## HEALTH AUTHORITY PERSONNEL

The responsibilities for children with special educational needs given to the health authorities under the 1981 Act are less far-reaching than those given to education authorities. The health authorities have a duty to identify children under the age of five years, and to pass this knowledge on to the education authority. They have a duty to write advice on children whom the education authorities have decided to assess under the formal procedures of the 1981 Act. They do not have the ultimate responsibility to ensure that children with special educational needs who have a Statement are supplied with the provision described in the Statement. This responsibility lies with the education authority. However, there is some moral pressure for health authorities to make provision available if they control resources without which children's needs will not be met.

Health authorities have a history of co-operation with social services departments through joint funding arrangements, but their experience with education departments is relatively recent, since the joint funding arrangements with LEAs were only set up in 1983. However, they have a history of co-operation with education departments in the identification and assessment of children with special educational needs.

The way in which education authorities have involved health authorities in planning for, and implementation of, new procedures in line with the demands of the 1981 Education Act has been described more fully in Chapter 6. The extent to which the health authority was consulted and involved in planning will have some bearing on the evaluations which are given of the new procedures. Most health authorities do not appear to have extensive involvement in the joint planning of services for children with special educational needs. In our detailed study of authorities, only one of the five had a multi-service panel which met regularly to discuss policy and planning for special needs. In the other areas, consultation between the two authorities appeared to be minimal, and evidence from our studies of rural authorities indicates that separate development is the norm. Given the structural and political differences between the two authorities described in Chapter 4, this is, perhaps, not surprising. However, Circular 1/83 stresses the importance of close co-operation between the education, health and social services:

> Inter-authority and inter-professional co-operation and collaboration are essential for effective assessment. The precise arrangements for co-operation and collaboration between health and local authorities will need to be worked out at the local level. All services should therefore review their patterns of work and agreed procedures, which will avoid unnecessary duplication of work and delays, and which will help to ensure that the appropriate professionals can be involved quickly at any stage. The Secretaries of State hope that effective and constructive co-operation will help to make the best use of available skills and resources in providing for children with special educational needs under the Act. (Para. 75)

The inter-service meetings for administrators held as part of our research strategy were attended by representatives of medical, speech therapy, physiotherapy and nursing disciplines. These groups were also represented at meetings held in rural shires. Since these heads of service represent practitioners, we will not present the views of professionals separately from those of administrators.

We have already noted that health authorities adopted varying procedures for the collation of advice from professionals in the health service. The preferred option of professionals appeared to be that their advice be forwarded verbatim to the education authorities and that, if a summary were needed, it should be made by the advising professional, rather than the designated medical officer. This arose out of a concern that the implications of the advice might not be understood by the medical officer and, therefore, distortions might occur. So, in this sense, practitioners were worried that the new procedures under the Act would inhibit the efficient exchange of information between health professionals and education officers. They were also concerned that, in many cases, they were not given any feedback on the results of a multi-professional assessment and, therefore, could not monitor the children for whom they had provided advice. They felt that two-way communication between themselves and the education authorities was non-existent. Once they had given advice, they were no longer involved by the LEAs, unless they were called upon to provide a service.

Doctors, particularly, felt that the new procedures had placed restrictions upon their communication with parents. They had been used to suggesting placements in particular special schools, and were now told by the LEAs that this was no longer acceptable. Other professional groups within the health authorities, who had been used to a much more informal system of referral, also found the bureaucracy attached to the provision of help for children with special needs somewhat irksome. For example, health visitors could no longer ask nursery schools to take children who they thought would benefit from educational help for social reasons. They now had to refer such children through official channels for assessment.

Most health personnel did not consider the risk of breaches of confidentiality by the exchange of information with education authorities to be a serious problem. If they had information to impart that they did not wish parents to see, they would make a telephone call, or write it in a separate note.

There were some difficulties in obtaining reports from hospital consultants, and these sometimes introduced long delays into the procedures, if such reports were seen to be crucial by the parents or the medical advisers. There seemed to be no way of getting consultants to give information speedily when delays did occur.

The main effect of the 1981 Education Act on the work of health authority personnel was perceived to be an increase in demand for services, which they found difficult to cope with. There was an increased awareness on the part of parents of the importance of speech therapy and physiotherapy for children's educational progress, and so they were putting pressure on the services to provide this. At the same time, the placement of more children with special needs in mainstream schools had meant that the traditional ways of delivering the services to groups of children in special schools were being altered by demands for therapists to visit children in mainstream. Not only was this seen as less cost effective, but very often the facilities available in mainstream were not suitable.

There was also perceived to be a greater administrative burden as a result of the new procedures, with no increase in clerical or administrative staff to cope with it.

All these new pressures came at a time when resources were fully stretched, and government spending and manpower restrictions meant that community health services could not readily respond to increased demands. Many health service personnel felt that children's needs were being left unmet because the resources simply were not available, and that the procedures of the 1981 Education Act were not likely to produce extra resources. In fact, they were diverting resources away from meeting children's needs.

## SOCIAL WORKERS AND THE 1981 EDUCATION ACT

Social services have been given a statutory role in the procedures for formal assessment under the 1981 Education Act. When the local education authority notify parents of their decision to make an assessment, they are obliged to send copies of the notification to the health authority and the social services authority (Education (Special Educational Needs) Regulations (3)). However, unlike the health authority's involvement, there is no precise instruction about what a social services department should do when it receives such a notification. This vagueness appears to have led to confusion and a lack of involvement of social services in decision-making about children with special educational needs.

Circular 1/83 explains the reasons for sending the notification to social services:

> This is intended to enable . . . social services to consider whether they know of any problems affecting the child in their . . . sphere and to indicate to the LEA whether they have information relevant to the assessment of the child's special educational needs. (Para. 31)

Paragraph 74 of the Circular urges health authorities, local education authorities and social services departments to nominate officers to act as points of contact for the purpose of assessments of special educational needs. In Chapter 7, we noted the difficulties we experienced in contacting social workers to take part in one of our research exercises. There seemed to be no clear idea in social services departments about who had responsibility for co-ordinating information about children with special educational needs.

Whether or not this is the case, it is our impression that, on the whole, social services departments are not playing an active role in assessments. There appear to be several reasons for this. One is that, in many cases, even though a family may be known to social services, the child being assessed is not the social worker's client and, therefore, it is not immediately apparent to the social worker what information may be relevant to the assessment. Allied to this is the worry on the part of social workers that to pass on information about family circumstances may be a breach of confidentiality.

Secondly, there appears to be a tradition of difficulty of understanding between education and social services, and in some cases social workers feel uncertain about the motives of education departments wishing to assess children. This is particularly true of the type of children who are likely to be their clients, i.e. children with behavioural problems or with moderate learning difficulties.

Another major reason for the lack of involvement of social services is that they have been bombarded with several major pieces of legislation in recent years, some of which are more crucial to their operations than the 1981 Education Act, and they simply have not had the time to become familiar with the legislation or to understand the implications which it might have for their work. There appears to have been very little in-service training for social workers about the 1981 Education Act. Only one-third of the authorities who answered our questionnaire had arranged any training for social services personnel about their new procedures for implementing the 1981 Education Act.

Among those social workers who had become familiar with the legislation and had been involved in the assessment procedures, several concerns were expressed. Social workers seemed to be more concerned with parental rights than any of the other professional groups we had contact with. They were worried that the form of the procedures did not allow parents to express their views adequately. The fact that the 'named person' was a local education authority employee meant that parents had no independent support for their point of view. In the case of children in care who were being assessed, they felt that it would be appropriate to appoint a 'guardian *ad litem*' to look after the child's interests. They also felt that it would be a good idea for parents to be able to nominate their own 'named person'.

Like other professional groups, social workers were concerned that lack of resources was inhibiting the meeting of children's needs. The disputes between education and social services departments about financial responsibility for certain types of provision could be due to concerns about keeping within departmental budgets. These disputes often concerned whether a child needed residential provision for 'educational' or 'social' reasons, and whether such provision should be made available during school holidays as well as term time. Social services questioned what they saw as the very narrow definition of 'special educational needs' employed by some LEAs.

Those social workers who were interested in and knowledgeable about the 1981 Education Act saw it as a very useful piece of legislation and regretted that more social workers were not involved with children with special needs and their parents. They saw a role for social workers to act in support of parents during the procedures and to help with any subsequent liaison between the parents and the LEA. Certainly the marginal role played by many social services departments at present was not what was envisaged when the 1981 Education Act was placed on the statute book.

## SUMMARY AND CONCLUSIONS

Despite having many negative issues to raise, there is no doubt that those having to work with the new legislation are fundamentally in agreement with its aims and philosophy. Professionals and administrators in health, education and social services considered that the new rights given to parents to be consulted and involved were a positive advance, even if they created more work. They also felt that the formal assessment procedures, though bureaucratic, resulted in a better assessment of children's needs. The days had gone when a child could simply be placed in a special school by making a phone call.

The difficulties which were being experienced by those working with the new legislation were mainly due to local factors, particularly the shortage of resources available to meet children's needs adequately; the Act had exposed the deficiencies in local provision. The extra demands created by increased parental pressure, and by the heightened awareness of teachers of children's special needs, had led to dilemmas for all concerned if adequate resources could not be made available.

Such shortages led to frustration and anxiety for parents who were worried about their children; to moral dilemmas for professionals who had to disguise the extent of the mismatch between needs and provision; and to stress for administrators who had to arbitrate between conflicting demands.

There has been a major change in the way in which children with special educational needs are assessed and allocated provision. There has also been some reallocation of resources within LEAs. Whether children's needs are being more adequately met is open to question, at least on the evidence of those who have given us their views in the course of this research.

# Chapter 9

## The Effects of the 1981 Education Act: Implications for the Future

INTRODUCTION

In Chapter 1 we discussed the 1981 Education Act in terms of its underlying principles. Those were:

(i)   principles concerned with the *nature* of special educational needs
(ii)  principles concerned with the *rights* of those with special educational needs — and their parents
(iii) principles concerned with the *effectiveness* of identifying, assessing and meeting special educational needs.

We noted the changes in thinking about special education which had led to the setting up of the Warnock Committee, and the subsequent translation of some of the Committee's recommendations into a legislative framework. We also noted aspects of the 1981 Act which were less than a full response to the principles outlined and which might cause difficulties for those attempting to achieve the aims implicit in those principles. In Chapter 4, we described the organizational, political and economic constraints which might lead to differences in the levels of achievement of those aims by local authorities.

In this chapter we attempt to assess the findings of our research into the effects of the Act on local and health authority policies and practices and to suggest ways in which the difficulties which have been experienced in the implementation of some aspects of the legislation might be overcome.

We will consider the interpretations of the new ideas of special education outlined in Chapter 5 and the operationalization of those ideas as revealed in the LEAs' policies and practices (outlined in Chapters 6 and 7). We will also consider the effects of those ideas, policies and practices on the experiences of those involved in the identification, assessment and meeting of children's special educational needs (Chapter 8).

The findings will be considered within the framework of the three groups of principles outlined above: concepts of special educational needs; rights and accountability; and concern for effective education.

## CONCEPTS OF SPECIAL EDUCATIONAL NEEDS

The relative definition of special educational needs, introduced by the 1981 Education Act to replace the categories used under the previous legislative framework, received a broad welcome by those working in education and health authorities. There was a common acceptance that the previous system was not sufficiently flexible to allow an individual response to children's needs and that the categories were not helpful in describing the functional implications of specific disabilities.

It appeared to those working within LEAs that there was a growing awareness at all levels of the existence of children with special educational needs in the broadest sense and a corresponding awareness of the obligation to meet those needs. Respondents to our questionnaire indicated that this growing awareness of special educational needs had been one of the major factors influencing change in special needs provision in local authorities.

This awareness also manifested itself in a substantial increase in the proportion of children with special educational needs receiving education in mainstream schools, reported by 76 per cent of those authorities responding to our questionnaire. There is no doubt that this indicates a shift in emphasis away from meeting needs within segregated provision and towards a more flexible response to provision for children with special educational needs.

Another indicator of the growing awareness of special educational needs, and a flexible response to them, was the number of LEAs who reported an increase in provision for pre-school children, particularly of Portage-type schemes and counselling and play advice.

The abolition of categories of handicap had led to a less stereotyped view of need, so that, for example, children with Down's Syndrome, whose parents we interviewed, were placed in a wide range of provision, from mainstream schools, through schools for children with moderate learning difficulties, to schools for children with severe learning difficulties.

It appeared that a large number of the authorities with whom we came into contact were willing to be flexible and to experiment with new ways of meeting needs. Nevertheless, staff in local and health authorities found several difficulties with the new definition of special educational needs.

One of the difficulties was that, though the definition proposes an interactive view of children's needs, the implications for the terms in which assessments of needs are made do not seem to have been grasped by many of those involved. Most of the Statements which we have seen in the course of our research concentrated their attention on deficits within the child which led to special needs, with very little attention given to the child's environment, whether at home or at school. The fact that a child's needs are often couched in terms of what the school cannot offer, for example, 'small class sizes', 'a structured environment' or 'teachers skilled in teaching basic subjects', does imply that a school lacks resources. However, such observations are usually taken to imply that the child should be moved to a school where such resources are available and that the child, rather than the school, has failed. This lack of attention to the child's environment when assessing special educational needs appears to be a major factor in causing the issue of a Statement still to be very much identified with a move to relocate the child out of mainstream and into a segregated setting. Although DES figures indicate that there are some authorities which have large proportions of their children with Statements in mainstream schools, these are still only a minority of LEAs. As was pointed out in Chapter 5, only about a quarter of LEAs placed more than 23 per cent of their children with Statements in mainsteam schools.

The very narrow definition of 'needs', in terms of needs for resources, is counter to the advice given in Circular 1/83. This suggests that there are three aspects of needs which should be considered:

(i)   descriptions of the child's functioning
(ii)  the aims of provision
(iii) the facilities and resources recommended to achieve those aims.

In the Statements to which we had access, the inclusion of (ii) was often lacking, so that the connection between (i) and (iii) gave rise to the deficit model of need, and often a lack of direction in the Statement about what the future goals for the child should be.

Another problem with the relative definition of special educational needs is that it defines needs in terms of calling for provision which is additional to that 'made generally' in local authority schools. This means that the threshold at which children will be considered for a statutory assessment, and possible Statement, will vary between LEAs and even within LEAs if there are differences in levels of provision in different areas. This would not be a significant problem if the Statements were used to allocate additional resources to children on an individual basis according to their needs and the facilities available to meet those needs. However, many local authorities have intervened in this infinitely flexible system, by having policies about which types of provision will be made available through a Statement and which will not. Therefore, the criterion for issuing a Statement is not whether or not a child's needs are able to be met within available resources, but whether the child's needs fall within one of the categories specified by the LEA for which provision is made available through the issue of a Statement.

The adoption of such policies appears to be a response to a need, on the part of professionals and administrators, to have some firm guidelines about what is meant by 'generally available'. The arguments surrounding the High Court action *R.* v. *Hampshire ex parte J.* have prompted many local authorities to reassess their criteria. Even before this, staff in some LEAs had been of the opinion that they would have to issue Statements for far more than the 1.8 per cent of their school populations that had been envisaged by the drafters of Circular 8/81. This does not yet appear to have been reflected in official DES statistics of proportions of children with Statements (see Chapter 5), but this may be due to the fact that it will apply to new Statements, and not to children already in special schools on April 1 1983. Therefore, it may be several years before such a trend will be picked up by DES statistical returns. Nevertheless, it appears that some clarification by the DES is necessary to indicate to LEAs the meaning of 'educational provision made generally' in relation to special educational needs, and the point at which the LEA has to determine the provision to be made. At the moment, the range of practice which we encountered extended from one LEA where any provision in mainstream was not the subject of a Statement, no matter how severe or complex the child's needs, to another where provision given in disruptive units and reading centres (excluded by the Circular) could only be made through a Statement. Guidance needs to be given about whether 'generally available' means 'available to every pupil', 'available in every school' or 'available through a service to which every school has access'.

The fact that the LEA is only required to determine the special educational provision for those children who require resources 'additional to or otherwise different from' those generally available has, to some extent, diverted attention away from the obligation on schools to provide for *all* those registered pupils who have special educational needs. The focus has been on 'the 2%'; the needs of 'the 18%', though recognized, have not been given the same status. Therefore, children whose special needs provision has been 'determined by the LEA', and whose provision to meet those needs has been protected by a Statement, form a separate group from those who have special needs, but who do not have Statements.

A further difficulty encountered by those attempting to provide a service for children with special educational needs is that the abolition of categories has made it difficult to monitor the incidence of particular needs and to plan provision to meet them. The relative definition of needs creates problems for those who have the responsibility for planning the allocation of resources for groups of children, and also have to make resources available to meet needs on an individual basis. This is especially the case when resources are limited. These difficulties and possible solutions will be discussed in more detail in a later section. However, it is the case that many LEAs have taken the step of introducing a set of new descriptive terms to replace the former categories, and that these are often used as a form of shorthand by those working with children. The DES itself laid the foundations for such actions by providing a list for LEAs to use when filling in form 7M.

Despite the difficulties encountered by those attempting to work with the new relative definition of special educational needs and all that it entails in terms of changes in attitudes and practices among a wide range of people, including professionals, administrators and parents, there is no doubt that change has occurred and, according to respondents to our questionnaire, it has been largely the demands of the new legislation which have brought about change. Whether such changes have also come about in the area of the new rights given to children and parents and the new levels of openness and accountability demanded by the statutory assessment procedures will be considered in the next section.

## RIGHTS AND ACCOUNTABILITY

The right of children with special educational needs to receive their education in ordinary schools, mixing with children who do not have special educational needs, is the way in which the 1981 Education Act codifies the principles of equality of opportunity and the right to education in the least restrictive environment, which form the basis of much of the current thinking in this field. The right of parents to make their views known to the LEA and to receive written copies of the evidence upon which the LEA bases its decisions about their children's education similarly reflects the growing acceptance of the principle that consumers of services should have some say in the way in which those services are delivered. The statutory assessment procedures and the Statement of Needs are the mechanisms whereby children's rights to have their special educational needs identified, assessed and met are safeguarded. Because there is a potential conflict between parents' rights to involvement in decision-making and children's rights to have their needs met, the Secretary of State has the ultimate power to decide whether the provision offered by the LEA for a child is acceptable. These, then, are the basic principles and the framework designed to support them, from which the more detailed procedures of the Act follow.

**Statements of Needs**

The outcome of the statutory procedures is usually the production of a Statement of Needs. The Statement of Needs serves two functions. First, it provides an open record of decision-making which holds the LEA accountable to the child and its parents, and second, this record of decision-making also renders the LEA accountable to the community for its decisions about the allocation of resources and for its upholding of the basic principle of equitable treatment for its children. It could be, as Welton (1983) has observed, 'a powerful and subtle document'.

However, as reported in Chapter 7, many of the Statements that we saw in the course of our research were far from being powerful or subtle. They had been rendered impotent by the use of vague and generalized descriptions of children's needs and the provision required to meet their needs. As noted in the previous section, contributors to Statements find difficulty in separating the specification of needs from the provision required to meet needs, and they tend to pay little attention to anything other than within-child factors. They tend not to articulate in any systematic way the aims for the child which the provision is designed to achieve. Obviously Statements of this kind do not protect children's rights to have their individual needs met, and, if they are so generalized as to commit the LEA to no particular resource (as were those from one LEA which we studied), they cannot perform their function as instruments of accountability.

The bland and stereotyped nature of some Statements may reflect a fear in local authorities that they will be led to commit themselves to resources which they cannot provide. This applies also to non-educational provision, which, if it appears on the Statement, the LEA has the ultimate responsibility to provide. It has been suggested that the Statement should expose the gap between the child's needs and the LEA's capacity to make provision, and that parental pressure, through appeals, would force LEAs to provide a better service. It seems to us, and to many working within LEAs, that this is a wholly unsatisfactory way of providing a dynamic for provision, since the onus for ensuring change falls on individual families who may already be vulnerable. Other methods should be found. Suggestions for the setting up of channels of communication between education, health and social services authorities and for monitoring and planning allocation of resources will be elaborated in the next section.

Another reason for the lack of an individualized description of children's needs on the Statement may be the pressure under which the LEA staff are working to produce them. It appears from responses to our questionnaire, and from the detailed study interviews, that the statutory assessment procedures have generated a great deal of paperwork, and that many LEA officers are experiencing difficulties in completing Statements within a reasonable time. In such circumstances, slotting in an agreed formula of words to produce the desired outcome would obviously be one way to cut down on workload. However, as already pointed out, if children's rights are to be safeguarded, the onus is left with LEAs to employ sufficient staff and to produce efficient methods of organizing the procedures, so that satisfactory, accountable Statements can be produced.

It would appear that there is a need to establish a code of good practice for the writing of Statements and for in-service training to ensure that those responsible for this task understand the functions of the Statement as part of the process of meeting children's needs.

## Safeguarding the rights of children

The success of the 1981 Education Act in safeguarding children's rights to have their needs identified, assessed and met has been called into question by much of what has been written so far in this report. As we have pointed out, there is no doubt that there is now a greater awareness of special needs and the obligations to meet them, and also a great deal of commitment on the part of those working in education and health authorities. However, there are still major difficulties to be overcome. Most of these appear to stem from lack of adequate resources in LEAs to meet needs, and from this spring many of the shortcuts and difficulties in achieving good practice which we have noted.

For example, Circular 1/83 stipulates criteria for the use of provisional placements, which would restrict them to children whose needs require a long period of assessment, or to those who have emotional and behavioural problems, where such a placement would be part of the assessment. However, we have found a widespread use of provisional placements of children in special schools pending the issue of Statements for reasons which were more concerned with the lack of any suitable alternative provision in mainstream, or where a child had been experiencing learning difficulties in mainstream for some time, and these difficulties had not been identified and no provision to meet the needs been made, so that the situation had become a crisis referral.

Ideally, children should have their needs assessed within their normal environment and provision should be made within mainstream, if parents agree and if the three provisos in Section 2 (3) of the Act are observed. However, for many children this is not an option, particularly for children under the age of 5, where the majority of provision appears to be in a segregated setting. We came across several examples of young children for whom education in mainstream had not been considered as an option by LEA staff, even though the parents had wanted it and made those views known to the LEA officers concerned. There is a risk that children's rights to education in mainstream are undermined if they are placed in a segregated setting for assessment and for their first formal educational experience. We have noted, earlier in this chapter, that education for the under-fives was one area where there had been a substantial increase in provision recorded by many LEAs. However, attention needs to be drawn to the dangers of developing segregated, rather than integrated, forms of provision for pre-school children.

As far as the education of older children is concerned, LEAs have reported that one major stimulus for changes in allocation of resources for children with special needs has been a move towards more provision in mainstream. This has been a response to parental demand as well as to professional attitudes. However, as noted earlier, the majority of children with Statements are not placed in mainstream schools. It is too soon to say whether the shift towards more mainstream placement marks a fundamental change and a recognition of the right of children to have their needs met in the least restrictive environment. It may be that the DES will need to clarify the provisos inhibiting the placement of children in mainstream schools and, in particular, what is meant by 'the efficient use of resources'. There needs to be some guidance to LEAs about what should be taken into account when assessing this.

Once children are receiving their special educational provision, they have a right to a regular review of their progress. The annual review provides an opportunity for those concerned with the child's education to assess whether it is meeting the aims set out in the Statement. Of course, all that we have said concerning Statements, and the way in which they are drafted, will have a bearing on whether the annual review can ensure that the child's right to effective monitoring can be safeguarded. However, despite the problems caused by vague or stereotyped wording in Statements, there is evidence that special schools have welcomed the annual review as a monitoring device, and that many LEAs have made efforts to ensure that annual reviews are carried out with due recognition for accountability to children, parents and the community. It may be that some LEAs need to pay more attention to the involvement of parents as active participants in annual reviews, not as mere passive receivers of a report. It would also enhance the rights of children if they were asked, in appropriate circumstances, to give their views on the aims set for them, whether these were realistic, and whether the provision made had helped them to achieve the aims.

The other major review of the progress of children with Statements takes place between the ages of 12 and 14 years. This re-assessment, 'the 13+', has the specific aim of considering the transition from school to work or to other forms of education or training. It would seem particularly appropriate to seek the views of children at this review. This does not appear to happen in the majority of LEAs at the moment.

A particular problem arises for those children who are assessed for the first time after the age of 13. We found that the parents of these children were worried about what would happen to them after they had left school. It would seem that some attention should be given to post-school goals for these children during their statutory assessment.

## Safeguarding the rights of parents

The statutory procedures for the assessment of children with special educational needs contain requirements to inform, involve and give time for parents to consider the decisions made by LEAs. Professionals and administrators working in education, health and social services have expressed worries that the formalities introduced in order to safeguard these rights have led to the procedures becoming impersonal and cumbersome. They fear that informing parents of their rights to appeal, for example, will cause conflict. However, we do not have any evidence to support this view. Many of the parents whom we interviewed had negative issues to raise and felt that the access they had to LEA decision-making had made them aware that there were some aspects of that process which had been unsatisfactory. Nevertheless, these problems were not created by the procedures, but by the way that some LEAs had carried them out.

Another cause for concern among those working in local authorities was that the delays introduced in the procedures, to allow parents time to consider their response to the proposal or to the draft Statement, would prolong the assessment to an unacceptable degree. However, delays in completing Statements, which caused parents a lot of worry, were not usually due to these factors and would have been less problematic if parents had been kept informed of the reasons for delay.

The formality of the wording of letters from the LEA did not appear to worry parents; it was something which they expected in their dealings with official bodies, and they found nothing strange about it. However, parents were upset if they felt that LEA staff were attempting to manipulate them or to withhold information. The parents felt that this happened when the LEA was attempting to force them to accept provision which they did not want, or where the LEA staff were uncertain about the needs of their child or the best provision to meet the needs. One of the problems with involving parents in the decision-making for the Statement was that LEAs often did not have a choice of provision to offer; therefore, in a sense, there was very little decision-making to be done once the child had been identified. Also, parents cannot make informed choices if they are given very little information. There seems to be a conflict between the advice in Para. 35 of Circular 1/83, which says that advisers to the LEA should not suggest particular schools to parents, and Para. 49, which suggests that parents should be taken to see the suggested school at the draft Statement stage. By this stage, the decision about the placement has already been taken. Therefore, it is presented to the parents as a '*fait accompli*'.

We found that the presentation and content of many of the booklets designed to inform and involve parents made them difficult to understand and follow. The language of the booklets was difficult, and many LEAs had made no provision for the translation of booklets or letters into the languages of minority communities. However, we also saw some very good booklets for parents, over which obvious care had been taken. It seems that such booklets are an essential part of taking positive steps to inform parents of their rights and to involve them fully in the assessment procedures. It would be helpful if LEAs, DHAs, SSDs and voluntary organizations could co-operate to produce booklets to inform all those concerned with special educational needs, including parents, of the authorities' approaches to meeting needs and the procedures which they follow. Such booklets should include information about the range of provision available from the education, health and social services and from the voluntary organizations. The planning of such a booklet might also be a valuable way for the organizations concerned to share information about the provision they offer, and might be a basis for the more rational planning of services suggested in the next section.

The full involvement of parents as 'partners' in the decisions about their children's education is still far from being realized, though the possibility for change has been created by the 1981 Education Act. Parents appear to need positive help and encouragement to take a more active part in the procedures, and the recommendations of the Warnock and Fish Reports for a 'named person' or 'parent supporter' should be considered. The voluntary organizations could have an important role to play in providing impartial help and support for parents. It is all too common at present for voluntary organizations to be called on by parents when relations between them and the LEA have broken down. This is a cause of regret to the voluntary organizations, and those whose representatives we have talked to would welcome the opportunity to play a more positive role.

The last resort for parents who cannot resolve their differences with the LEA is to appeal. The outcomes of local appeals and those to the Secretary of State were considered in Chapter 7. We also noted that appeals are not considered by LEA officers to be a satisfactory method of resolving conflict and that many parents who are unhappy with their child's provision do not appeal. It seems, then, that none of those concerned feel that appeals should be undertaken unless there is no alternative. Local appeals are a public review of the evidence upon which the local authority has based its decisions about the nature of a child's needs and the allocation of resources to meet those needs. It is through such appeals that the LEA can be made accountable for its decisions to the community which it serves. Since this is the case, appeals committee decisions should be binding upon LEAs. If appeals committees are to be given this power, they should also be chosen to be representative of the community, and the balance of numbers within their membership should not be in favour of the LEA.

## THE CONCERN FOR EFFECTIVE EDUCATION

At the heart of the obligation to meet children's needs is the principle that educational aims are the same for all children, and that education is a compensatory resource to enable all children to achieve those aims as far as possible. Our research was not concerned with the evaluation of the quality of the educational provision made in schools, except in so far as the 'coping threshold' of schools has a bearing on the threshold of referral of children for statutory assessment. We were more concerned with the effectiveness of the procedures for ensuring the identification, assessment and provision for children with special educational needs.

### Identification of children with special educational needs

The majority of LEAs had produced information for their staffs about the new procedures to be followed for statutory assessment. Many had also produced new guidelines about the identification and referral of children whose special needs might require the LEA to determine the provision to be made. These guidelines tended to emphasize the role which teachers in mainstream schools had to play in meeting needs. At the same time, many LEAs had changed the way in which support for children in mainstream schools was delivered. As already noted, special needs support services were now more likely to offer support for teachers to make provision for such children themselves, thus extending the 'coping capacity' of class teachers.

### The statutory assessment procedures

We have already noted the perception among some LEA and DHA staffs that the 1981 Act procedures are cumbersome and cause delays. One of the main causes of delay appears to be the time taken by professionals to assess children and to forward their advice based on this assessment to the LEA. There has also been some concern expressed by professionals that if advice is summarized by the designated officer, rather than sent verbatim to the LEA, the implications of the advice may not be understood. Some professionals also expressed worries about confidentiality and the difficulty of passing on sensitive information. They were also concerned that there was often no feedback to advising professionals about the outcome of assessments. All this points to the need for improvements in communication between professionals and administrators, both within and between services.

Another cause of delays in allocating provision to children (and this was seen as especially crucial for very young children) was that in some LEAs all extra provision was tied to Statements. The Act allows flexibility in the assessment and the form in which Statements are produced for those under the age of two, with the safeguard that an assessment can only take place if parents agree. It may be possible to introduce a similar flexibility for older children, in those cases where parents are in agreement with the LEA, in order to be able to make provision available more quickly for those children whose needs would otherwise not be met for a prolonged period. Again, there would have to be the safeguard that parents could refuse such an assessment and have the right to a full assessment under the 1981 Act procedures, if they wished. There would also have to be help for parents to play a full role in any decision-making about their children's education, and the role of the 'parent supporter' described in the previous section would be essential in protecting parents' rights and ensuring that parents were not pressurized into agreement at a time when they might be especially vulnerable.

### Monitoring the evaluation of service delivery

In the previous section on 'Rights and accountability', we discussed the role of Statements as standards against which service delivery for individual children can be measured. There are, however, broader issues concerned with the effective monitoring of services for children with special educational needs. These include the planning and delivery of such services, both by the education authorities and by health authorities and social services departments. At present, there appears to be very little joint planning of these services, and later in this chapter we will make suggestions about how effective joint planning and evaluation could be carried out.

### The implications for training

The 1981 Education Act has highlighted the gap between aims and achievement for many children in our education system. There is a growing awareness that a large minority of children in our schools have special educational needs, and that, for many, the resources to meet those needs are not available. The Warnock Committee suggested that one in five of all children would experience learning difficulties at some stage in their school career. The proportion of those children who are given Statements will reflect the availability of resources to meet those needs within the provision 'generally made' in an authority's schools.

Under the 1981 Education Act, school governors have been given the duty of ensuring that schools have set up systems to identify children with special educational needs, and that any child who has special educational needs receives provision to meet those needs. The governors also have to ensure that all those likely to teach the child are aware of his or her special educational needs. This places the onus to provide effective education very firmly on the schools and governors.

Such increased awareness and expectation of effective intervention has led to an increasing emphasis on improving the skills and knowledge of teachers and others who provide services for children with special needs. There have been moves within LEAs and teacher training institutions to provide in-service training specifically for those who teach children with special needs in mainstream schools. This training has been studied in detail by a research project directed by Seamus Hegarty at the NFER[1]. Designating a part of LEA funding to such in-service training represents the only specific resource initiative taken by central government in relation to the 1981 Act.

An innovative scheme for training a wide range of professionals involved with children with special educational needs was the development of a Modular Diploma in Special Educational Needs by Manchester University and Manchester Polytechnic, in conjunction with a number of higher education establishments in the north-west. This is not the place to comment on their findings, but they indicate the importance of in-service training for ensuring the effective education of children with special educational needs[2].

Some LEAs appear to have given governors very little training or information to help them fulfil their duties under the Act effectively. In one LEA, a member of the research team was involved in training for governors and elected members about the Act and its implications, but such examples are rare. This is one area where thought could be given to providing training.

There is obviously a need to provide training for all levels of staff in LEAs, DHAs and SSDs who are involved in meeting special educational needs. These will include those who plan services and allocate resources, as well as professionals working with children. Further research is under way at the University of London Institute of Education into the most effective ways of organizing training for those who are involved in planning and managing special needs services[3].

**Implications for co-operation between the education, health and social services**

Most LEAs had disseminated information about the Act to those who would be involved in the new procedures under the Act. The majority had provided some training for all heads of mainstream schools (84 per cent) and for designated special needs teachers (71 per cent). Rather fewer had provided any training for DHA or SSD staff (38 and 33 per cent respectively). This lack of joint training for other services reflects the predominant pattern which emerged when we investigated LEAs' preparation for the implementation of the Act. Only a minority of LEAs had provided an active role for DHA or SSD staff in the formulation of their new procedures for the identification assessment and provision for children with special needs. We have described the approaches used in some detail in Chapter 6.

This, perhaps, reflects the difficulties inherent in attempting to co-ordinate services between education, health and social services which were analysed in Chapter 4. As we suggested earlier in this chapter, channels need to be set up to provide regular opportunities for administrators and professionals from the three services to discuss all aspects of special needs service delivery. A model for this might be the 'Board' and 'Panel' system adopted in one of our detailed study authorities. The Panel met regularly to make decisions about initiating statutory procedures, and about the contents of draft Statements. The Board met less frequently, but would monitor the Panel decisions and make longer-term strategic plans based on information about trends in decision-making about special needs. Such regular inter-service meetings, focusing on the implications of decisions about individual children for the planning of services, would help to overcome some of the problems we found in LEAs which did not have such regular contact. For instance, shortages in non-educational provision, particularly speech therapy, were undermining the effectiveness of educational provision for special needs in many authorities. If some realistic estimate of demand could be made by a regular inter-service review, it might be that a more responsive system could operate.

Another advantage of such an exchange of information is that it would provide an opportunity for the three services to avoid duplicating services, and to plug gaps in existing provision. In a time of scarce resources, it is important to use them efficiently, and education, health and social services might find mutual benefits to be gained by closer collaboration of this kind. The government has paved the way for this by extending the joint funding arrangements between health authorities and the social services departments to include the education authorities.

As suggested earlier in this chapter, the inclusion of voluntary organizations in such planning activities would widen the range of facilities and expertise that could be made available.

Closer co-operation between the three services might also facilitate communication between their staffs at all levels with respect to service delivery of special needs. If staffs within the different services understand each other's roles and responsibilities, it is less likely that the kinds of misunderstandings about client needs which we have observed in the course of our research will occur.


CONCLUSIONS

The overwhelming impression gained during our research was that those involved in all aspects of providing for children with special educational needs were in fundamental agreement with the principles which underpin the legislation and were attempting to put them into effect. The difficulties which they encountered were due partly to aspects of the legislation which cause problems in themselves, such as the relative definition of special educational needs, partly to the differences in structures and perspectives of the organizations called upon to co-operate in meeting needs and partly due to national funding policies over which they had no control. A major thread running through all comments upon the effectiveness of the service was the inadequacy of resources available to carry out to the full the obligation to meet children's needs. Despite these limitations, there has been a major shift in thinking about special needs and the ways in which these can best be met, and movements in some areas to put these new ideas into practice.

## NOTES

(1)    See Moses, D. and Hegarty, S. (eds) (1987) *Developing Expertise — A Study of INSET for Special Needs*. Windsor: NFER/Nelson.
(2)    See Sebba, J. and Robson, C. (1987) '*The development of short school-focussed studies in special educational needs.*' *Research Papers in Education* **2**, 1.
(3)    See Evans, J. (1987) *Decision-making for Special Needs: Key Considerations and Implications for Services*. London: University of London Institute of Education.

# Chapter 10

## The Role of Legislation in Changing Policy and Practice

'Today's structures are monuments to yesterday's problems.'

### INTRODUCTION

This final chapter attempts to assess the extent to which the policies and practices discussed in this report are the result of the passage of the legislation and how far they are the result of other influences, such as public opinion, changing professional views, financial policies and pressure group campaigns.

The view of policy implementation described in Chapter 2 would indicate that there is no simple, direct link between policy statements enshrined in legislation and policy outcomes evidenced by behaviour in individual situations. Policy implementation is a complex interaction between ideas, structures, systems, groups and individuals. We have adopted a model of the policy process, based on Whitmore's model of policy formulation and implementation, which attempts to draw these factors together (Whitmore, 1984). The application of this model to the particular case of the development of special education policy in England and Wales is illustrated in Table 1, Chapter 2. The process is viewed as being subject to a number of constraints, which steadily refine the policy until the point at which it is translated into action by individuals. The questions posed by this model are therefore:

(i) Can we identify the crucial factors which influence policy formulation and implementation?

(ii) How far are any changes that are observed due to legislation and how far are they due to other factors?

As noted in the previous chapter, there have been a number of changes in LEA and DHA policies regarding provision of services for children with special educational needs, and there is a great variety of change between local authorities, and in some cases within local authorities. Some authorities were much further along the road towards changing their policies in the direction that the Act indicated than others. This would confirm our view that the Act was one part of a shift in paradigm, which had already begun to influence LEA policies.

However, the differences between LEAs and the extent to which local factors acted as inhibitors to change in some areas indicate that the 1981 Act, reflecting the shift in paradigm, was not the only influence on special education policy. We have noted the difficulties that implementers in some areas encountered in trying to negotiate new procedures with the various professional groups. We have also noted the difficulties of attempting to re-allocate resources tied up in one form of provision to forms which are more in line with the Act's philosophy. It seems that the status quo is a powerful inhibiting force, and that an LEA's past history of special needs services is a powerful influence on the direction, extent and pace of change that it can sustain.

The question must also be posed: to what extent do the changes that have been reported constitute *real* or *fundamental* change and to what extent are they cosmetic or symbolic?

In Chapter 4 we discussed the ideas of special education and the way they had been understood and interpreted in local authorities. We concluded that there were conceptual areas in which those working with the Act had not internalized the new ideas. Although they had adopted the new statutory assessment procedures, they were often using them to relocate children from mainstream to special education in the same way as the SE procedures had been used. Similarly, though most authorities recorded a positive attitude to the concept of integration, for the majority of children with Statements the only available provision is still segregated.

In this chapter we will attempt to comment on the nature of change associated with the Act, and the factors that inhibit and facilitate change, using Whitmore's framework. We will also make suggestions about what legislators and policy-makers at central and local levels can do to influence change.

## THE CORE DIMENSION

In Whitmore's framework, the 'core dimension' means the fundamental problem to be addressed. In this particular instance the problem can be expressed as: 'What arrangements need to be made for dealing with those children who pose a problem for the education system?' From the tortuous way in which we had to frame that question, it can be deduced that it is very difficult to conceptualize such a problem, except in terms of some frame of reference — a policy paradigm — which directs the thinking and language to be used in formulating the problem and, therefore, to some extent the solutions to the problem. In the past, when our education system was less well developed and the demands made on children to achieve certain standards were differentiated through selection and exclusion, many of the children who are now identified as 'problems' would not have been seen as such. The frames of reference of those who identify and describe the problem, in this case predominantly those in the medical, educational and social work professions, have a powerful influence upon shaping the policy paradigm.

## THE POLICY PARADIGM

As indicated above, the policy paradigm is the way in which the problem and solutions to the problem are defined. Kirp (1982) has suggested that the British approach to special education was to conceive it in terms of a problem to be tackled by means of the input of professional 'expertise', and that the role which could be played by other forces, such as legal or bureaucratic ones, has been minimized. However, there are signs that the dominant role played by professionals in defining the problem of special educational needs, and the solutions to it, is being challenged. The new rights of parents, given by the legislation, have introduced the concept of a more proactive role for 'consumers' in the delivery of services. The role of parents as a pressure group has already contributed to some fundamental changes in special needs policy, such as the provision of education for severely mentally handicapped children and the current emphasis on integration of children with special needs into mainstream schools. There are also indications that the new legal framework is being tested by parents in the courts, as well as through the appeals process. Professionals are now more aware of the rights of parents to be involved in decision-making about their children, but it may be some time before the dominance of the professionals gives way to a more equal partnership.

Chapter 5 indicated the extent to which those concerned with the education of children with special needs have adopted the paradigm proposed by the Act, and the difficulties which some have had in translating ideas into action. At the same time, the existence of the legislation and the new practices which have evolved from it will provide a new focus for debate, and eventually for the emergence of a new paradigm. In order for this to happen, there is a need to provide a forum for continued debate, and to allow as wide a constituency as possible to be involved. Debate among policy-making professionals and administrators needs to be informed by the views of the practitioners and consumers of the services.

A National Advisory Committee for Special Education, one of the Warnock Committee's proposals which was not implemented, would appear to be one way to provide a forum for such debate. We therefore recommend reconsideration of the need for such a committee (see Voluntary Council for Handicapped Children, 1984).

## THE MONITORING FRAMEWORK

As already noted, the monitoring framework (that is, the Acts, Regulations and Circulars issued by central government in order to steer the actions of those in local authorities in the directions mapped out in the policy paradigm) is itself the result of a complex series of negotiations and consultations between the government and the interest groups involved. These are described in more detail in Chapters 1 and 2. After the passage of the legislation, further changes can be expected in response to a build-up of 'case law', indicating the extent to which the legislation has been effective in changing practices in LEAs in line with the policy paradigm, and to shifts in the paradigm itself as the social, economic, political and educational climates change. One explanation of the problems which local and health authorities have found in attempting to resource special needs under this new framework is that the policy paradigm was formulated in a time of expansion in educational spending, and the Act was implemented in a very different economic climate. It is always likely to be the case that legislation will lag behind prevailing opinion, and that changes will have occurred, not only in the paradigm, but also in the political and economic situations into which the legislation which codifies it is delivered.

## THE INTER-ORGANIZATIONAL RESOURCE DEPENDENCIES

The different political, organizational and resourcing structures of the local and health authorities, and the problems to which these give rise in the implementation of any legislation which requires co-operation between them, are described in some detail in Chapter 4. The relationship of central to local government is also considered in that chapter. The difficulties which local authorities and health authorities have encountered in providing a co-ordinated, well-planned response to the legislation have been one of the dominant themes of this report. Some authorities have attempted to overcome these difficulties by setting up structures for the planning and monitoring of services, as described in this report, but the problems of different structures and funding mechanisms remain. Until there is a more rationalized system of providing welfare services of all kinds, based on co-terminous or, at the very least, co-ordinated local administrative areas, with similar funding arrangements, a great deal of time and energy will have to be spent in devising ways for the different organizations to relate to one another. There have been developments in joint funding and in the requirement for local areas to set up Joint Consultative Committees to discuss local authority and health authority joint planning. A recent draft circular from the DHSS has indicated the way in which the government wishes such planning to be monitored.

As well as differences in administrative structures and funding arrangements, the local authorities and health authorities are staffed by a number of different professional groups, each with its own perspectives and paradigms. We have noted, in our report, the different emphases placed on special educational needs by education, health and social services personnel. Those attempting to implement policies within large and complex organizations, particularly where more than one organization is involved, will need to take such factors into account and to ensure that thorough and extensive negotiations have taken place in order to achieve a common understanding of the policy and its implications. Joint training of personnel, both initial and in-service, would appear to be an essential pre-requisite for fostering such understandings.

## ADMINISTRATIVE STRUCTURES AND PROCESSES

This dimension of the model considers actions by personnel at the local level to attempt to implement the legislation. It concerns the setting up of new administrative procedures, and the attempts of senior personnel to change the behaviour of their subordinates in order to conform to the requirements of the new sets of arrangements. Several strategies which LEAs used in order to do this were noted in Chapter 6. The most successful appeared to be those where a wide range of opinion was canvassed before new procedures were decided upon. Nevertheless, the most common strategy used was a top-down model, which gave those who were actually working with the new procedures very little say in their design. Most change within local authorities appears to be incremental and carried out within a restricted budget, so that it is often difficult for LEAs to consult a wide range of opinion. However, it appears that, if such consultations are possible, many of the difficulties which are encountered when trying to change administrative procedures could be avoided. There appears to be a need for the development of 'management of change' techniques in all services, particularly those where new demands and initiatives are constantly giving rise to organizational and administrative changes.

## THE PROFESSIONAL INTERFACE WITH THE CONSUMER

This is the point at which the constraints upon action focused down through the policy-implementation chain are made manifest. It is at this level that the policy and all the influences which have shaped it since its inception will be experienced. Weatherley's concept of the 'street level bureaucrat' implies that professionals have great power, at this level, to shape policy. It may appear that this is an overstatement, since professionals are also constrained by all that has gone before. It is the case that individual professionals can thwart the intentions of policy-makers by refusing to implement the 'spirit' of the legislation, although we found little evidence of this, since the majority of those we talked to were very much in agreement with the legislation's aims. However, Weatherley's argument is that those charged with delivering services operate a kind of rationing system when resources are limited, and it is this which distorts practice. This has been confirmed by our research, since we found that the main reason for poor service and bad practice was not a lack of commitment to the legislation, but difficulties in meeting the level of demand for services.

## CONCLUSION

We have held back in this report from making a simplistic recommendation about the need for more resources for special educational needs, as we realize that a responsible critique must involve looking at the disposition as well as the level of resourcing. We have noted that LEAs have increased resourcing for special needs, both in absolute and in relative terms. There is no doubt, however, that the Act required a redistribution of resources in favour of children with special educational needs. Within fixed levels of resources, this inevitably implies a reduction of resources for the remainder of the school population. Policy-makers will have to decide whether this is what they intend. Furthermore, policy-makers must look more closely at the funding implications of major policy initiatives. Change itself has cost implications; lack of funding for the change process may result in LEAs having to keep resources tied up in obsolete or unsuitable provision.

We have described the ways in which people at all levels in the education, health and social services have attempted to come to terms with major changes in the way they deliver a service to children with special needs and their parents. We have studied local authorities and health authorities at a time when they have been under great pressure to innovate and at the same time to limit expenditure. It is probably too soon to assess fully the extent of change that has taken place — the experience of similar legislation in the United States suggests that such policies take up to 10 years to effect major change. Perhaps in 1993 we shall be able to look back and see how far we have come. We might also be able to see how far we have yet to go.

# Appendix A

## Membership of Advisory Bodies

### (a) DES Steering Committee

HMI Mr TI Ambrose
Mr EL Basire, DES (until 10.12.85)
Mr AJ Bowers, Cambridge Institute of Education
Miss AF Brown, DES
Mr K Cornwall, Principal Educational Psychologist, Hampshire LEA (until 6.12.84)
Dr R Davie, Director, National Children's Bureau
Mr M Dunning, DHSS
Miss C Edwards, DES
Dr D Ernaelstein, DHSS
SSI Mr FH Green, HMI (until 21.5.84)
Mr J Gunner, Head Teacher, Hampshire LEA
Mr RM Harvey, Education Officer, ILEA
SI Mr CP Marshall, HMI
Mr BC Peatey, DES
SI Mr AJ Rose, HMI
Mrs A Smith, Deputy Head Teacher, Croydon LEA
Miss S Stanton, DES

### (b) Project Advisory Group

Dr M Berger, St. George's Hospital, Surrey
Dr PN Christie, Tolworth Hospital, Surrey
Mr JM Conway, Adviser, Barnsley LEA
Mr M Dunning, DHSS
Dr C Gipps, University of London, Institute of Education
Mr FH Green, Spastics Society (from 23.5.84)
Mrs M Leah, Lecturer, King Alfred's College, Winchester

SI Mr CP Marshall, HMI
Mr P Newell, Children's Legal Centre (until 16.12.85)
Mrs LS Pearson, Principal Educational Psychologist, Birmingham LEA
Mr BC Peatey, DES
Mr K Pocklington, University of Cambridge, Department of Education
Mrs P Russell, Voluntary Council for Handicapped Children
Mr C Stiles, Education Officer, Stockport LEA

# *Appendix B*

# Questionnaire

**University of London Institute of Education**

59 Gordon Square, London WC1H 0NT      Telephone 01-636 1500

## Policy and Provision for Special Needs Project

## Administration of Special Needs Service under the 1981 Education Act. (Autumn, 1985)

For the purpose of this questionnaire,

1.    1st April, 1983 is used to indicate the introduction of the new legislation.

2.    The term 'Parents' is used to mean parents and/or Guardians.

3.    'Children with special needs' is used to mean children for whom different or addi-
      tional provision is made who were ascertained under the SE procedure before
      1st April, 1983, or are the subject of a Statement under the 1981 Education Act.

4.    'Change' is used to mean change within the LEA even where it may be limited
      to only some areas within it.

5.    Where information of the type requested is not readily available, e.g. it would require
      prolonged clerical activity to produce it, THE QUESTION SHOULD BE
      CROSSED OUT.

6.    Please complete the questionnaire by circling the answer appropriate to your LEA.
      Space for additional comment/information is available for those who require it
      at the end of each section **and** at the end of the questionnaire.

— 2 —

**A. Substantial Changes in Special Educational Needs STAFFING since 1st April, 1983.**

1. Please indicate (i) any major change in the NUMBER OF STAFF *and* (ii) if the change/s involved were MAINLY achieved by redeployment.

**Please circle to indicate staff changes.**

| Staff | No staff of this type | (i) Increased | (i) Decreased | (i) Unchanged | (ii) Redeployed | |
|---|---|---|---|---|---|---|
| Administrator | 0 | 1 | 2 | 3 | 1 | 6-7 |
| Clerical Officer | 0 | 1 | 2 | 3 | 1 | 8-9 |
| Psychologist | 0 | 1 | 2 | 3 | 1 | 10-11 |
| Inspector/Adviser (SEN) | 0 | 1 | 2 | 3 | 1 | 12-13 |
| Peripatetic Advisory/Support Teacher | 0 | 1 | 2 | 3 | 1 | 14-15 |
| Mainstream-based SEN Teacher | 0 | 1 | 2 | 3 | 1 | 16-17 |
| Special Unit Teacher | 0 | 1 | 2 | 3 | 1 | 18-19 |
| Special School Teacher | 0 | 1 | 2 | 3 | 1 | 20-21 |
| Special School Teacher providing mainstream support | 0 | 1 | 2 | 3 | 1 | 22-23 |
| Welfare Assistant/Non Teaching Auxiliary | 0 | 1 | 2 | 3 | 1 | 24-25 |
| Other, please indicate: | | | | | | |
| ............................................ | — | 1 | 2 | — | 1 | 26-27 |
| ............................................ | — | 1 | 2 | — | 1 | 28-29 |
| ............................................ | — | 1 | 2 | — | 1 | 30-31 |

| | Yes | No | |
|---|---|---|---|
| 2. Has the LEA appointed or designated a "Statementing Officer"? | 1 | 2 | 32 |

If 'Yes' please indicate:

(i) Title of Post: ....................................................................

(ii) Level of Appointment: ...............................................................

(iii) Brief Job Description: ................................................................
................................................................
................................................................
................................................................

Any additional Comment on implications of the 1981 Act for staffing special needs services.
................................................................
................................................................
................................................................
................................................................

— 3 —

**B. FUNDING for Special Educational Needs since 1st April, 1983**

FUNDING MAY OR MAY NOT BE LIMITED TO THAT PROVIDED BY A SPECIFIC SPECIAL
EDUCATION BUDGET.

**Please circle**

1. Has the *proportion* of the total Education Budget
directed to Special Educational Needs since 1983:

| | |
|---|---|
| remained the same | 1 |
| decreased | 2 |
| increased | 3 |

33

2. Has *spending* (£GROSS) on Special Educational
Needs since 1983:

| | |
|---|---|
| remained the same | 1 |
| decreased | 2 |
| increased | 3 |

34

If 'Increased' has the increase:

| | |
|---|---|
| kept pace with inflation | 1 |
| failed to keep pace | 2 |
| exceeded the rate of inflation | 3 |
| don't know | 4 |

35

3. Have the priorities for spending WITHIN Special
Educational Needs since 1983:

| | |
|---|---|
| remained the same | 1 |
| changed | 2 |

36

If priorities have 'Changed', please indicate those aspects of special needs service which have been allocated
proportionately increased OR decreased funds:

| | Funding | |
|---|---|---|
| | Increase | Decrease |
| Designated special schools | 1 | 2 | 37 |
| Designated special units | 1 | 2 | 38 |
| Peripatetic advisory/support services | 1 | 2 | 39 |
| Mainstream-based SEN Teachers | 1 | 2 | 40 |
| Special School Teachers providing mainstream support | 1 | 2 | 41 |
| Schools Psychological Service | 1 | 2 | 42 |
| Inspector/Adviser SEN | 1 | 2 | 43 |
| Welfare Assistant/Non-Teaching Auxiliary Service | 1 | 2 | 44 |
| SE Provision in other LEA(s) | 1 | 2 | 45 |
| Independent SE Provision | 1 | 2 | 46 |
| SE Provision in FE Colleges | 1 | 2 | 47 |

Other: please indicate MAJOR fund users only.

. . . . . . . . . . . . . . . . . . . . . . . . . . . . . . . . . . . . . . . . . . . . . . . . . . . . . . . . . . . . . . . . . . . . . . . . . . . . . . . . . . . . . . . . . . . . . .    48-49

. . . . . . . . . . . . . . . . . . . . . . . . . . . . . . . . . . . . . . . . . . . . . . . . . . . . . . . . . . . . . . . . . . . . . . . . . . . . . . . . . . . . . . . . . . . . . .

4. Does the LEA carry out joint financial planning of services for Special Needs? Where 'Yes', please indicate the nature of such planning.

**Please circle**

| | Yes | | | | No | |
|---|---|---|---|---|---|---|
| | Routine and extensive | Routine but limited | Ad hoc but common | Ad hoc and rare | No joint planning | |
| with other LEA(s)? | 1 | 2 | 3 | 4 | 5 | 50 |
| with DHA(s)? | 1 | 2 | 3 | 4 | 5 | 51 |
| with SSD? | 1 | 2 | 3 | 4 | 5 | 52 |
| with Voluntary Organization(s)? | 1 | 2 | 3 | 4 | 5 | 53 |
| with other bodies? | 1 | 2 | 3 | 4 | 5 | 54 |

Please (i) indicate which other bodies .................................................................

.........................................................................................................

.........................................................................................................

.........................................................................................................

and (ii) give example(s) of such joint planning bodies, e.g. District Handicap Team

.........................................................................................................

.........................................................................................................

.........................................................................................................

5. Does the LEA share financial arrangements for special needs, (i.e. shared building use, staff working in other service provision, split funded provision inside/outside LEA)?

| | Yes | No | |
|---|---|---|---|
| | 1 | 2 | 55 |

Where 'Yes' (i) does this include joint funding with:

| | | | |
|---|---|---|---|
| other LEA(s)? | 1 | 2 | 56 |
| DHA(s)? | 1 | 2 | 57 |
| SSD? | 1 | 2 | 58 |
| Voluntary Organisations? | 1 | 2 | 59 |
| Other: please indicate which organisations | 1 | 2 | 60 |

.........................................................................................................

.........................................................................................................

.........................................................................................................

(ii) Please indicate the nature of *major* joint funded SE provision ................................

.........................................................................................................

.........................................................................................................

Any additional Comment on implications of 1981 Act for funding of special needs services: ..................

.........................................................................................................

.........................................................................................................

.........................................................................................................

.........................................................................................................

— 5 —

| | | | | |
|---|---|---|---|---|

1-5

## C. Changes in Special Educational Needs PROVISION SINCE 1st April, 1983.

1.  Please indicate *any major change* in the proportion of children with special needs receiving different types of special needs provision.

**Please circle to show change/s in** *proportion* **of children in receipt of provision**

| (a) PRE-SCHOOL CHILDREN WITH SPECIAL NEEDS aged 0-2 | | No provision of this type | Increase | Decrease | No change | Don't know | |
|---|---|---|---|---|---|---|---|
| Parental Play Advice/Counselling | | 0 | 1 | 2 | 3 | 4 | 6 |
| LEA Home Tuition Service | | 0 | 1 | 2 | 3 | 4 | 7 |
| LEA *Special* Nurseries | | 0 | 1 | 2 | 3 | 4 | 8 |
| LEA Day/Residential Schools for | SLD | 0 | 1 | 2 | 3 | 4 | 9 |
| LEA Day/Residential Schools for | MLD | 0 | 1 | 2 | 3 | 4 | 10 |
| LEA Day/Residential Schools for | EBD | 0 | 1 | 2 | 3 | 4 | 11 |
| LEA Day/Residential Schools for | Visually Impaired | 0 | 1 | 2 | 3 | 4 | 12 |
| LEA Day/Residential Schools for | Hearing Impaired | 0 | 1 | 2 | 3 | 4 | 13 |
| LEA Day/Residential Schools for | Physically Handicapped | 0 | 1 | 2 | 3 | 4 | 14 |
| LEA Day/Residential Schools for | Delicate | 0 | 1 | 2 | 3 | 4 | 15 |
| LEA Hospital Schools | | 0 | 1 | 2 | 3 | 4 | 16 |
| Other LEA Special Schools | | 0 | 1 | 2 | 3 | 4 | 17 |
| LEA Designated Special Units for | SLD | 0 | 1 | 2 | 3 | 4 | 18 |
| LEA Designated Special Units for | MLD | 0 | 1 | 2 | 3 | 4 | 19 |
| LEA Designated Special Units for | EBD | 0 | 1 | 2 | 3 | 4 | 20 |
| LEA Designated Special Units for | Visually Impaired | 0 | 1 | 2 | 3 | 4 | 21 |
| LEA Designated Special Units for | Hearing Impaired | 0 | 1 | 2 | 3 | 4 | 22 |
| LEA Designated Special Units for | Physically Handicapped | 0 | 1 | 2 | 3 | 4 | 23 |
| LEA Designated Special Units for | Delicate | 0 | 1 | 2 | 3 | 4 | 24 |
| LEA Mainstream Nurseries | | 0 | 1 | 2 | 3 | 4 | 25 |
| LEA Mainstream Schools | | 0 | 1 | 2 | 3 | 4 | 26 |
| SE Provision in other LEA(s) for | SLD | 0 | 1 | 2 | 3 | 4 | 27 |
| SE Provision in other LEA(s) for | MLD | 0 | 1 | 2 | 3 | 4 | 28 |
| SE Provision in other LEA(s) for | EBD | 0 | 1 | 2 | 3 | 4 | 29 |
| SE Provision in other LEA(s) for | Visually Impaired | 0 | 1 | 2 | 3 | 4 | 30 |
| SE Provision in other LEA(s) for | Hearing Impaired | 0 | 1 | 2 | 3 | 4 | 31 |
| SE Provision in other LEA(s) for | Physically Handicapped | 0 | 1 | 2 | 3 | 4 | 32 |
| SE Provision in other LEA(s) for | Delicate | 0 | 1 | 2 | 3 | 4 | 33 |
| Independent SE Provision for | SLD | 0 | 1 | 2 | 3 | 4 | 34 |
| Independent SE Provision for | MLD | 0 | 1 | 2 | 3 | 4 | 35 |
| Independent SE Provision for | EBD | 0 | 1 | 2 | 3 | 4 | 36 |
| Independent SE Provision for | Visually Impaired | 0 | 1 | 2 | 3 | 4 | 37 |
| Independent SE Provision for | Hearing Impaired | 0 | 1 | 2 | 3 | 4 | 38 |
| Independent SE Provision for | Physically Handicapped | 0 | 1 | 2 | 3 | 4 | 39 |
| Independent SE Provision for | Delicate | 0 | 1 | 2 | 3 | 4 | 40 |
| DHA Paediatric Assessment Centre | | 0 | 1 | 2 | 3 | 4 | 41 |
| DHA other provision, please specify ............................ | | 0 | 1 | 2 | 3 | 4 | 42 |
| SSD Day Nursery | | 0 | 1 | 2 | 3 | 4 | 43 |
| Opportunity Play Groups | | 0 | 1 | 2 | 3 | 4 | 44 |
| Portage Schemes | | 0 | 1 | 2 | 3 | 4 | 45 |

— 6 —

**Please circle to show change/s in *proportion*
of children in receipt of provision**

| (b) PRE-SCHOOL CHILDREN WITH SPECIAL NEEDS aged 2-5 | No provision of this type | Increase | Decrease | No change | Don't know | |
|---|---|---|---|---|---|---|
| Parental Play Advice/Counselling | 0 | 1 | 2 | 3 | 4 | 6 |
| LEA Home Tuition Service | 0 | 1 | 2 | 3 | 4 | 7 |
| LEA *Special* Nurseries | 0 | 1 | 2 | 3 | 4 | 8 |
| LEA Day/Residential Schools for SLD | 0 | 1 | 2 | 3 | 4 | 9 |
| LEA Day/Residential Schools for MLD | 0 | 1 | 2 | 3 | 4 | 10 |
| LEA Day/Residential Schools for EBD | 0 | 1 | 2 | 3 | 4 | 11 |
| LEA Day/Residential Schools for Visually Impaired | 0 | 1 | 2 | 3 | 4 | 12 |
| LEA Day/Residential Schools for Hearing Impaired | 0 | 1 | 2 | 3 | 4 | 13 |
| LEA Day/Residential Schools for Physically Handicapped | 0 | 1 | 2 | 3 | 4 | 14 |
| LEA Day/Residential Schools for Delicate | 0 | 1 | 2 | 3 | 4 | 15 |
| LEA Hospital Schools | 0 | 1 | 2 | 3 | 4 | 16 |
| Other LEA Special Schools | 0 | 1 | 2 | 3 | 4 | 17 |
| LEA Designated Special Units for SLD | 0 | 1 | 2 | 3 | 4 | 18 |
| LEA Designated Special Units for MLD | 0 | 1 | 2 | 3 | 4 | 19 |
| LEA Designated Special Units for EBD | 0 | 1 | 2 | 3 | 4 | 20 |
| LEA Designated Special Units for Visually Impaired | 0 | 1 | 2 | 3 | 4 | 21 |
| LEA Designated Special Units for Hearing Impaired | 0 | 1 | 2 | 3 | 4 | 22 |
| LEA Designated Special Units for Physically Handicapped | 0 | 1 | 2 | 3 | 4 | 23 |
| LEA Designated Special Units for Delicate | 0 | 1 | 2 | 3 | 4 | 24 |
| LEA Mainstream Nurseries | 0 | 1 | 2 | 3 | 4 | 25 |
| LEA Mainstream Schools | 0 | 1 | 2 | 3 | 4 | 26 |
| SE Provision in other LEA(s) for SLD | 0 | 1 | 2 | 3 | 4 | 27 |
| SE Provision in other LEA(s) for MLD | 0 | 1 | 2 | 3 | 4 | 28 |
| SE Provision in other LEA(s) for EBD | 0 | 1 | 2 | 3 | 4 | 29 |
| SE Provision in other LEA(s) for Visually Impaired | 0 | 1 | 2 | 3 | 4 | 30 |
| SE Provision in other LEA(s) for Hearing Impaired | 0 | 1 | 2 | 3 | 4 | 31 |
| SE Provision in other LEA(s) for Physically Handicapped | 0 | 1 | 2 | 3 | 4 | 32 |
| SE Provision in other LEA(s) for Delicate | 0 | 1 | 2 | 3 | 4 | 33 |
| Independent SE Provision for SLD | 0 | 1 | 2 | 3 | 4 | 34 |
| Independent SE Provision for MLD | 0 | 1 | 2 | 3 | 4 | 35 |
| Independent SE Provision for EBD | 0 | 1 | 2 | 3 | 4 | 36 |
| Independent SE Provision for Visually Impaired | 0 | 1 | 2 | 3 | 4 | 37 |
| Independent SE Provision for Hearing Impaired | 0 | 1 | 2 | 3 | 4 | 38 |
| Independent SE Provision for Physically Handicapped | 0 | 1 | 2 | 3 | 4 | 39 |
| Independent SE Provision for Delicate | 0 | 1 | 2 | 3 | 4 | 40 |
| DHA Paediatric Assessment Centre | 0 | 1 | 2 | 3 | 4 | 41 |
| DHA other provision, please specify ................................................ | 0 | 1 | 2 | 3 | 4 | 42 |
| SSD Day Nursery | 0 | 1 | 2 | 3 | 4 | 43 |
| Opportunity Play Groups | 0 | 1 | 2 | 3 | 4 | 44 |
| Portage Schemes | 0 | 1 | 2 | 3 | 4 | 45 |

— 7 —

|   |   |   |   |   |
|---|---|---|---|---|

1-5

**Please circle to show change/s in** *proportion*
**of children in receipt of provision**

| (c) **PRIMARY AGED CHILDREN WITH SPECIAL NEEDS**<br>(First/Infant/Junior/Primary/Middle (Junior)) | No provision<br>of this type | Increase | Decrease | No change | Don't know | |
|---|---|---|---|---|---|---|
| Parental Play Advice/Counselling | 0 | 1 | 2 | 3 | 4 | 6 |
| LEA Home Tuition Service | 0 | 1 | 2 | 3 | 4 | 7 |
| LEA *Special* Nurseries | 0 | 1 | 2 | 3 | 4 | 8 |
| LEA Day/Residential Schools for SLD | 0 | 1 | 2 | 3 | 4 | 9 |
| LEA Day/Residential Schools for MLD | 0 | 1 | 2 | 3 | 4 | 10 |
| LEA Day/Residential Schools for EBD | 0 | 1 | 2 | 3 | 4 | 11 |
| LEA Day/Residential Schools for Visually Impaired | 0 | 1 | 2 | 3 | 4 | 12 |
| LEA Day/Residential Schools for Hearing Impaired | 0 | 1 | 2 | 3 | 4 | 13 |
| LEA Day/Residential Schools for Physically Handicapped | 0 | 1 | 2 | 3 | 4 | 14 |
| LEA Day/Residential Schools for Delicate | 0 | 1 | 2 | 3 | 4 | 15 |
| LEA Hospital Schools | 0 | 1 | 2 | 3 | 4 | 16 |
| Other LEA Special Schools | 0 | 1 | 2 | 3 | 4 | 17 |
| LEA Designated Special Units for SLD | 0 | 1 | 2 | 3 | 4 | 18 |
| LEA Designated Special Units for MLD | 0 | 1 | 2 | 3 | 4 | 19 |
| LEA Designated Special Units for EBD | 0 | 1 | 2 | 3 | 4 | 20 |
| LEA Designated Special Units for Visually Impaired | 0 | 1 | 2 | 3 | 4 | 21 |
| LEA Designated Special Units for Hearing Impaired | 0 | 1 | 2 | 3 | 4 | 22 |
| LEA Designated Special Units for Physically Handicapped | 0 | 1 | 2 | 3 | 4 | 23 |
| LEA Designated Special Units for Delicate | 0 | 1 | 2 | 3 | 4 | 24 |
| LEA Mainstream Nurseries | 0 | 1 | 2 | 3 | 4 | 25 |
| LEA Mainstream Schools | 0 | 1 | 2 | 3 | 4 | 26 |
| SE Provision in other LEA(s) for SLD | 0 | 1 | 2 | 3 | 4 | 27 |
| SE Provision in other LEA(s) for MLD | 0 | 1 | 2 | 3 | 4 | 28 |
| SE Provision in other LEA(s) for EBD | 0 | 1 | 2 | 3 | 4 | 29 |
| SE Provision in other LEA(s) for Visually Impaired | 0 | 1 | 2 | 3 | 4 | 30 |
| SE Provision in other LEA(s) for Hearing Impaired | 0 | 1 | 2 | 3 | 4 | 31 |
| SE Provision in other LEA(s) for Physically Handicapped | 0 | 1 | 2 | 3 | 4 | 32 |
| SE Provision in other LEA(s) for Delicate | 0 | 1 | 2 | 3 | 4 | 33 |
| Independent SE Provision for SLD | 0 | 1 | 2 | 3 | 4 | 34 |
| Independent SE Provision for MLD | 0 | 1 | 2 | 3 | 4 | 35 |
| Independent SE Provision for EBD | 0 | 1 | 2 | 3 | 4 | 36 |
| Independent SE Provision for Visually Impaired | 0 | 1 | 2 | 3 | 4 | 37 |
| Independent SE Provision for Hearing Impaired | 0 | 1 | 2 | 3 | 4 | 38 |
| Independent SE Provision for Physically Handicapped | 0 | 1 | 2 | 3 | 4 | 39 |
| Independent SE Provision for Delicate | 0 | 1 | 2 | 3 | 4 | 40 |
| DHA Paediatric Assessment<br>Centre | 0 | 1 | 2 | 3 | 4 | 41 |
| DHA other provision, please specify<br>...................................................... | 0 | 1 | 2 | 3 | 4 | 42 |
| SSD Day Nursery | 0 | 1 | 2 | 3 | 4 | 43 |
| Opportunity Play Groups | 0 | 1 | 2 | 3 | 4 | 44· |
| Portage Schemes | 0 | 1 | 2 | 3 | 4 | 45 |

— 8 —

**Please circle to show change/s in** *proportion*
**of children in receipt of provision**

**(d) SECONDARY AGE CHILDREN WITH SPECIAL**
**NEEDS**

| | No provision of this type | Increase | Decrease | No change | Don't know | |
|---|---|---|---|---|---|---|
| LEA Day/Residential Schools for SLD | 0 | 1 | 2 | 3 | 4 | 6 |
| LEA Day/Residential Schools for MLD | 0 | 1 | 2 | 3 | 4 | 7 |
| LEA Day/Residential Schools for EBD | 0 | 1 | 2 | 3 | 4 | 8 |
| LEA Day/Residential Schools for Visually Impaired | 0 | 1 | 2 | 3 | 4 | 9 |
| LEA Day/Residential Schools for Hearing Impaired | 0 | 1 | 2 | 3 | 4 | 10 |
| LEA Day/Residential Schools for Physically Handicapped | 0 | 1 | 2 | 3 | 4 | 11 |
| LEA Day/Residential Schools for Delicate | 0 | 1 | 2 | 3 | 4 | 12 |
| LEA Hospital Schools | 0 | 1 | 2 | 3 | 4 | 13 |
| Other LEA Special Schools | 0 | 1 | 2 | 3 | 4 | 14 |
| LEA Designated Special Units for SLD | 0 | 1 | 2 | 3 | 4 | 15 |
| LEA Designated Special Units for MLD | 0 | 1 | 2 | 3 | 4 | 16 |
| LEA Designated Special Units for EBD | 0 | 1 | 2 | 3 | 4 | 17 |
| LEA Designated Special Units for Visually Impaired | 0 | 1 | 2 | 3 | 4 | 18 |
| LEA Designated Special Units for Hearing Impaired | 0 | 1 | 2 | 3 | 4 | 19 |
| LEA Designated Special Units for Physically Handicapped | 0 | 1 | 2 | 3 | 4 | 20 |
| LEA Designated Special Units for Delicate | 0 | 1 | 2 | 3 | 4 | 21 |
| LEA Home Tuition Service | 0 | 1 | 2 | 3 | 4 | 22 |
| LEA Mainstream Schools | 0 | 1 | 2 | 3 | 4 | 23 |
| LEA Sixth Form Colleges | 0 | 1 | 2 | 3 | 4 | 24 |
| LEA Colleges of F.E. | 0 | 1 | 2 | 3 | 4 | 25 |
| SE Provision in other LEA(s) for SLD | 0 | 1 | 2 | 3 | 4 | 26 |
| SE Provision in other LEA(s) for MLD | 0 | 1 | 2 | 3 | 4 | 27 |
| SE Provision in other LEA(s) for EBD | 0 | 1 | 2 | 3 | 4 | 28 |
| SE Provision in other LEA(s) for Visually Impaired | 0 | 1 | 2 | 3 | 4 | 29 |
| SE Provision in other LEA(s) for Hearing Impaired | 0 | 1 | 2 | 3 | 4 | 30 |
| SE Provision in other LEA(s) for Physically Handicapped | 0 | 1 | 2 | 3 | 4 | 31 |
| SE Provision in other LEA(s) for Delicate | 0 | 1 | 2 | 3 | 4 | 32 |
| Independent SE Provision for SLD | 0 | 1 | 2 | 3 | 4 | 33 |
| Independent SE Provision for MLD | 0 | 1 | 2 | 3 | 4 | 34 |
| Independent SE Provision for EBD | 0 | 1 | 2 | 3 | 4 | 35 |
| Independent SE Provision for Visually Impaired | 0 | 1 | 2 | 3 | 4 | 36 |
| Independent SE Provision for Hearing Impaired | 0 | 1 | 2 | 3 | 4 | 37 |
| Independent SE Provision for Physically Handicapped | 0 | 1 | 2 | 3 | 4 | 38 |
| Independent SE Provision for Delicate | 0 | 1 | 2 | 3 | 4 | 39 |
| DHA Provision, please specify ...................................................... | 0 | 1 | 2 | 3 | 4 | 40 |
| SSD Provision, please specify ...................................................... | 0 | 1 | 2 | 3 | 4 | 41 |

2. Please suggest up to four reasons for any *major* changes that have taken place in the LEA pattern of provision for special educational needs since 1st April, 1983.

.................................................................................. 42-43

.................................................................................. 44-45

.................................................................................. 46-47

.................................................................................. 48-49

Additional comment on implications of the 1981 Act for special needs provision.

..................................................................................

..................................................................................

..................................................................................

..................................................................................

**D. Implementation of the 1981 Act**

**Please circle**

1. In addition to any written information provided, has the LEA given specific training to help implement the 1981 Education Act?

|  | Yes | No |  |
|---|---|---|---|
|  | 1 | 2 | 50 |

If 'Yes' please indicate the audience/s for such training:

| | | |
|---|---|---|
| Administrators | 1 | 51 |
| Clerical Officers | 1 | 52 |
| Psychologists | 1 | 53 |
| Inspectors/Advisers | 1 | 54 |
| Peripatetic Advisory/Support Teachers | 1 | 55 |
| EWO/ESW's | 1 | 56 |
| **Mainstream:** Headteachers | 1 | 57 |
| SEN Teachers | 1 | 58 |
| Other Teachers | 1 | 59 |
| Governors | 1 | 60 |
| **Special Unit:** Unit Heads | 1 | 61 |
| Unit Teachers | 1 | 62 |
| **Special School:** Headteachers | 1 | 63 |
| Teachers | 1 | 64 |
| Governors | 1 | 65 |
| Welfare Assistants/Non-Teaching Auxiliaries | 1 | 66 |
| DHA(s) Personnel | 1 | 67 |
| SSD Personnel | 1 | 68 |
| Parents | 1 | 69 |
| Voluntary Organisations | 1 | 70 |

2. When did the LEA replace SE procedures by those of the 1981 Education Act?

Date of introduction ☐☐☐    71-72

Any additional comment on the implementation of the 1981 Act.

..................................................................................

..................................................................................

..................................................................................

..................................................................................

**E. Statement Procedure under the 1981 Act**

1. Please indicate how long the statementing procedure takes, i.e. from the *sending of the letter* to inform    1-5
parents of the LEA proposal to assess to the *child receiving provision.*

| | | |
|---|---|---|
| The shortest time | weeks | 6-7 |
| The longest time | weeks | 8-9 |
| Estimate of average time | weeks | 10-11 |

—10—

*a)*

2. Does the LEA make use of provision/assessment placement under the Act?    **Please circle**

| | |
|---|---|
| Always | 1 |
| Often | 2 |
| Sometimes | 3 |
| Never | 4 |

12

3. Are the statutory consultation periods built into the Act appropriate?    **Yes**    **No**

| | | |
|---|---|---|
| "the 29 days" | 1 | 2 |
| "the 15 days" | 1 | 2 |

13
14

Any additional comment on the consultation periods.

............................................................................

............................................................................

............................................................................

............................................................................

4. Are any other aspects of the 1981 Act procedures causing delay in the completion of Statements?    1    2    15

If 'Yes' please indicate possible causes of delay:

............................................................................    16-17

............................................................................    18-19

............................................................................    20-21

............................................................................    22-23

5. .Who in the LEA takes the decision to INITATE the 1981 Act procedures (i.e. that a letter be sent to parents informing them of the proposal to assess the child?).

| | | |
|---|---|---|
| Administrator alone (e.g. AEO) | 1 | 24 |
| Psychologist alone | 1 | 25 |
| Inspector/Adviser SEN alone | 1 | 26 |
| Panel of professionals: | 1 | 27 |

please indicate who is involved

..........................................................

..........................................................    28-29

Other(s) please indicate

..........................................................

..........................................................

..........................................................    30-31

6. Does the LEA accept *direct referral* to the person(s) initiating the procedures from:    **Yes**    **No**

| | | |
|---|---|---|
| Mainstream Headteacher | 1 | 2 | 32 |
| DHA(s) Paramedical Staff | 1 | 2 | 33 |
| DHA(s) Medical Staff | 1 | 2 | 34 |
| SSD Staff | 1 | 2 | 35 |

—11—

**Please circle**

| | Pre-School Children | School Age Children | |
|---|---|---|---|
| 7. How is the letter informing of the LEA proposal to assess USUALLY delivered to parents? | | | |
| By Post | 1 | 1 | 36-37 |
| By hand | 2 | 2 | |
| If 'By Hand' who will deliver it? | | | |
| Health Visitor | 1 | 1 | 38-39 |
| EWO/ESW | 1 | 1 | 40-41 |
| Psychologist | 1 | 1 | 42-43 |
| Other please indicate who | 1 | 1 | 44-45 |

..............................................................................

8. To which officer(s) of the authority (Section 5:3) are parents
directed for further information at this stage?

| | | |
|---|---|---|
| Administrator (e.g. AEO) | 1 | 46 |
| Clerical Officer | 1 | 47 |
| Psychologist | 1 | 48 |
| EWO/ESW | 1 | 49 |
| Headteacher/Teacher | 1 | 50 |
| Other(s) please indicate whom | | 51-52 |

..............................................................................

..............................................................................

| | Yes | No | |
|---|---|---|---|
| 9. Does this person remain the person to contact throughout the assessment/statementing? | 1 | 2 | 53 |
| If 'No please indicate contact(s) for later stages. | | | 54-55 |

..............................................................................

..............................................................................

10. What action is taken if the home language of parents is NOT English?

..............................................................................

..............................................................................

..............................................................................

..............................................................................

11. Where parents have ASKED for a Section 5 Assessment, does the LEA
carry out a full (Section 5) assessment?

| | | |
|---|---|---|
| Always | 1 | |
| Often | 2 | 56 |
| Sometimes | 3 | |
| Never | 4 | |

If assessment is made otherwise than under Section 5, what action is taken?

..............................................................................

..............................................................................

..............................................................................

. , ..............................................................................

—12—

**Please circle**

12. Where parents have ASKED FOR/AGREED TO the assessment, does the LEA wait 29 days before formally seeking educational, medical, psychological and other advice?

| | | |
|---|---|---|
| Always | 1 | |
| Often | 2 | 57 |
| Sometimes | 3 | |
| Never | 4 | |

13. What help is available to parents in making representation or providing written evidence at this stage? ...............................................................................
............................................................................................
............................................................................................

14. Do parents provide evidence at this stage?

| | | |
|---|---|---|
| All | 1 | |
| Most | 2 | 58 |
| Some | 3 | |
| None | 4 | |

| | Yes | No | |
|---|---|---|---|
| Unless 'None', do ALL appropriate professionals receive copies of the parental evidence BEFORE completing their Advice? (Regulation 4:4) | 1 | 2 | 59 |

15. How is the advice from professionals *usually* co-ordinated! (Circular 1/83, para. 34-35)

| | | |
|---|---|---|
| At a meeting of professionals who *know* the child? | 1 | |
| At a meeting of *representatives* from different services? | 2 | 60 |
| Advice from individual professionals sent *direct* to LEA for co-ordination? | 3 | |
| Advice from individual professionals *collated* by LEA, DHA(s), SSD administrator(s) before being sent to LEA? | 4 | |

Otherwise: please indicate how ...................................
............................................................................
............................................................................
............................................................................

16. Who *most commonly* determines the child's NEEDS as described on the Statement?

| | | |
|---|---|---|
| Administrator alone (e.g. AEO) | 1 | |
| Clerical Officer alone | 2 | |
| Psychologist alone | 3 | 61 |
| Inspector/Adviser (SEN) alone | 4 | |
| Panel of professionals | 5 | |

Other(s) please indicate post(s) ................................
............................................................................
............................................................................

| Where a 'Panel of professionals,' please indicate whether staff are involved from: | Yes | No | |
|---|---|---|---|
| SSD | 1 | 2 | 62 |
| DHA | 1 | 2 | 63 |

—13—

Please circle

17. Who *most commonly* decides that a STATEMENT should be made?

Administrator alone (e.g. AEO)     1

Clerical Officer alone     2

Psychologist alone     3      64

Inspector/Adviser (SEN) alone     4

Panel of Professionals     5

Other(s) please indicate post(s)

.........................................................

.........................................................

18. Who *most commonly* decides upon the PROVISION to be made available on the Statement?

Administrator alone (e.g. AEO)     1

Clerical Officer alone     2

Psychologist alone     3      65

Inspector/Adviser (SEN) alone     4

Panel of Professionals     5

Other(s) please indicate post(s)

.........................................................

.........................................................

19. Are there special circumstances where provision may be decided by others? (Qv Question 18)

                  Yes     No

                  1      2      66

If 'Yes', (i) what are these special circumstances?

Child under 2 years                   1      67

Child under 5 years                   1      68

Child over 16 years                   1      69

Placement in residential school        1      70

Provision not primarily on educational grounds      1      71

Other reasons: please indicate what these are:

..................................................................     72-73

..................................................................

(ii) Please indicate who then decides upon the provision to be made. .....

.................................................................................

.................................................................................

20. Who *most commonly* decides WHERE the provision is to be made?     1-5

Administrator (e.g. AEO)     1

Clerical Officer     2

Psychologist     3      6

Inspector/Adviser (SEN)     4

Panel of Professionals     5

Other(s) please indicate post(s)

.........................................................

.........................................................

—14—

Please circle

21. Who *most commonly* DRAFTS the proposed STATEMENT?

| | | |
|---|---|---|
| Administrator (e.g. AEO) | 1 | |
| Clerical Officer | 2 | 7 |
| Psychologist | 3 | |
| Other(s) please indicate post(s) | | |

.................................................................

.................................................................

22. Is the DRAFT STATEMENT routinely submitted to any other body for approval?

| | | |
|---|---|---|
| Panel of Professionals | 1 | 8 |
| Panel of elected members | 1 | 9 |
| Other(s) please indicate post(s) | | |
| | | 10-11 |

.................................................................

.................................................................

23. Who SIGNS the *final Statement?*

| | | |
|---|---|---|
| Chief Education Officer | 1 | 12 |
| Administrator (e.g. AEO) | 1 | 13 |
| Psychologist | 1 | 14 |
| Other: please indicate | | |
| | | 15 |

.................................................................

.................................................................

24. Who RECEIVES a copy of the *final Statement*

| | | |
|---|---|---|
| Parents | 1 | 16 |
| School Psychological Service | 1 | 17 |
| Advising Psychologist | 1 | 18 |
| Inspector/Adviser (SEN) | 1 | 19 |
| DHA Administrator | 1 | 20 |
| DHA Advising Professionals | 1 | 21 |
| SSD Administrator | 1 | 22 |
| SSD Advising Professinals | 1 | 23 |
| Receiving School | 1 | 24 |
| Other: please indicate ........................................ | | |
| | | 25-26 |

.................................................................

.................................................................

Any additional comment on the introduction of 1981 Act procedures.

.................................................................................

.................................................................................

.................................................................................

.................................................................................

## F. Annual Review (Schedule 1, Part II, Para. 5)

| | Yes | No | |
|---|---|---|---|
| 1. Does the LEA offer schools advice/guidance on how the annual review should be conducted? | 1 | 2 | 27 |
| If 'Yes' does the LEA expect advice to be taken from: | | | |
| those giving the original advice? | 1 | 2 | 28 |
| the parents? | 1 | 2 | 29 |
| the child? | 1 | 2 | 30 |

—15—

2.  If parents are not invited to attend what arrangements are made for their involvement? . . . . . . . . . .
. . . . . . . . . . . . . . . . . . . . . . . . . . . . . . . . . . . . . . . . . . . . . . . . . . . . . . . . . . . . . . . . . . . . . . . . . . . . . . . . . .
. . . . . . . . . . . . . . . . . . . . . . . . . . . . . . . . . . . . . . . . . . . . . . . . . . . . . . . . . . . . . . . . . . . . . . . . . . . . . . . . .

**Please circle**

| | Yes | No | |
|---|---|---|---|
| 3.  Are copies of review documents routinely sent | | | |
| to the LEA? | 1 | 2 | 31 |
| to the parents? | 1 | 2 | 32 |

Any additional comment on Annual Review. . . . . . . . . . . . . . . . . . . . . . . . . . . . . . . . . . . . . . . . . . . . . . . . .
. . . . . . . . . . . . . . . . . . . . . . . . . . . . . . . . . . . . . . . . . . . . . . . . . . . . . . . . . . . . . . . . . . . . . . . . . . . . . . . . .
. . . . . . . . . . . . . . . . . . . . . . . . . . . . . . . . . . . . . . . . . . . . . . . . . . . . . . . . . . . . . . . . . . . . . . . . . . . . . . . . .
. . . . . . . . . . . . . . . . . . . . . . . . . . . . . . . . . . . . . . . . . . . . . . . . . . . . . . . . . . . . . . . . . . . . . . . . . . . . . . . . .

### G. Mandatory 13 + Reassessment (Regulation 9)

| | Yes | No | |
|---|---|---|---|
| 1.  Has the LEA a specified procedure to be followed in the case of 13 + reassessments? | 1 | 2 | 33 |
| Where 'Yes' is this identical to the procedure for Section 5 assessment? | 1 | 2 | 34 |

2. Please indicate those who are ROUTINELY expected to contribute to a
13 + reassessment:

| | | |
|---|---|---|
| Headteacher/Teacher | 1 | 35 |
| Psychologist | 1 | 36 |
| Inspector/Adviser (SEN) | 1 | 37 |
| EWO/ESW | 1 | 38 |
| DHA(s) representative | 1 | 39 |
| SSD representative | 1 | 40 |
| Specialist Careers Adviser for handicapped | 1 | 41 |
| Careers Adviser | 1 | 42 |
| Parents | 1 | 43 |
| Child | 1 | 44 |
| Other: please indicate | | |

. . . . . . . . . . . . . . . . . . . . . . . . . . . . . . . . . . . . . . . . . . . . . . . . . . . . . . . . . .      45-46
. . . . . . . . . . . . . . . . . . . . . . . . . . . . . . . . . . . . . . . . . . . . . . . . . . . . . . . . . .
. . . . . . . . . . . . . . . . . . . . . . . . . . . . . . . . . . . . . . . . . . . . . . . . . . . . . . . . . .

Any additional comment on 13 + Reassessment. . . . . . . . . . . . . . . . . . . . . . . . . . . . . . . . . . . . . . . . . . .
. . . . . . . . . . . . . . . . . . . . . . . . . . . . . . . . . . . . . . . . . . . . . . . . . . . . . . . . . . . . . . . . . . . . . . . . . . . . . . . . .
. . . . . . . . . . . . . . . . . . . . . . . . . . . . . . . . . . . . . . . . . . . . . . . . . . . . . . . . . . . . . . . . . . . . . . . . . . . . . . . . .

### H. Ceasing to Maintain a Statement

| | Yes | No | |
|---|---|---|---|
| 1.  Is it *usual practice* to withdraw the Statement if a child is moved from special to mainstream school? | 1 | 2 | 47 |

—16—

|  | | Please circle | | For Research Use Only |
|---|---|---|---|---|

2. Has the LEA a *procedure* to be followed when a Statement is no longer to be maintainted?

Yes 1      No 2      48

If 'Yes', please indicate who will ROUTINELY be consulted:

Parent(s)      1      49

Headteacher/Teacher      1      50

Psychologist      1      51

Inspector/Adviser /SEN)      1      52

EWO/ESW      1      53

DHA Professionals      1      54

SSD Professionals (where they advised)      1      55

Other: please indicate post(s)

...............................................................      56-57

...............................................................

Any additional comment on ceasing to maintain a Statement.

...............................................................................

...............................................................................

...............................................................................

### I. Local Appeals (Section 8/1981, Part 1, Schedule II/1980)

1. What is the size of the Local Appeals Committee?

Not Applicable, No Local Appeals Committee      0

3 members      1      58

5 members      2

7 members      3

**IF NO LOCAL APPEALS HAVE BEEN HEARD GO ON TO Section J. Page 17.**

2. For the MOST RECENT LOCAL APPEAL which has been heard, please indicate the presence on the committee of the following:

LEA Committee Member (elected/co-opted)      1      59

Other Local Authority Member      1      60

LEA Teacher      1      61

Parent of Child in LEA School      1      62

3. Did the MOST RECENT LOCAL APPEALS COMMITTEE include a member with knowledge of Special Education?

Yes 1      No 2      63

4. How many Appeals have been heard by the Local Appeals Committee since the Act was implemented?

[ ]      64-66

5. How many Appeals resulted in

(a) a request to amend the Statement?      [ ]      67-69

(b) the amendment of a Statement by the LEA?      [ ]      70-72

(c) an Appeal to the Secretary of State (Section 8)?      [ ]      73-75

Any additional Information on Appeals Procedures ...........................................

...................................................................................

...................................................................................

### J.  Additional Information

1.  This Questionnaire was completed by

...................................................................................

post...............................................................................

LEA ................................................ Date ...................

Please use the space below to give any additional information about the 1981 Education Act, the way in which it has been implemented, its effect upon services for children with special needs and those involved with the procedures and any suggestions you may have for the amendment of the Act, Regulations and Circulars of Guidance.

Please return this questionnaire, together with documents listed on the attached check list, in the SAE provided. Any additional postage required will be paid by the receiver.

**THANK YOU FOR YOUR HELP**

# References

Abrams, P. (1984) 'Realities of neighbourhood care: the interactions between statutory, voluntary and informal social care'. *Policy and Politics* **12**(4), 413–49.

Adams, F. (ed.) (1986) *Special Education*. Harlow: Longman.

Baroness Young (1980) Address to White Paper Conference, University of London Institute of Education, 28 November 1980.

Barrett, S. and Hill, M. (1984) 'Policy bargaining and structure in implementation: towards an integrated perspective'. *Policy and Politics* **12**(3), 219–240.

Charnley, H. (1983) 'Who decides what: a case study of decision-making in a District Health Authority'. University of Surrey M.Sc. dissertation (unpublished).

Corwin, R.G. (1981) 'Patterns of organisational control and teacher militancy: theoretical continuities in the idea of loose-coupling'. *Research in the Sociology of Education* **2**, 261–291.

Court Report (1976) *Fit for the Future*. London: HMSO.

*Education* (1985), 26 July, p. 99.

Elmore, R. (1980) 'Backward mapping: implementation research and policy decisions.' *Political Science Quarterly* **94**(4), 601–616.

Evans, J. (1987) *Decision-making for Special Needs: Key Considerations and Implications for Services*. London: University of London Institute of Education.

Gipps, C., Gross, H. and Goldstein, H. (1987) *Warnock's 18% — Children with Special Needs in Ordinary Schools*. Basingstoke: Falmer Press.

Griffiths, R. (1984) *NHS Management Inquiry Report*. London: HMSO.

Hill, M. (1981) 'The policy-implementation distinction: a quest for rational control?' in Barrett, S. and Fudge, C. (eds) *Policy and Action*. London: Methuen.

Holland, W. *et al*. (1983) 'Geographical variation in mortality from conditions amenable to medical intervention in England and Wales'. *Lancet*, 26 March.

Houlihan, B. (1984) 'The regional offices of the DOE — policemen or mediators — A study of local housing policy. *Public Administration* **62**, 401–421.

ILEA (1985) *Educational Opportunities for All?* The Report of the Fish Committee. London: ILEA.

Jones, N. (1982) 'Children with Special Educational Need: the legislative framework' in Welton *et al*. (1982) (see below).

Jones, N. (1983) 'An Integration Approach to Special Educational Needs'. *Forum* **25**(2).

Kirp, D. (1982) 'Professionalisation as policy choice: British special education in comparative perspective'. *World Politics* **34**(2), 137–174.

Law Society Group for the Welfare of People with Mental Handicap (1985). Report of a working party on the 1981 Education Act. London: Law Society.

Layfield Report (1976) *Committee of Enquiry into Local Government Finance*. Cmnd 6453. London: HMSO.

Levitt, R. (1976) *The Reorganised National Health Service*. London: Croom Helm.

Moses, D. and Hegarty, S. (eds) (1987) *Developing Expertise — A Study of INSET for Special Needs*. Windsor: NFER/Nelson.

National Association of Principal Educational Psychologists (1985) *Survey of LEA Principal Educational Psychologists September, 1983: LEA Psychological Service and the Act*. London: NAPEP.

Newell, P. (1983) *ACE Special Education Handbook: The New Law on Children with Special Needs*. London: Advisory Centre for Education.

Newsom Report (1963) *Half Our Future*. London: HMSO.

Nichols, R. (1983) *Survey of the Role of the Adviser in the Implementation of the Education Act (1981)*. London: National Association of Advisory Officers in Special Education.

Pearson, L. (1986) *Report of the Survey of LEA Psychological Services and the 1981 Education Act, Autumn 1984*. London: NAPEP.

Plowden Report (1967) *Children and Their Primary Schools*. London: HMSO.

Rogers, R. (1986) *Caught in the Act*. London: CSIE/Spastics Society.

Sandow, S. *et al*. (1986) 'Parental perceptions and the 1981 Education Act'. *British Journal of Special Education* 13(1), 19–21.

Sebba, J. and Robson, C. (1987) '*The development of short school-focussed studies in special educational needs*'. *Research Papers in Education* 2.1.

Self, P. (1972) *Administrative Theories and Politics*. London: Allen and Unwin.

Swann, W. (1985) 'Is the integration of children with special needs happening? An analysis of recent statistics of pupils in special schools'. *Oxford Review of Education* 11(1).

Tomlinson, S. (1985) 'The expansion of special education'. *Oxford Review of Education* 12(2), 157–165.

Townsend, P. and Davidson, N. (1982) *Inequalities in Health: The Black Report*. Harmondsworth: Penguin.

Voluntary Council for Handicapped Children (1984) *A National Advisory Committee for Special Educational Needs: Report of a Working Party*. London: VCHC.

Warnock Report (1978) *Special Educational Needs*. London: HMSO.

Weatherley, R. (1979) *Reforming Special Education: Policy Implementation from State Level to Street Level*. Cambridge, MA. and London: MIT.

Wedell, K. (1981) 'Concepts of Special Educational Need'. *Education Today* 31, 3–9.

Wedell, K. (1983) 'Assessing Special Educational Needs'. *Secondary Education Journal* 13, 14–16.

Wedell, K. *et al*. (1981) *The Assessment of Special Educational Needs. Final Report to the Department of Education and Science*. London: University of London Institute of Education.

Welton, J. (1983) 'Implementing the 1981 Education Act'. *Higher Education* 12, 597–607.

Welton, J. *et al*. (1982) '*Meeting Special Educational Needs: The 1981 Act and Its Implications*'. Bedford Way Paper No. 12. London: Heinemann.

Whitmore, R. (1984). 'Modelling the policy/implementation distinction: The case of child abuse'. *Policy and Politics* 12(3), 241–267.

Whittington, C. (1983) 'Social work in the welfare network: negotiating daily practice'. *British Journal of Social Work* 13, 265–286.

Wilding, P. (1982) *Professional Power and Social Welfare*. London: Radical Social Policy.

Wilson, M. (1986) 'The Education Act 1981'. *Health Visitor, Midwife and Community Nurse Journal* 22(7): 218–221.

Wingham, G. (1986) 'Closed worlds? — A study of the relationship between social workers and the special education system'. Dissertation submitted as course requirement of the CNAA M.Sc. in Sociology, Polytechnic of the South Bank.

Wolfendale, S. (1985) 'Involving parents in assessment'. In De'Ath, E. *et al*. (eds) *Working Together with Children with Special Needs: Implications for Pre-School Services*. Partnership Paper No. 3. London: National Children's Bureau.

# Legislation, Statutory Instruments, Circulars and White Papers

**Acts:**

Education Act (1921). London: HMSO.
Education Act (1944). London: HMSO.
Education Act (1980). London: HMSO.
Education Act (1981). London: HMSO.
Local Government Act (1972). London: HMSO.
Education (Handicapped Children) Act 1970. London: HMSO.

**Regulations and Statutory Instruments:**

Education (Special Educational Needs) Regulations 1983. London: HMSO.
Statutory Instrument 1983 No. 29. London: HMSO.

**Circulars:**

Circular 2/75. The Discovery of Children Requiring Special Education and the Assessment of Their Needs. London: DES.
Circular 8/81. The Education Act 1981. London: DES.
Circular 1/83. Assessments and Statements of Special Educational Needs. (Joint Circular with DHSS Health Circular HC(83)3 and Local Authority Circular LAC (83)2). London: DES.

**White Papers:**

Special Needs in Education (1980). White Paper Cmnd 7996. London: HMSO.
Educational Reconstruction. White Paper 1943. London: HMSO.

# Name Index

# Subject Index